INDIAN WOMEN
EDUCATION AND EMPOWERMENT

INDIAN WOMEN
EDUCATION AND EMPOWERMENT

Volume Two

DR. ANITA ARYA

GYAN PUBLISHING HOUSE
New Delhi-110002

INDIAN WOMEN

EDUCATION AND EMPOWERMENT

[*Women Study, Mass Media, Political Science*]

ISBN: 81-212-0626-X (Set)
ISBN: 81-212-0690-1

Published in 2000 in India by
Gyan Publishing House
5, Ansari Road
New Delhi 110 002

Laser Typeset at Alphabet, Delhi
Printed at Mehra Offset Press, New Delhi.

Contents

Foreword

I feel great pleasure and honour, while penning down this Foreword for Dr. Anita Arya's first book. I am further happy that this book is on women's studies, which must be the natural forte of a female social activist and a popular leader, which she certainly is.

For years, I have watched Anita Arya growing into a good leader, concerned with basic and vital social issues. She has come a long way from an humble party worker to her present status as Member of Parliament. In between she represented her people in the civic body and rose to become the first citizen of Delhi, as its Mayor. Since her entry in public life, she has never looked back.

It gave me an immense pleasure when I went through her lengthy work: INDIAN WOMEN spread over three volumes. The one thousand or so pages exposed me to a new world, which the women's world is. The way she has treated the subject and handled the material available is really remarkable. What pains she must have taken in collecting material and laying hands upon the original sources over the years, is another story. No doubt, she must be praised for her meritorious work.

Anita Arya, while preparing this book has worked in a large spectrum, which shows her clear understanding of the issues involved and her prowess to overcome the resisting factors whatsoever these were.

The peculiar speciality with Dr. Anita Arya is that she speaks politely, negotiates gently, debates strongly, concludes wisely and acts firmly.

Over a decade or so, I have seen her participating in meetings arguing the matters and making her points assertively. I have always marked her concern for the Indian women. She has her own ideas — based on observations and findings of course — on problems and perspectives, in regard to Indian women, a result of which is the present study.

Here, I take liberty to say that this book by Dr. Anita Arya is a different book on the subject, as it has the support of the experiences of a grassroot worker, practically involved in social activities and mixed up with masses. In this manner, this book has earned a status of a first hand study.

I believe — and quite strongly — that the scholars and readers will find the book thought provoking and eye opening and this is a fact which guarantees her success as an able editor and a good authoress.

As far as I know this gentle lady, known as Dr. Anita Arya, I can say without any fear of contradiction that she will rise steadily in life and career, scaling new heights year after year and achievement after achievement.

I wish her all success and look forward to her vital role as a parliamentarian during the next millennium.

Jagmohan

Preface

Women's world is a world in itself. Similarly, Women studies, as a branch of knowledge has become vast like an ocean. I am proud of being a student of this vital discipline, which has a large room for contribution and work. This effort of mine is a small step in the same direction.

Over thousand of years, our society has changed, a new civilization has replaced the old ones, people have developed culturally, economically and socially but an unfortunate section of the society in the East in general and in our country in particular is still living under the same circumstances, that is women. Their lot is same and they—barring a few fortunate ones—are either shackled, chained and bonded or they are bound to live under the dominance of the men, as ever. Ironically, that's true, in spite of the guarantee of the constitution, protecting laws and all the sincere efforts of various governments over the years. In fact, we cannot change the lot of a community or the whole social system altogether, in one go. Social change has to come from within and it takes its own time.

Throughout my two-decade involvement with women's problems and issues and my search for remedies for them, I have always found it challenging to work in these areas. As a grassroot worker and a down to earth social activist, since my student days, I have felt debted to do some thing for this happless group. I have done only a bit so far but I determine to do a lot in the years to come, in and outside Parliament. I have no illusions and realise that the path is ardous thorny and long enough. However, we have to assert and strive.

As my first humble contribution to women's studies, I am presenting this book of mine. Honestly, I was a bit confused when Gyan Publishing House urged me to compile and edit a book on Women and left the choice of the topic to me only. I had to think for weeks and months, before I decided to bring out a book on Indian women, covering all the concerning aspects. Hence this bulky study, spanning over one thousand odd pages and comprising three volumes. Notably each of these volumes is an independent book in itself.

Study of the prevailing status of women in our society is one of the core areas in women studies today. In order to make the work exhaustive and more comprehensive, I have divided it into three separate volumes, titled: (1) Society and Law, (2) Education and Empowerment, and (3) Work and Development.

The first volume approaches the study of women problems and prospects and the legal aspects have been examined in the socio-cultural settings.

The second volume provides information on women education and empowerment in a historical perspective.

The third volume is designed to provide information on gender and economic participation and the related problems of working women at various levels.

This voluminous book is the outcome of a painstaking research for years and compilation of materials from hundreds of sources, spread all over. In fact, I had begun this project, nearly a decade ago and finished it in over a five year period. So, for the last five years or so it has been lying for a thorough revision of the whole work, an excercise, which I carried out in the previous year only and that too at a fast pace, thanks to my overwhelming engagements in public life. One confession, I wish to make here is that I have not been able to devote my full attention to this work in its last phase and could not collect new data and other latest figure. I am afraid, if I would have opted for it, perhaps this book would not have been able to see the light of the day for another five years. So, I had to make a compromise and I regret for it. Truly speaking, this is the price, we 'politico-academics' have to pay, as public life is always taxing upon one's scholarly pursuit.

I hope this petty contribution of an humble fellows, would at least be able to stir the calm waters, create a sort of awareness among men and women and appeal to those who matter in our political and social system. If this much is done, I should feel honoured and privileged to have played a small role in the continuous process of social change and be apart of an ongoing historic struggle which is slated to be extended to the next millennium.

Dr. Anita Arya

Introduction

Emancipation and empowerment of women is not so easy. For raising the status of a section of our society, we need a great will, social awareness, a determination and an initiative, which should come from within. First of all, we have to alarm the society and prepare it for a change. Needless to say that a change needs an awakening which comes through education alone. That's why education is the most important factor, working behind any movement or struggle for women's lib and women's rights.

Indian women have been lagging behind in the sphere of education, for the last many centuries. Although, there has been considerable progress in the field of education of women, yet a lot has to be done for women education in India and its a long road to go.

As is well known, women in India have always been on the academic scene. Our history has produced a number of female scholars during all ages. We had good female scholars, authoresses and poetesses in ancient India, we had great female scholars and ladies of letters in medieval India — the list includes names like Meera Bai — and a lot of them in modern period.

The awakening among women — as in case of man — came first in Bengal, which produced good women scholars in 18th and 19th centuries, well before the commencement of general awareness at an all India level in the beginning of 20th century, Broadly speaking, the development in the educational status of women in India during 20th century can be classified into three periods viz, the first two decades, the third, fourth and the fifth decade (upto 1947) and the post-independence period.

During the pre-independence period. The educationists worked hard for the popularization of education among girls and women. They opened schools and colleges all over the country. These institutions changed the scenario to a great extent. Then came independence and the Government came on the scene and with that the educational development caught momentum. No doubt, we have achieved a lot, still a lot has to be done.

Currently, if we look at the women's education scenario in India, we find this area cluttered with contradictory complexes, theories, opposed to each other and a number of streams.

The irony of the situation is that our country has a large mass of people, which is least interested in education. The rest are either ignorant or half-heartedly interested in education of women.

Here, I would also like to discuss the purpose of education for women. In our country most of women go for education to get married properly. Among the rest a majority receive education, as per their needs, as they want employment on the basis of their qualification. Lastly, only a small minority opts for education for academic purposes or for their enlightenment.

However, there is a ray of hope at the end of the tunnel. There has been a tremendous and rapid growth in the number of women students in schools and colleges in the whole country after independence.

In 1947 there were only 9.3 per cent female students at the higher level, but this figure rose to 34.1 per cent in 1995-1996. Expectedly, this must have risen during last three or four years, though the data are not available.

The purpose of this study is to create an awakening among men, regarding the education and emancipation of women and among women themselves. This volume, particularly provides information on women education, empowerment and mass media in a historical perspective.

Editor

List of Tables

One

Women and Education

Women constitute almost half of the human race. Education has been recognized as an essential agent of social change and development in any society. Hence to think of harmonious development without educating women is an impossibility. Moreover it has been rightly said that to educate a woman is to educate the whole family.

Therefore, the emphasis with regard to women's education should be to equip her for the multiple roles as citizens, housewives, mothers, contributors to family income and builders of the new society.

In realisation of the importance of education in general and the need for equality in opportunities for the intellectual development of men and women, successive Five-Year Plans have consistently placed special emphasis on the acceleration of women's education. The emphasis with regard to women's education has all along been to equip her for the multiple roles as citizens, housewives, mothers, contributors to family income and builders of the new decades of planned development — to enrol more girls in schools; to encourage girls to stay in schools; to continue their education as long as possible; and to provide non-formal educational opportunities for women. The Draft Fifth Five-Year Plan has declared that "the outlays for the education of girls will be stepped up ....". The fulfilment of the constitutional directive in respect of providing free and compulsory education up to the age of 24 years has been included as one of the components of the Minimum Needs Programme.

These efforts have had a significant impact on the progress of women's education in India. For example, there is a primary school within easy walking distance from the home of almost all the children. This has resulted in an increase in the enrolment of girls in classes I-V as a percentage of total enrolment in these classes from 28.1 in 1950-51 to 37.6 in 1973-74. In respect of classes I-VIII, IX-X/XII and university education also there has been an appreciable increase in the percentage of girls' enrolment to total enrolment, between the years 1950-51 and 1973-74 (Table 1.1). In fact, girls' enrolment is observed to be growing at a faster rate than those of boys.

TABLE - 1.1

ENROLMENT TARGETS AND ACHIEVEMENTS IN THE FOURTH PLAN

(Figures in lakhs)

Age Group Classes	*1968-69*		*1963-74* (Target)*		*1973-74 (Likely Position)*	
6-11/I-V						
Boys	342.10	(93)	412.50	(105)	393.53	(100)
Girls	201.70	(57)	273.30	(73)	244.01	(66)
Total	543.89	(76)	685.80	(90)	637.54	(84)
11-14/VI-VIII						
Boys	87.11	(45)	121.90	(56)	104.92	(48)
Girls	33.40	(18)	59.10	(29)	45.37	(22)
Total	120.51	(32)	181.00	(45)	150.29	(36)
14-17-18/IX-XI/XII						
Boys	50.90	(29)	70.00	(35)	61.60	(31)
Girls	17.40	(10)	26.90	(14)	23.40	(12)
Total	68.30	(20)	96.90	(25)	85.00	(22)
17-23/University Stage						
Total	16.90	(2.9)	26.60	(3.9)	30.00	(4.4)

*In the case of secondary and university education these are estimates.

Note: Figures in parenthesis indicate enrolment as percentage of the relevant age group.

Despite these encouraging trends and marked progress made in respect of women's education, the education status of women is still far from satisfactory for the following reasons:

(a) Literacy among women is generally lower than that among men. According to the 1971 Census data, only 13.4 per cent of women in this age group of 25+ are literate. (Table 1.2)

(b) Enrolment of girls in classes I to V is only 66.4 per cent of girls in the corresponding age group, i.e., 6 to 11 years; while in respect of boys the relevant percentage is 100.2 (Table 1.3).

(c) Drop-out rate is also very high in classes I to V. A recent study has shown that the drop-out rate especially accentuated in the case of girls from rural areas and from the less privileged sections of society, is as heavy as 42.85 per cent between classes I and II.

(d) In classes VI to VIII, percentages of enrolment of girls and boys to the total girls and boys in the relevant age group (i.e. 11 to 14 years) are 22.2 and 48.3 respectively (Table 1.3)

(e) At the secondary stage, i.e., classes IX to XI/XII girls enrolled constitute only 12 per cent of girls in the relevant age group 14 to 17 years as against 31 per cent in respect of the enrolment of boys in this age group (Table 1.3).

(f) Enrolment of girls in Post-Matric classes constitutes only 2.3 per cent of girls in the concerned age group 17 to 23 years; while the enrolment percentage of boys in this age group is 7.5 (Table 1.3).

TABLE - 1.2
ENROLMENT IN PRIMARY EDUCATION AS PERCENTAGE OF THE POPULATION IN THE CORRESPONDING AGE GROUP

Year	*Primary Stage Classes (I-IV)*			*Middle Stage Classes (V-VII)*		
	Boys	*Girls*	*Total*	*Boys*	*Girls*	*Total*
1950-51	55.0	20.1	37.8	20.8	4.6	13.0
1955-56	59.5	25.0	42.6	25.6	6.9	16.5
1960-61	74.0	35.0	54.8	35.5	12.5	24.3
1965-66	90.2	47.6	69.2	49.9	20.7	35.6
1970-71	109.8	68.6	89.7	66.7	33.0	50.7
1975-76 (Estimated)	109.7	97.2	106.4	81.9	55.7	69.2

* Includes repeaters and other average students.
Source: Ministry of Education, Government of India.

It should be noted that the targets of Planning Commission for the IV five-year plan were considerably lower than those set by the National Committee on Women's Education.

TABLE - 1.3
SECONDARY STAGE

Year	*(Classes VII to X)*			*(Classes IX to XI)*		
	Boys	Girls	Total	Boys	Girls	Total
1950-51	10.9	1.8	6.5	3.3	0.5	1.9
1955-56	14.9	3.3	9.3	5.2	0.9	3.1
1960-61	20.8	5.4	13.1	8.0	1.6	4.9
1965-66	28.7	9.1	19.1	11.5	2.3	7.0
1970-71	34.2	12.2	23.4	14.6	3.5	9.2
1975-76	40.8	16.9	29.1	17.0	4.8	11.0

Source: Ministry of Education, Government of India.

Factors Retarding the Progress of Women's Education

Girls and women in India have thus not been able to take full advantage of the available opportunities/facilities for intellectual development. This is mainly because of several social and cultural factors in addition to various other reasons. Action plans and strategies for women's education should, therefore, aim at neutralizing the effects of the factors which have retarded the progress of women's education in India. With a view to facilitating the formulation of such a plan of action, in what follows, some of the major reasons which have operated against girls/women in taking full advantage of educational opportunities/facilities, are listed below:

(a) General indifference to education of girls.
(b) Social resistance arising out of fears and misconceptions that education might alienate girls from traditions and social values and lead to maladjustments, conflicts and non-conformism.
(c) Early marriage and social inhibitions against girls pursuing education after marriage.
(d) Prevalence of child labour among girls belonging to weaker sections and the hard domestic chores which some of the unmarried girls — even in the middle-class families are required to perform.
(e) The prevailing notion that the sole occupation of women is to bear children, look after her husband and children, and thus be restricted to domestic work.

*Promotional and Motivational Measures**

(v) School timings should be flexible, as many of the girls in this age group are required to help their mothers in routine domestic chores.
(vi) Adoption of multiple entry and part-time courses are recommended.
(vii) Incentive like mid-day meals, scholarships, free school uniforms, free books and study materials, stipends, awards, etc., should be extended to all girls in the rural areas and slums in the urban areas.

* Draft Fifth Fiye-Year Plan 1974-79, Planning Commission, Government of India, 1974, p. 197.

(b) Middle School - Girl Drop-outs

Alternative measures

(viii) For school drop-outs of girls, pre-vocational training programmes should be organized on an extensive scale to cover all girls in the rural areas and in the slums of urban areas. The objectives of such training should be to render them self-sufficient in home management, and help them to achieve economic independence. With this in view, such training programmes should include courses in sewing, knitting, cooking, nutrition, minor repairs of the house, motherhood, child care, etc.

(c) *Girls Who Never Attended Schools*

(ix) For the non-student girls in this age group, the objective should be to provide adequate preparation in life through a combined three-year course in general education and vocational training. Vocational training should be on the lines of pre-vocational training mentioned above.

(x) Such training programmes should be extended to all girls in the rural areas. In the urban areas, preference should be given to girls in slum areas and destitute girls.

Education for Girls in the Age Group 14-17 Years

Girls in this age group also can be classified into three groups:

(a) Girl students with motivation to attend secondary schools
(b) Girl drop-outs from classes VI to VIII
(c) Non-student girls, i.e., students who never attended schools

Girl Students

The action plans under this category should emphasize more on:

(i) facilitating more girls to pursue education at the secondary stage, and
(ii) strengthening the content in terms of both life and work relevance.

The following action plans are suggested:

Administrative and Structural Measures

(i) Separate girls' schools or separate sections should be started where the social/cultural environment demands them.

(ii) In co-educational schools special attention should be given to the provision of adequate toilet, rest and recreation facilities, separately for girls.

(iii) State Governments which have not yet made high school education free for girls should do so on a priority basis.

(iv) Multiple entry system and part-time education may be provided.

Promotional and Motivational Measures

(v) All courses of training in vocational and technical schools at the secondary stage should be open to both boys and girls. There should be no discrimination in this regard.

(vi) Liberal incentives in the form of book allowances, book-bank facilities, etc., should be extended to encourage more girls in rural areas and backward areas to pursue secondary education.

(vii) Separate hostel facilities should be provided particularly in rural areas and residential scholarships should be offered.

Pedagogical Measures

(viii) The curriculum should be more diversified taking into consideration the various occupational opportunities available to women and the interests and aptitudes of girls.

Girl Drop-outs

Alternative Measures

(ix) Condensed courses of education started in 1958 were found very useful. Under this scheme women in the age group 13-30 years who have had some schooling are prepared for middle school, matriculation or equivalent examination within a period of 2 years' duration. The minimum age limit here should be reduced to 15 years. This scheme should be extended to cover all rural areas and weaker sections of the urban community.

(x) The condensed courses should be organized for smaller groups, say 5 to 7 persons, using the community resources like girls' high schools and girls' colleges.

(xi) Apart from imparting general education, condensed courses should also aim at imparting job-oriented training with the active cooperation of existing vocational training institutions.

(xii) Correspondence courses and self-study programmes may be introduced.

(xiii) Efforts should be made to cover at least about 215 lakh of girls in the age group 15-30 under the condensed courses programme during the Fifth Plan period.

(c) *Non-student Girls*

(xiv) Fourth Plan introduced a programme of functional literacy with the objective of imparting elementary general education and vocational training — related to the functions performed — to men and women in the rural areas who never attended schools. This programme should be expanded to cover all rural areas.

(xv) Apart from imparting general elementary education and knowledge about farming techniques, the curriculum for women should include courses of training in occupational skills like kitchen, gardening, food processing, poultry keeping, animal husbandry: household arts like cooking, nutritional values of foods, locally available, sewing, knitting, etc., and motherhood, childcare and family planning as also electronics and such like fields.

(xvi) Similar programmes should also be designed for girls — in this age group and under this category — belonging to urban areas.

Education for Girls in the Age Group 17 Years and Above

Education for girls in this age group also can be divided into three groups, as in the case of other age groups:

(a) Education for girls at the higher education stage.
(b) Education for girl drop-outs from the educational system beyond secondary stage.
(c) Education for non-student girls — girls who never had any education.

In respect of the last category here, i.e., education for non-student girls, action plans are the same as those concerning non-student girls in this age group 14-17 years. Hence, this category is not dealt with separately here.

(a) *Education for Girls at the Higher Education Stage*

Action plans in this area should aim at-

(a) making higher education available to the less privileged sections of the society, particularly girls from the rural areas; and

(b) making the curriculum more relevant and responsive to the cultural and occupational needs of women.

The following action plans may be taken up for consideration:

Administrative and Structural Measures

(i) The general policy here should be to discourage separate institutions for women and to promote co-educational facilities. However, in areas where separate institutions are required to promote education of women, they may be permitted on the merits of such cases.

(ii) Vocational counselling and guidance services should be organized in a more meaningful way to help girls — in colleges and universities — opt for suitable courses relevant to their talent, interests and needs.

Promotional and Motivational Measures

(iii) Incentives like scholarships, freeships, etc., should be provided to enable girls from rural areas to pursue higher education.

(iv) For girls belonging to weaker sections, in addition to freeships and scholarships, bursaries should also be provided-to meet their expenses on food and lodging.

(v) Provision of self-cooking facilities in hostels for girls should also be considered.

(vi) Girls pursuing higher education should be provided easy access to text books and other reference material through book bank facilities.

(vii) Girls should be encouraged to enter professional courses. If necessary, reservation of seats for girls in professional courses may be considered.

Pedagogical Measures

(viii) Diversification of courses at the junior college level and undergraduate level should be undertaken on a priority basis, with a view to preparing the girls for the various employment opportunities open to them.

(b) *Education for Girls Drop-outs*

Girls in this age group drop-out of educational system for various reasons. Marriage is one of the reasons which force girls in this age group to discontinue further formal education. Economic hardship is another reason which forces some girls to drop out and seek jobs, with a view to supporting their families. Social prejudices and cultural attitudes also force some of the girls to leave the formal educational system. For girls in this category, therefore, the policy should be to extend non-formal educational facilities on a large scale.

The following actions are suggested:

(i) Facilities for part-time self-study and correspondence courses should be expanded on a large scale to enable working girls and non-working — married and unmarried — girls to enhance their educational qualifications.

(ii) In addition to courses leading to degree / diploma, short courses in specific subjects through summer schools/session, ad hoc programmes like seminars, laboratory work, workshop experience, etc., should be organized for working girls, with a view to upgrading their professional skills and qualifications. Facilities for further education not necessarily leading to a degree, but for upgradation of knowledge and skills could be provided.

(iii) While the initiative for organizing such programmes should be taken by the Central and State Governments, the employees should also be increasingly involved.

(iv) Pre-examination training facilities should be organized on a large scale for educated women from the rural areas and those belonging to weaker sections with the objective of equipping them to successfully compete in examination for public jobs.

(v) Entrepreneurship development programmes should be

organized separately for educated women in the age group 18-30 years with a minimum of matriculation level of education. The objective of such training programmes should be:

(a) to make them aware of the various opportunities for self-employment;
(b) to motivate them to take up self-employment;
(c) to impart needed skills/training; and
(d) to promote achievement motivating among them.

Administrative Measures

To make the various action plans successful and to achieve a real breakthrough in women's education, there is need for a matching and effective administrative set up, both at the Central and State Levels. With this in view, the following suggestions are made:

(i) In the Union Ministry of Education and Social Welfare, a special unit/cell may be set up to be in charge of women's education, to review and initiate follow-up action.
(ii) In each State education department, a senior officer should be placed in charge of girls' education in order that it may receive adequate emphasis, execution and coordination.
(iii) As the district is the operational unit for all educational programmes and as the needs of girls vary in extent and kind from area to area, within a district, a separate cell for girls' education — formal and non-formal — may be created within the purview of the district educational officer at the district headquarters.
(iv) School supervisory system should be staffed with more women.
(v) A suitable machinery may be set up at the Centre and the States to help in the formulation of plans for women's education — formal and non-formal — to monitor, coordinate and evaluate progress of women's education from time to time, to create public opinion in favour of women's education etc.

Two

Educational Development

Emphasis on different arguments justifying the value and necessity of education from the point of view of the individual as well as society has varied according to the historical needs of any society in different stages of its evolution. The first argument regards education as a value in itself, since it develops the personality and the rationality of individuals. The assumption here is that society, recognizing the innate value of rationality and learning, accords a high status to the educated. The second argument emphasizes the usefulness of educated persons to society at large. Their knowledge, by serving a social purpose, raises their status in society. From the point of view of the individual, education provides the necessary qualification to fulfil certain economic, political and cultural functions and consequently improves his socio-economic status.

With the recognition of the need to direct the process of social change and development towards certain desired goals, education has come to be increasingly regarded as a major instrument of social change. According to the *Education and National Development* Report of the Indian Education Commission:

> The realization of the country's aspirations involves changes in the knowledge, skills, interests and values of the people as a whole. This is basic to every programme of social and economic betterment of which India stands in need .... If this 'change on a grand scale' is to be achieved without violent revolution (and even for that it would be necessary) there is one instrument, and one instrument only, that can be used: Education.

One of the expectations from this directed use of education is that it will bring about reduction of inequalities in society, on the assumption that education leads to equalization of status between individuals coming from hitherto unequal socio-economic strata of society. It was on this argument that the Universal Declaration of Human Rights included education as one of the basic rights of every human being. The Constitution of the UNESCO directs its effort to achieve 'the ideal of equality of educational opportunity without regard to race, sex or any distinctions, economic or social'.

Education and Women's Status — The 19th Century View

The history of the movement for improving women's status all over the world shows emphasis from the beginning on education as the most significant instrument for changing women's subjugated position in society. Increase of educational facilities and opportunities, and the removal of traditional bars on entry of women to particular branches and levels of education, came to be supported by all champions of women's emancipation from the 19th century onwards. Social reformers in India, whether they were modernizing liberals or revivalists also emphasized the crucial importance of education of women to improve their status in society.

However, when we look into their justification for this departure from the tradition then prevalent in the country, we notice certain significant omissions. According to the reformers, the main purpose for educating women was not to make them more efficient and active units in the processes of socio-economic or political development, but to make them more capable of fulfilling their traditional roles in society as wives and mothers. The opposition of the orthodox conservatives was countered by the argument that women's education would strengthen the bonds of tradition and the family as the chief unit of social organization. In their view, the denial of education and early marriage prevented the development of the personality and rationality of women. Stunted and crippled personalities affected the harmony of the family atmosphere, weakening the bonds of the family. Education for women was regarded as a means to improve their status within the family, and not to equip them to play any role in the wider social context. The absence of any economic compulsion was, in fact, the main reason for the slow progress of women's education in this country.

Because of their reluctance to interfere in social matters, the colonial authorities generally supported this purely humanitarian and limited view of women's education. The problem of reaching education and health services to the women of this country led to a realization of the need for women teachers and doctors. Since this was impossible without training women in these professions the importance of these two vocations outside the familiar roles had to be incorporated in the programmes for women's education.

Post Independence Era — New Roles and Rights

In the discussions on women's education in the post-independence era, a new dimension appeared due to the acceptance of equality of women and their need to play multiple roles in society. According to the First Five-Year Plan (1951) :

> The general purpose and objective of women's education cannot, of course be different from the purpose and objective of men's education.... At the Secondary and even at the University stage women's education should have a vocational or occupational bias.

According to Report of the Secondary Edducation Commission, Government of India, 1953:

> In a democratic society where all citizens have to discharge their civic and social obligations, differences which may lead to variation in the standard of intellectual development achieved by boys and girls cannot be envisaged.

Report of the Committee on differentiation of Curricula for boys and girls :

> In the progressive society of tomorrow, life should be a joint venture for men and women. Men should share the responsibility of parenthood and home-making with women and women in their turn should share the social and economic responsibilities of men.

The emphasis on education equipping women to carry out their multiple roles as citizens, housewives, mothers, contributors to the family income and builders of the new society is consistent with the trend of discussions in international agencies on women's education as a basic ingredient for improvement of their status.

Traces of Ambivalence between old and new views

In spite of the growing recognition of importance of women's education, traces of the earlier view which supported it mainly as an equipment for their roles as wives and mothers without conceding any position of equality with men in other spheres of life, can still be found not only in the opinions of individuals, but even in the statements of official agencies. According to the Report of the University Education Commission (1949) :

> Women's and men's education should have many elements in common, but should not in general be identical in all respects, as is usually the case today. A woman should learn something of problems that are certain to come up in all marriages, and in the relations of parents and children, and how they may be met. Her education should make her familiar with problems of home management and skilled in meeting them, so that she may take her place in a home with the same interest and the same sense of competence that a well trained man has in working at his calling.

An understanding of this ambivalence between the traditional and the new attitudes on women's education is essential for examining the progress of women's education in this country, because it has an impact on academic planning, allocation of resources and development of values in society for both men and women. It lies at the root of all discussions regarding differentiation of curricula between the two sexes and continues to affect social attitudes regarding women's education, its social use and women's roles in society. This in turn has an impact on the class composition of women who are recipients of education. The achievements or the failures in the use of this instrument for transforming women's status have to be measured by these social indicators as well as quantitative ones like enrolment out-turn, number of institutions and teachers, literacy rates and total stock of educated women at different levels and in the light of the stated national objectives. According to the National Policy on Education (1967) :

> The educational system must produce young men and women of character and ability committed to national service and development. Only then will education be able to play its vital role in promoting national progress, creating a sense of common citizenship and culture and strengthening national integration.

Progress of Women's Education in India: The Formal Education System

The Constitution of the Republic of India guarantees equality of opportunity to all citizens irrespective of race, sex, caste and communities and directs the States to "Endeavour to provide within a period of ten years from the commencement of this Constitution for free and compulsory education for all children until they complete the age of 14 years". The Indian Education Commission in its Report (1966) regretted the failure to achieve this target. It emphasized the crucial importance of fulfilling this directive in the coming decades. In view of the immense resources needed for this purpose, the Commission recommended phasing of this programme in the following manner :

(i) by providing five years of effective education to all children by 1975-76 and seven years of such education by 1985-86;

(ii) by making part-time education for about one year compulsory for all children in the age group 11-14, who have not completed the lower primary stage and are not attending schools. The aim, will be to make these children functionally literate and stop all further additions to the ranks of adult non-literates; and

(iii) by efforts to liquidate adult illiteracy.

The following review will indicate that even the targets recommended by the Education Commission have not been achieved, particularly in the case of women. The enrolment targets set for the Third Plan by the National Committee on Women's Education (1959) were equal numbers with boys in the age group 6-11, at least half that of the boys in the age group 11-14 and least one-third that of boys in the age group 14-17. As indicated in Table 1.1 the targets for the age groups 6-11 and 11-14 have not been reached even at the end of the Fourth Plan. The expected proportion of one-third in the age group 14-17 set for the Third Plan has however been exceeded slightly by the end of the Fourth Plan. The Fifth Five-Year Plan notes that in spite of substantial progress in the expansion of educational facilities, the targets laid down for both elementary and secondary education registered a shortfall in enrolment, while those in higher education were exceeded. "But shortfalls have been particularly large in the case of elementary education, more so in the case of girls.

Educational experts now admit that the delay in the achievement of the Constitutional directive is mainly due to the slow progress of education among girls, Scheduled Castes and Scheduled Tribes. The discrepancy in the progress of education between boys and girls may be seen in the marked difference in the percentage of boys and girls of the corresponding age groups enrolled in primary, middle and secondary schools.

Development in the Pre-Independence Period

The foundations of the formal system of education, sponsored and supported by the State, and divided into three well-defined stages (primary, secondary and university) and two main streams (general and vocational) were laid during the first half of the nineteenth century. It was created essentially for men with the ultimate objective of utilizing them as government servants. In the initial years girls had little or no access to it, partly because society at that time could not imagine them as government servants. However, as the formal system of education began to spread, the role of education as a liberating influence came to be recognized and increasingly accepted. Thus began the advocacy of the access of girls and women to the formal system of education spearheaded by national leaders, missionaries and a few enlightened officials. It received little response. Only a few thousand girls, mostly belonging to urban upper and middle-class families entered, the formal system of education between 1850 and 1870. As women teachers became available and social forces like: a rise in the age of marriage, urbanization and the demand for educated wives began to gather momentum during the last hundred years, this movement steadily grew and today the total enrolment of girls in the formal system of education at all stages and in all streams, is more than thirty-two million.

The movement naturally began in the cities, and then spread to the towns and villages. It began among the Christians, Anglo-Indians, Parsees and upper caste Hindus. Wealth played an ambivalent role; while middle-class families were generally more favourable to the education of girls, some of the richer and more aristocratic families remained aloof and do so even today.

The mass awakening during the freedom movement, and the role that women played in the struggle had a great impact on women's education, and it began to increase at a much faster pace. In 1854, the total enrolment of girls in the formal system was only about 1,97,000 all in primary schools. But over the following nine decades, it grew significantly as indicated in Table 2.1.

TABLE - 2.1

EDUCATION OF GIRLS AND WOMEN IN PRE-INDEPENDENCE PERIOD

		Enrolment of girls in				
Year	*Percentage of Literacy for Women*	*Primary Schools*	*Secondary Schools*	*Colleges & Universities*	*Other Institutions*	*Total*
(1)	(2)	(3)	(4)	(5)	(6)	(7)
1881-82	0.2	124,291	2,054	6	515	127,066
1901-02	0.7	344,712	9,075	256	2,370	365,413
1921-22	1.8	1186,224	26,163	905	10,836	1224,128
1946-47	6.0	3475,165	602,280*	23,207	56,090	4156,742
No. of girls enrolled per 100 boys		36	22 for middle schools 14 for secondary schools	12 for general education 7 for vocational education	12	30

* This includes 3,21,508 girls enrolled in middle schools The enrolment in secondary schools proper is thus only 2,80,772.

Source: Ministry of Education, Government of India.

The expansion of women's education began at the primary stage and was mostly confined to it for quite some years. In 1947, 83 per cent of all girls enrolled were in primary schools (about half of them in class I only). Expansion at the secondary stage was slow to start and slow to spread. In 1947, only 7 per cent of the girls enrolled were in secondary school. However, contrary to what happened in Western countries, the admission of women to Indian universities presented no problem. Calcutta University permitted women candidates to appear for the Entrance and B.A. examination as early as 1877 and 1878 respectively. Bombay University followed in 1883. The first two women graduates of Calcutta received their degrees in 1883, the year of the University Silver Jubilee. Congratulating them and the University for 'this memorable event', the Vice-Chancellor described it as a paving stone to "A general recognition of the right of the women of this country to education, and of the duty of the men of this country to provide it from them." Even with the removal of the ban, the spread of higher education among women remained slow. In 1947 the total enrolment in higher education was only about 23,000 which was 1/2 per cent of all girls enrolled in the educational system.

Development in the Post-Independence Period

Since independence, the education of women at various levels has expanded more rapidly, but is still far from satisfactory (Table 2.2).

TABLE - 2.2
EDUCATION OF GIRLS AND WOMEN IN THE POST-INDEPENDENCE PERIOD

Year	*Enrolment of Girls in*			
	Primary School Classes (I-V)	*Middle School Classes (VI-VIII)*	*Secondary School Classes (IX-XI)*	*Colleges and Universities (General Education)*
1946-47	34.75 (36)	3.22 (22)	2.81 (14)	0.20 (12)
1950-51	53.85 (39)	5.34 (20)	1.61 (15)	0.40 (14)
1955-56	76.39 (44)	8.67 (25)	3.18 (21)	0.84 (17)
1960-61	113.47 (48)	16.70 (32)	5.41 (23)	1.50 (22)
1965-66	182.93 (57)	28.46 (37)	11.72 (30)	3.24 (28)
1968-69	199.36 (59)	34.93 (39)	15.60 (32)	4.32 (30)
1973-74	244.01 (62)	45.37 (43)	23.40 (36)	9.00 (31)
(Estimated) 1978-79 (Projected Target)	318.90 (69)	72.50 (51)	31.70 (39)	16.00 (34)

Notes: (1) The statistics of 1946-47 refer to enrolments in primary, middle and secondary schools and not in classes I-V, VI-VIII and IX-XI and hence are not strictly comparable. The comparable figures would more probably be 36.8 lakh at the primary stage, 3.2 lakh at the middle stage and 0.8 lakh at the secondary stage.

(2) Figures in parentheses indicate the number of girls for every 100 boys enrolled.

(3) Figures in the last column relate to enrolment at undergraduate, post graduate and research stages in general education — arts, science and commerce courses.

Sources: (1) Figures for school enrolment in 1950-51, 1960-61, 1965-66, 1968-69 are from Ministry of Education, Form A.

(2) Figures for school enrolment in 1973-74 and 1978-79 (target) are from 'Draft Fifth Five Year Plan, 1974-79, Vol. II, p. 197.

(3) Figures of enrolment in colleges and universities are taken from Ministry of Education, Form A, for all years up to 1968-69.

Differences in the Enrolment of Boys and Girls

During the year of independence, i.e., 1947-48, the total number of boys enrolled at various levels of the educational system was 1,11,34,665 while the girls were only 35,50,503 indicating an excess of 75,84,162 boys over girls. Table 2.3 indicates the relative expansion in the enrolment of boys and girls at all levels of the educational system.

TABLE - 2.3

TOTAL ENROLMENT IN THE EDUCATIONAL SYSTEM ALL LEVELS

Year	*Boys*	*Girls*	*Excess of boys over girls*
1950-51	1,91,42,009	64,00,763 (33)	1,27,41,246
1960-61	3,37,04,897	1,42,59,505 (42)	1,94,45,392
1970-71	5,57,12,623	3,00,30,484 (54)	2,56,82,139

(Figures within parentheses indicate the number of girls enrolled per 100 boys.

TABLE - 2.4

PERCENTAGE DISTRIBUTION OF BOYS AND GIRLS IN DIFFERENT STAGES OF THE EDUCATIONAL SYSTEM

Year	*Pre-primary*	*Primary*	*Secondary**	*University*	*Professional schools*	*Total*
1950-51						
Boys	0.1	70.0	20.9	2.0	7.0	100.0
Girls	0.2	82.4	12.7	0.6	4.1	100.0
1960-61						
Boys	0.3	67.3	24.7	2.7	5.0	100.0
Girls	0.6	76.7	18.4	1.3	3.0	100.0
1970-71						
Boys	0.3	66.3	26.4	4.5	2.5	100.0
Girls	0.5	74.3	19.5	2.4	3.3	100.0

* (Secondary includes middle, high and higher secondary)

As already indicated in Tables 1.2 and 1.3, the percentage of enrolment to the population in the corresponding group also shows a marked difference between boys and girls in all these years. Table 2.4 indicates the percentage distribution of boys and girls in different stages of education.

Present Position

In classes I-V, the total enrolment is 244 lakh or 66 per cent of the total population in the age group 6-11. One girl out of every three is thus still out of school. What is worse, the drop-out rates are very high : of every 100 girls enrolled in class I, only about 30 reach class V. Classes VI-VIII, the total enrolment is 45.37 lakh or only 22 per cent of the total population in the age group 11-14. Only one girl out of 5 is at school in this age group. As universal education in the age group 6-14 is the national objective, it is obvious that considerable headway is still to be made in the expansion of education for the age group 6-11 and especially for the age group 11-14.

The enrolment of girls at the secondary stage at present is 23.4 lakh or 12 per cent of the total population in the age group 14-17 (as against 31 per cent for boys) (Table 2.5). The proportion of girls enrolled now drops down to 1 in 8. Secondary education, even now, is largely confined to the upper and the middle classes, urban areas. In the rural areas, it mainly utilized well-to do families, particularly from the middle-classes.

TABLE - 2.5
PERCENTAGE DISTRIBUTION OF ENROLMENT OF BOYS AND GIRLS IN SECONDARY SECTIONS

	Percentages enrolment of		
Areas	*Boys*	*Girls*	*Total*
Rural	83.42	16.58	100.00
Urban	71.31	28.69	100.00
Total	76.64	23.36	100.00

Source: Second All-India Educational Survey — National Council of Educational Research and Training, 1967, p. 62.

At the university stage, the total enrolment in general education, i.e., in Sciences, Humanities and Social Science is about 9 lakh or about 1.3 per cent of the age group 17-23 (about 31 girls for every 100 boys enrolled). A stagewise analysis, however, shows that the proportion of women to men is higher at the postgraduate than at the undergraduate level and is showing a rapid increase. In professional education, women have substantial enrolments in teaching, medicine, and fine arts; but their enrolment in other courses like commerce, law, agriculture or engineering is still very small. Higher education is mostly confined, even more than secondary education, to urban upper and middle-classes. Tables 2.6 and 2.7 give the position of enrolment of Women in University Education between 1950-51 to 1970-71.

TABLE - 2.6
ENROLMENT OF WOMEN IN UNIVERSITY EDUCATION
(ALL LEVELS INCLUDED) - (FACULTY-WISE) (U.P. BOARD INCLUDED)

Faculty	*1950-51*			*1960-61*			*1970-71*		
	Total	*Women*	*No. of Women per 100 Men*	*Total (T)*	*Women (W)*	*No. of Women per 100 Men*	*Total*	*Women*	*No. of Women per 100 Men*
Arts	1,82,005	29,262	16.1	4,86,228	1,19,687	24.6	13,29,626	4,21,850	31.7
Science	1,27,168	9,046	7.1	3,02,700	31,696	10.5	9,48,009	1,68,540	17.8
Commerce	34,067	189	0.6	90,214	831	0.9	3,44,108	12,675	3.7
Education	4,135	1,339	32.4	19,005	6,230	32.8	56,922	20,799	36.5
Eng/Tech.	12,094	19	0.16	45,389	403	0.89	90,034	910	1.0
Medicine	15,260	2,493	16.3	35,215	7,714	21.9	97,601	22,296	22.8
Agriculture	4,744	8	0.17	27,584	124	0.45	43,352	169	0.4
Veterinary Science	1,101	5	0.45	5,385	38	0.71	6,222	44	0.7
Law	13,649	290	2.1	27,251	815	3.0	70,618	2,626	3.7
Others	2,522	475	18.8	10,893	2,917	26.8	14,800	5,913	40.0
All faculties	3,96,745	43,126	10.9	10,49,864	17,0455	16.2	30,01,292	6,55,822	21.9

Source: 1950-51 and 1960-61, Ministry of Education and Social Welfare U.G.C.

TABLE - 2.7

ENROLMENT FOR UNIVERSITY EDUCATION (ALL FACULTIES INCLUSIVE) STAGEWISE (U.P. BOARD INCLUDED)

Stage	*Undergraduate*			*Postgraduate*			*Research*			*All levels*		
Year	*Women (T)*	*Wx 100 (W)*	*Total T*	*Women (T)*	*Wx 100 (W)*	*Total T*	*Women (T)*	*Wx 100 (W)*	*Total T*	*Women (T)*	*Wx 100 (W)*	*Total T*
1950-51	375,319	40,499	10.8	19,922	2,425	12.1	1,434	202	14.1	396,745	32,126	10.9
1960-61	985,872	159,491	16.2	58,909	10,170	17.3	5,083	794	15.6	1049,864	179,455	16.2
1970-71	2826,799	611,553	21.6	161,182	41,516	25.8	13,311	2,753	20.7	3001,292	655,822	21.9

* includes P, UC, PP, C.

£ Included the Research enrolment of Commerce, Education, Engg/Tech. and Medicines.

Source: 1950-51 and 1960-61—Education in Universities in India-Annual Publication of the Union Ministry of Education and Social Welfare.
1970-71— University Development in India - Basic Facts and Figures - U.G.C., - Annual Publication.

TABLE - 2.8

QUINQUENNIAL GROWTH IN ENROLMENT BY STAGE EDUCATION - 1960-61 TO 1970-71

Stage	*1960-61 to 1965-66 Quinquennial Growth Rate*			*1965-66 to 1970-71 (75) Quinquennial Growth Rate*		
	Boys	*Girls*	*Total*	*Boys*	*Girls*	*Total*
Pre-Primary	45.0%	43.9%	47.0%	29.9%	19.0%	24.8%
Primary	34.9%	56.1%	41.8%	20.6%	30.7%	24.2%
Secondary	49.7%	70.6%	54.7%	18.2%	30.5%	21.5%
University	76.3%	119.4%	83.5%	57.3%	78.4%	61.5%
Professional and special school	16.5%	74.6%	1.6%	3.9%	34.6%	9.3%
All Stages	37.1%	60.1%	44.0%	20.5%	31.5%	24.2%

The National Committee on Women's Education had reviewed the progress of women's education before, during and after independence and concluded that in spite of the direct action taken by the States for this purpose after independence, "the education of women has not made satisfactory progress between 1947 and 1957. Even today there is a very wide disparity between the education of men and that of women and only 36 girls are under instruction for every hundred boys at schools. The targets fixed for the First and Second Plans even tend to widen this disparity and the education of women has made very slow progress in rural areas where it is needed most."

The Committee had, therefore, strongly recommended "that the education of women should be regarded as a major and a special problem in education for a good many years to come and that a bold and determined effort be made to face its difficulties and magnitude and to close the existing gap between the education of men and women in as short a time as possible; that the highest priority should be given to schemes prepared from this point of view; and the funds required for the purpose should be considered to be the first change on the sums set aside for the development of education." Following this recommendation, efforts to bridge the gap between boys and girls in education were stepped up from 1960. The growth rate of boys and girls enrolment at different levels in the next quinquennium again indicates slackening of the efforts.

It is to be noted that the rate of growth is much higher in the university and the vocational stages than in the primary and secondary stages. Interpreted in the context of Indian social conditions, this indicates that the expansion of women's education is much faster when the beneficiaries are from the urban middle class (Table 2.8).

Enrolment as an Index of Educational Advance: Problems of Retention, Wastage and Stagnation

While educational statistics have always tended to use enrolments as the main indicator of measuring progress, in the Committee's experience this suffers from certain limitations. Since the quantum of grants for all educational institutions is linked to enrolment figures, there is an inevitable tendency to attach undue importance to mere enrolment. These statistics do not, however, indicate whether all children on a school register in fact attend school even for a short time. As observed by the Education Commission "the task of universal education begins when children are enrolled in Class I. It is completed only when they are successfully retained till they complete class VIII".

The problem of drop-outs of enrolled children as well as the problem of stagnation have contributed to the unreliability of enrolment statistics as a valid measure of progress.

The National Committee on Women's Education, while admitting that these were general problems of the educational system, had indicated that the extent of wastage or drop-outs was much higher in the case of girls. The all-India average of drop-outs at the primary stage was 74 per cent for girls while that of boys was 62.4 per cent. The Education Commission reporting in 1966 found wastage at the lower primary stage to be 56 per cent for boys and 62 per cent for girls, about two-thirds of this wastage occurring in class I. At the higher primary stage wastage was 24 per cent for boys and 34 per cent for girls. A study conducted by the NCERT on the problem of wastage and stagnation in primary and middle schools also corroborates this finding. (Sharma and Sapra, 1971)

> The differences between the rate of wastage and stagnation for boys (62.30%) and girls (71.36%) are highly significant. The rate for boys is 37.59% between grades I and II, 10.53% between grades II and III, 7.14% between grades III and IV, and 7.04% between grades IV and V. For girls it is 42.85% between grades I and II, 12.12% between grades II and III, 8.51% between grades III and IV and 78.8% between grades IV and V. This indicates that except for grades I and II, the differences in the rates of wastages and stagnation for boys and girls in other grades are minor.

One of the causes for this large wastage in class I is the prevalent practice of enrolling children in class I throughout the year. In spite of repeated recommendations against this practice we regret to find it to be still prevalent in many States. For example, in Madhya Pradesh an enrolment drive was undertaken just 5 weeks before the end of the session.

The economic and educational causes of wastages and stagnation are well recognized. In case of girls, however, social factors like marriage, betrothal and parental apathy to girls education also play a major part. The National Committee on Women's Education has estimated that 25 to 30 per cent of cases of wastages among girls fell under this category. In our opinion the slow progress in enrolment and the high rate of dropouts and failures in the education of girls spring from the same reasons and ultimately affect the overall progress of women's education.

Out Turn

Turning from enrolment to the out turn of students from the schools and the university system we find that the progress is extremely slow. The significant features are the slower rate of increase in number of girls per 100 boys at the school final examinations, viz., Matriculation and Higher Secondary and the much faster rate of increase at the university stage, particularly in the first degree. This shows that the gap between men and women is narrowing more rapidly at the higher level than at the primary and secondary stages. Since higher education in India is still confined to a small minority of the population, the impact of this trend on the educational development of women as a whole cannot be described as high (Table 2.9).

In professional education, the only courses open to women before independence were medicine, education, nursing and law. Since very few women sought training in law, professional education for them was in fact confined to the first three. Admission to engineering and technology courses was thrown open to women only in 1948. Considering this late start, their success in these courses has been significant. Their representation in other professional fields, however, remains very slow. Similarly, women's entry into research is mainly a post independence development and the progress at this level is satisfactory. The earlier wide-spread belief that girl's had less aptitude and even intelligence than boys for pursuit of studies, particularly in subjects like Mathematics or Science, has been completely disapproved by their success at various examinations. At the university level in particular, the performance of girls in all subjects including Science and Mathematics has often outstripped that of boys. A general opinion of faculty members is that the average girl student is more conscientious and disciplined than the average male student. Table 2.10 gives the total number of

TABLE - 2.9
OUT TURN OF STUDENTS AT DIFFERENT STAGES OF THE EDUCATIONAL SYSTEM

Examination	*Matriculation and Equivalent*			*Higher Secondary and Equivalent*			*Pre-University*			*Intermediate*		
Year	*Boys*	*Girls*	*No. of Gs/100 Boys*	*Boys*	*Girls*	*No. of Gs/100 Boys*	*Boys*	*Girls*	*No. of Gs/100 Boys*	*Boys*	*Girls*	*No. of Gs/100 Boys*
1947-48	126885	15391	12	-	-	-	-	-	-	30898	4680	15
1950-51	210995	30148	14	-	-	-	-	-	-	63168	9517	15
1955-56	357166	72328	20	-	-	-	-	-	-	111818	19921	18
1960-61	452153	113966	25	46707	10290	22	71824	20650	29	92838	22893	25
1965-66	645552	202711	31	167852	39318	23	113094	39783	35	52306	16255	31

Examination	*B.A./B.Sc. Pass Hons.*			*M.A./M.Sc.*			*Doctorates Genl. and Professional Subjects*			*Professional Degrees and Equivalent Diploma only*		
Year	*Boys*	*Girls*	*No. of Gs/100 Boys*	*Boys*	*Girls*	*No. of Gs/100 Boys*	*Boys*	*Girls*	*No. of Gs/100 Boys*	*Boys*	*Girls*	*No. of Gs/100 Boys*
1947-48	15719	2867	18	3190	444	14	102	4	4	10173 (Break up is unavailable)	-	-
1950-51	27357	4881	18	6262	876	14	136	10	7	17892	1553	9
1955-56	44041	9948	23	9603	2166	23	321	29	9	31951	3821	12
1960-61	70757	22295	32	18570	5115	28	959	283	3	53045	7179	14
1965-66	89865	38589	43	25959	9628	37	808	99	16	67546	10721	16

educated persons by sex and levels according to cencus of 1971. Table 2.11 gives the total number of degree holders and technical personnel by sex according to Census of 1971.

TABLE - 2.10

ESTIMATED TOTAL STOCK OF EDUCATED PERSONS BY SEX & LEVELS

(Figures in Hundreds)

	Males	*Percentage of Total Male Population*	*Females*	*Percentage of Total Female Population*
Primary	334,989	11.9	165,115	6.3
Middle	207,089	7.3	76,930	2.9
Matriculation or Higher Secondary	134,733	4.8	37,365	1.4
Non-technical Diploma or Certificate	1,388	0.04	455	0.01
Technical Diploma or Certificate	3,048	0.1	1020	0.0003
Graduate	28,212	1.0	6,931	0.3

Source: Census of India 1971, Part II, Special-estimated from 1% sample data, p. 121.
Note: Percentages calculated.

TABLE - 2.11

DEGREE HOLDERS AND TECHNICAL PERSONNEL IN EACH SUBJECT FIELD, 1971

	Subject Field	*Persons*	*Males*	*Females*
	Total	2,191,300	1,782,300	4,09,000
1.	Arts/Humanities	1,139,900	8,43,800	2,96,100
2.	Commerce	172,000	1,68,100	3,900
3.	Agriculture	39,600	39,200	400
4.	Veterinary Science/Medicine	11,000	10,800	200
5.	Science	4,50,400	3,68,600	81,800
6.	Engineering & Technology	2,49,700	2,462,00	3,500
7.	Medicine (Allopathy)	68,400	55,100	13,300
8.	Medicine (Others)	23,200	20,400	2,800
9.	Nursing*	3,800	400	3,400
10.	Technical/Vocational trade	19,700	18,500	1,200
11.	Others	13,600	11,200	2,400

Source: Country Statement - India -Submitted to World Population Conference, Bucharest (Romania) 19-30 August 1974.

Note: During the 1971 Census, a schedule was distributed among degree holders and technical personnel for being filled by them and return to the census enumerators/census office. The above table is based on filled-in schedules received back.

* The degree course in nursing has started only recently, but, according to the draft Fifth Year Plan, the number of nurses by the end of 1973-74 is likely to be 88,000.

Growth of Institutions

The National Committee on Women's education had felt that provision of separate institutions of girls would help to break down the prejudice against their education, and provide more impetus to the spread of education among women. There is no doubt that in the period since 1960-61 there has been an enormous expansion in the number of these exclusive institutions. In 1947-48, institutions meant exclusively for women constituted only 10.3 per cent by 1967-68 they formed 29 per cent of the total. Out of the total number of educational institutions established during this 20-year period, slightly more than half came up between 1960-61 and 1967-68. In the case of institutions exclusively meant for women, however, more than three-fourths of the increase took place between 1960-61 and 1967-68 (Table 2.12).

TABLE - 2.12
GROWTH OF EDUCATIONAL INSTITUTIONS

Year	*Educational Institutions*		
	Total Number of Institutions	*Number of Institutions Exclusively for Girls*	*Percentage of Col. (3) to Col. (2)*
1	2	3	4
1947-48	1,64,553	16,951	10.3
1950-51	2,86,860	24,829	8.7
1955-56	3,66,641	24,873	6.8
1960-61	4,72,655	41,674	8.8
1961-62	6,85,602	1,16,150	16.9
1962-63	7,26,632	1,42,572	19.6
1963-64	6,91,986	1,22,784	17.7
1964-65	7,53,418	1,44,069	19.1
1965-66	7,27,262	1,81,238	24.2
1966-67	7,58,790	2,10,291	27.7
1967-68	7,93,799	2,30,032	29.0

Source: Ministry of Education.

While we welcome the growth of institutional facilities for the spread of education among women, we would like to point out certain adverse features of this rapid growth that have been brought to our notice. At the primary level, a large number of these schools are single teacher institutions, with obvious limitations on their teaching capacity. One of the reasons mentioned to us for low enrolment and high dropouts of girls was the wide prevalence of single teacher schools which frequently have to close due to the absence of the teacher. The problems become more acute when the teacher is on maternity leave, since provision of a substitute is tardy or absent.

At the middle and the secondary levels, there is frequent criticism of the low standard of teaching facilities, particularly for subjects like science and mathematics. The students' choice of subjects is very often determined, not by their aptitudes, but by institutional limitations.

At the college level the expansion has been most rapid, from 81 women's colleges in 1953-54 to 435 in 1971-72. 250 of these colleges, however, have an enrolment of less than 500 (55 have less than 100), which makes them non-viable from the point of view of resources, both financially and academically.

One of the results of the policy to encourage establishment of women's institutions has been relative lack of vigilance by the public and academic authorities regarding standards of these institutions. Eligibility conditions for recognition or for financial assistance through grants-in-aid have frequently been relaxed or waived altogether.

In our opinion the spread of substandard or limited education will not help the achievement of equality of opportunities, and may in the long run damage the cause of girls education. Vigilance regarding standards is imperative, particularly at the higher levels of the educational system and must form a part of the policy of encouragement and assistance.

Women Teachers

The need to increase the number of women teachers as an essential condition for the development of women's education has been long recognized in India. In recent years, this has been emphasized even more by the National Committee, the National Council for Women's Education and the Education Commission who recommended adequate provision for their training and recruitment. The Education Commission recommended that the employment of women teachers should be encouraged in all stages and all sections of education. In order to achieve this, the Commission suggested provisions of the following:

(a) opportunities for part-time employment on large scale;
(b) residential accommodation particularly in rural areas;

(c) special allowances for women teachers working in rural areas; and

(d) expansion of condensed courses for adult women and education through correspondence courses.

In 1947, 14.4 per cent of the school teachers in the country were women. In 1965-66, they formed 21.8 per cent. While the proportion of women teachers at different levels has increased very slowly as indicated in Tables 2.13 and 2.14, it may be noted that the percentage of trained teachers is higher among women than men.

TABLE - 2.13

NO. OF WOMEN TEACHERS EMPLOYED IN PRIMARY, MIDDLE AND SECONDARY SCHOOLS

Year	*Primary Schools*	*% Trained*	*Middle Schools*	*% Trained*	*Secondary Schools*	*% Trained*
1950-51	28,281 (18)	69.1	12,887 (18)	58.1	19,982 (19)	66.2
1955-56	1,17,067 (20)	73.7	23,844 (19)	63.2	35,085 (23)	72.9
1960-61	1,26,788 (21)	73.4	83,532 (32)	73.4	62,347 (22)	73.9
1965-66	1,80,315 (24)	73.1	1,38,539 (36)	79.0	1,10,703 (30)	76.3
1968-69	2,09,504 (26)	76.9	1,53,034 (36)	82.4	1,20,678 (30)	80.3
1973-74	2,50,000 (26)	77.0	1,99,000 (37)	83.0	1,50,000 (30)	81.0

Source: Ministry of Education, Form A, except for 1973-74 which are estimates.

Note: Figures in parentheses represent percentage of total teaching staff.

TABLE - 2.14

NUMBER OF WOMEN TEACHERS EMPLOYED IN COLLEGES AND UNIVERSITIES

Faculty	*No. of Women Teachers in Colleges and Universities*		
	1950-51	*1960-61*	*1970-71*
Arts	1,091 (11.4)	5,624 (14.9)	10,,136 (19.7)
Science	379 (6.3)	Included in Arts	5,381 (13.6)
Commerce	4 (0.4)	57 (2.1)	227 (3.2)
Education	130 (24.3)	448 (22.8)	924 (23.9)
Engg./Tech.	1 (neg.)	12 (0.3)	92 (1.2)
Medicine	173 (9.8)	731 (12.8)	2,236 (19.2)
Agriculture	1 (0.2)	21 (1.4)	49 (1.5)
Veterinary Science	12 (8.2)	11 (1.7)	18 (1.6)
Law	Nil	9 (1.2)	173 (10.8)
Others	24 (16.1)	10 (4.2)	154 (15.7)
All Faculties	1,815 (8.5)	6,923 (12.5)	19,390 (15.0)

Source: Ministry of Education and Social Welfare for 1950-51 and 1960-61 and University Grants Commission for 1970-71.

Note: Figures in parentheses represent percentage of total teaching staff.

Even in the States like Haryana, Punjab, Tamil Nadu where almost all the villages have been electrified and are connected to the cities by *pukka* roads, women teachers are still reluctant to serve in rural areas. The problem becomes more acute in States like Uttar Pradesh, Bihar, Madhya Pradesh, Rajasthan, Himachal Pradesh and Jammu & Kashmir where the villages are often situated in remote and inaccessible areas.

There is no public conveyance available and very often the villages can only be reached on horse back, by bullock cart or on foot. Some of the basic problems identified by women teachers, in almost all the states that the committee visited, are given below:

(a) Women teachers face a certain degree of resistance from their families to their working in rural areas, partly from the general apprehension against women working away from home and partly from a fear of personal insecurity in villages. This has been aggravated by the deteriorating law and order situation in villages. There is also a fear that rural society may be unfriendly and even antagonistic to outsiders. We would, however, like to mention that in some states we were told that rural society had now come to accept and even respect women teachers and doctors.

    Most of these attitudes are shared by thc teachers themselves. Added to them is another cause of resistance from the women, used to life in urban areas, that life in villages would be dull and unattractive.

(b) Apart from these factors, the lack of physical amenities like modern medical facilities, proper accommodation, toilets, transport and schooling for children are real difficulties that deter women from service in rural areas. Even when houses are provided, they are often outside the village, without any consideration for the problems of distance and insecurity that women have to face. If they are within the school, the teachers cannot bring their families. The problem of accommodation becomes still more acute with married women, if they have to work away from their husbands and families.

In our opinion these problems need to be solved on a priority basis in order to increase the supply of women teachers in rural schools. If this is not done, then the present imbalance in the development of women's education between urban and rural areas will increase. Added to this will be yet another imbalance, that of increasing unemployment among trained and qualified women teachers, whose reluctance to serve in rural areas prevents their employment. The beginnings of this imbalance are already noticeable in many States.

Inspection

The system of inspection of schools varies from State to State. The general complaint however, is that schools are not inspected regularly. In Himachal Pradesh a retired school teacher informed us that during her 24 years' service she had faced only three inspections. In some states like Uttar Pradesh and Bihar village schools to be inspected once a year are only those which are within easy reach. In most States all inspections cease during the rainy season.

There is an overall inadequacy of women on the inspecting staff. Insufficient numbers and over-large jurisdictions contribute to the general inefficiency of inspections. For women in particular, the problems of distance, and inadequate arrangement for transport and night halts create added difficulties. This leads sometimes to a reluctance to serve on the inspecting staff, and in the States where the grade of inspectors is the same as that of headmistress of a high school (e.g. Punjab), women members of the service prefer to remain as headmistresses. In Himachal Pradesh, we found that there was no women on the inspecting staff.

States like Himachal Pradesh and Madhya Pradesh do not have a separate women's cadre of inspectors, and girls schools are often inspected by male inspectors. In the case of single-teachers schools, this sometimes creates a problem. We received some complaints from teachers of misbehaviour, blackmail or exploitation on the part of inspectors.

Attitudes to the Education of Girls and Women

Social attitudes to the education of girls vary, ranging from acceptance of the need to one of absolute indifference. The Committee's survey reveals some interesting trends. A statement that girls should not be given any education received a categorical rejection by 77.8 per cent of the respondents. A small minority (16.8 per cent) did, however, agree with the view. In the case of higher education, however, we find a surprisingly hostile attitude since over 64.50 per cent responded that a girl should not be allowed to go for higher education even if she is very intelligent.

In view of the constitutional directive regarding free and compulsory education up to the age of 14, we tried to elicit public opinion on the question of making education compulsory. In response to our general questionnaire, 77.5 per cent of the respondents, male and female supported compulsory education for up to the 8th class. A separate questionnaire issued to educationists and administrators regarding measures necessary to improve girls' enrolment in schools also evoked a substantial support in favour of compulsion.

In urban areas, by and large, the acceptance of the need of education for girls is greater than in rural areas. Among the affluent there are two distinct attitudes. Some families are opposed to it for traditional reasons while others have welcomed it as an accomplishment and a symbol of modernization. Among the middle-classes the acceptance is the highest. The attitude among the lower-middle-class is more difficult to generalize because today's lower-middle-class consists of white collared as well as manual workers. Though economically one, socially they are two distinct classes, their attitudes being determined much more by their social background rather than their economic position. While an increasingly large section, conscious of economic necessity, is prepared to make substantial sacrifices for girls' education, a very large number still finds itself unable to do so for economic and social reasons. For the majority of the people who live below subsistence level, poverty is the predominant factor governing the attitude to girls' education.

Reasons for Slow Progress in Giirls' Education

Reasons for the variations in social attitudes and the consequent slow progress of women's education are both social and economic.

(a) Large majority of girls, by the time they reach the age of eight, are required to do various domestic chores, e.g., collecting firewood, coal waste, cow dung, fetching water, sometimes from long distances, washing, cleaning, cooking, reaching food and water to parents in their places of work, etc.

(b) Majority of girls of this age group have to look after the siblings, especially when their mothers are engaged in earning a livelihood.

(c) A substantial number of girls are engaged in contributing to the family income by their own labour. The prevalence of child labour has long been admitted as the greatest deterrent to the spread of education among children of the poor. The Committee was appalled by the extent and degree of use of young girls of five to fourteen working for twelve hours a day. One 12-year old girl in Andhra Pradesh informed us that she could not remember any other pattern of existence in her whole life. Similar is the case in fireworks, matches, weaving and many other industries, mostly in unorganized sector. A very large number of girls in this age group work as domestic servants — either as helpers or as independent earners. In Calcutta, we found one 12-year old supporting a family of six members by working in a number of houses as a part-time domestic servant. This was by no means an exceptional case. These girls are too exhausted at the end of their day's labour to attend evening classes even if they could be arranged.

In the agricultural sector, girls in the same age group do share the burden of field labour, but mostly in the peak seasons. Their hours of work being less, it is possible for them to attend school, if facilities were available. The school term should be adjusted according to the seasonal agricultural activities. It should be noted that the exclusion from education because of participation in labour is higher among girls than boys, as they constitute a higher proportion of the unpaid family workers. According to the National Sample Survey (1960-67) the labour participation rates for boys and girls in the age group 10-19 is on the decline in urban areas. In rural areas a similar trend is evident in the case of boys, but for girls this decline is negligible.

(d) Our Survey reveals several difficulties in the way of facilities for girls' education. Nearly 53 per cent of the respondents refer to shortage of schools in general, 57.65 per cent to absence of separate schools for girls in many places. 43.57 per cent to overcrowding in schools and 53.95 per cent to distance from house to school. While 39.41 per cent point to the absence of women teachers, 40.46 per cent do not regard this as a difficulty. Other difficulties brought to our notice are the lack of adequate transport arrangements and toilet facilities, as also the prevalence of single teacher schools.

(e) The irrelevance of education as imparted in schools today has been discussed at length by the Education Commission. While endorsing their views, we would like to add that this has a particularly adverse effect on parental attitude to the education of girls, especially in rural areas. Parents who have not as yet accepted the utility of educating girls find in its irrelevance a justification for their apathy. Mothers of young girls told us that except for reading and writing, which the girls could pick up in two or three years, schools taught very little that was useful. One peasant woman in a Punjab village felt that one way of making school education more meaningful would be to train girls to handle and repair tractors. Some women in the Kulu Valley wanted training in methods of fruit preservation, so that they could fully utilize the products of their orchards.

(f) Education in the rural areas often results in alienation of the girls from their habitat. While this criticism was voiced in many places, the most vocal opinion was expressed by women in the villages of Himachal Pradesh. Since the development of the State and the standard of living of its people depended on the continued efforts of women in agriculture, education in their opinion was becoming an adversary of progress. Girls who completed their formal education in the villages did not want to continue living in villages or take part in agricultural activities. The problem became more accrued when, owing to absence of secondary school in the villages, they had to study outside, in urban or semi-urban areas. Many of them found village life with its hardships intolerable afterwards. This was particularly brought to our notice in Nagaland and Himachal Pradesh. Most girls who complete secondary school develop a desire for white-collared jobs, or urban life in some form.

(g) While early marriage or betrothal was undoubtedly the greatest deterrent to progress of girls' education in the past, it is much less so now. Our survey indicates that only 38.1 per cent of the respondents find early marriage a genuine difficulty for girls' education while 41.5 per cent do not agree with this view. The average age at marriage has been rising steadily from 15.4 between 1941-51 to 18 in 1961-71. The national average for 1971 is 20 in urban and 18 in rural areas. The percentage of unmarried girls in the age group 10-14 rose from 77.63 to 86.21 in rural areas and from 93.01 to 95.79 in urban areas between 1961 and 1971. For the age group 15-19 this percentage changed from 14.2 to 36.91 in rural areas and 29.4 to 63.76 in urban areas. When we turn to the admittedly educationally backward States, however, we find this to be still a problem. The average age at marriage for women during 1951-61 was 14.81 in Bihar and Orissa, 13.87 in Madhya Pradesh, 14.22 in Rajasthan and 14.43 in Uttar Pradesh, when the national average was 16.3. During our tours we met a number of girls in their teens who were already married. The social restriction on girls pursuing their studies after marriage however has been rapidly breaking down. In one high school in Madhya Pradesh we found 10 per cent of the girls were married. At the higher levels of education the presence of young married women is a normal phenomenon. Nevertheless, the problem still continues to exist in certain communities and areas.

The strongest social support for girls' education continues to come from its increasing demand in the marriage market. According to our survey, 64.25 per cent of the respondents felt that education helped to improve marriage prospects of a girl. For example, when a residential school for tribal boys was started in Deomali (Arunachal Pradesh), the demand for a similar institution for girls came from totally illiterate tribal parents, as they apprehended that the boys, once educated would refuse to marry within the community if they did not find educated girls.

The influence of the marriage market is also restrictive in some ways. Since marriage within the community or caste continues to be the prevalent norm, in communities where education has not spread sufficiently among the men, the parents are reluctant to educate their girls beyond a certain level. It is taken for granted that the man has to be more educated than the woman. This has been intensified by the pressure of the dowry system which acts in two ways. On the one hand the search for bridegrooms for educated girls becomes confined to men with still higher education-whose demand for dowry is prone to be higher. On the other, the burden of the double expenditure on education as well as marriage acts as a deterrent to girls' education.

Literacy

Our review of the progress made by women within the formal system of education indicates its severe limitations. In spite of all the expansion, the system now covers only 10 per cent of the total female population. In the 15-25 age group however, the situation is much worse, as seen in Table 2.15. Less than 7 per cent of the 15-25 age group and less than 2 per cent of the 25 and above age group are now covered by the formal system. The vast majority are still illiterate. As for the literate section, the skill acquired may be illusory or temporary, as many of them do not succeed in retaining literacy. A study sponsored by UNESCO on retention of literacy in Malaysia and India (1970) found that literacy is not permanently retained without four years of formal schooling, or high proficiency in adult literacy courses (designated as grade III by the Literacy House, Lucknow). Two other factors contribute to the loss of literacy:- (a) lack of use in occupation, and (b) non-recognition of the value of literacy by the community. This study also indicated that the percentage of loss is higher among women in both urban and rural areas.

As pointed out elsewhere in our Report, illiteracy remains the greatest barrier to any improvement in the position of women in employment, health, the enjoyment and exercise of legal and constitutional rights, equal opportunity in education, and generally in attaining the equality of status that our Constitution has declared as the goal of the nation. The trend of discussion in the United Nations Commission on the Status of Women and various reports of the UNESCO over the last three decades, indicate that the achievement of high educational status by a minority produces little or no impact on the status of the large mass of women if they remain outside the reach of education or other instruments of modernization because of illiteracy.

The significant point to be noted is that, unlike the enrolment in the formal educational system, literacy did not increase at such a rapid rate after independence, either in absolute number or in relation to the growth of literacy among men. The enrolment of girls in primary education increased from 20.1 per cent in 1950-51 to 68.6 in 1970-71. This indicates that despite the progress in formal education, the proper sections of Indian women, the majority of whom have to labour for living, are still illiterate.

TABLE - 2.15

EDUCATIONAL LEVEL OF WOMEN BY AGE GROUP

(in Lakhs)

Educational level	*No. of Women*		*Total*
	Urban Areas	*Rural Areas*	
(Age Group (15-24)			
Illiterate	36	262	298 (67.5 p.c. of the total number of women in this age group)
Literate	7	21	28
Primary and Middle level	35	52	87
Matriculates and above	20	7	27 (6.2 p.c. of the total number of women in this age group)
Total of literate and educated	62	81	143
Age Group (25 and above)			
Illiterate	129	816	945 (88.6 p.c. of the total number of women in this age group)
Literate	17	29	46
Primary and Middle level	41	41	82
Matriculates and above	14	3	17 (1.6 p.c. of the total number of women in this age group)
Total of literate and Educated	72	74	146

N.B. The percentages of different age groups and different educational level (for women) were derived, in the first instance, from the one per cent Sample Data of the 1971 Census. These percentages were then applied to the total female population as given by the 1971 Census in order to arrive at the approximate figures presented above.

The advance of Indian women in this field can only be described as pitifully meagre as Table 2.16 indicates:

TABLE - 2.16
PROGRESS OF LITERACY — 1901-1971

(Number of Literate Females per 1000 Males)

Year	Total Literate Males	%age of Literate Males to Total Male Population	Total Literate Females	%age of Literate Females to Total Female Population	No. of Literate Females per 1000 Males
1	2	3	4	5	6
1901	14690080	9.83	996341	0.69	68
1911	16938815	10.56	1600763	1.05	94
1921	19841438	12.21	2782213	1.81	140
1931	23969751	15.59	4169105	2.93	132
1951	45610431	24.95	13650683	7.93	299
1961	77939833	34.44	27578928	12.95	354
1971*	111911000	39.51	48699191	18.44	435

* Provisional population totals, Paper I for 1971 supplement Census of India.

Source: Census of India 1961. Vol. I, Part II A, General Population Tables, p. 181, "Some Quantitative Indices of Social Change in India" Census Publication, p. 22.

The Education Commission had emphasized the imperative need "to liquidate adult illiteracy" and "to stop all further additions to the ranks of adult non-literates," — describing such measures as "transitional." In reality the number of illiterates has been increasing with such rapidity that the task of eradicating it is becoming more and more formidable with the passage of time.

TABLE - 2.17
NUMBER OF ILLITERATES BY SEX 1951-71

Census Year	Males	Females
1950-51	139,918,031	161,908,945
1960-61	148,206,268	185,211,889
1970-71	172,025,614	215,314,004

The challenge of the widening illiteracy gap will have to be borne in mind in determining priorities in educational development in the years to come. The claims of the formal educational system which can cater to the needs of only a minority for a long time will have to be balanced against the claims of eradication of illiteracy. This stands out as the most important and imperative need to raise the status of women who are already adults and constitute the largest group.

The enrolment figures under the programmes of adult literacy for women as given by the Ministry of Education are :- 2 million in 1950-51; 3 million in 1960-61; 6 million in 1965-66, and 3.2 million in 1968-69. This should not result in complacency. In the absence of specific evaluation of these programmes we have no evidence that enrolment necessarily resulted in these women becoming literate.

It is obvious that while the constitutional directive of universal education up to the age of 14 years must receive the highest priority in the formal system, the need of the large majority of adult women, illiterate or just literate, cannot be met by that system. An alternative system has, therefore, to be designed for this purpose to provide basic education to adult women, particularly in the 15-25 age group.

Imbalance in Educational Development

The sharp increase in the number of illiterate women in spite of the rapid expansion of education of women at various levels, points to severe imbalance in the distribution of edducational effort and resources among different sections of the population. Education is a double edged instrument which can eliminate the effects of socio-economic inequalities, but which can itself introduce a new kind of inequality between those who have it and those who do not.

The Education Commission had identified amongst other forms of educational inequalities, the wide disparity of educational development between the advanced and the backward classes. While agreeing with this view, we would like to emphasize another important factor which has a direct impact on the development of women's education, viz., regional differences. Imbalances in women's education and literacy are the consequences of great disparity of educational progress between rural and urban areas, between different sections of the population and between regions, which reflect, to a great extent variations in regional attitudes to women. Tables 2.18 to 2.25 attempt a comparison in the development of literacy and education at different levels for women in different States. They indicate dimensions of the imbalance.

TABLE - 2.18
ENROLMENT RATIOS (PERCENTAGE OF GIRLS IN RELEVANT AGE GROUP) BY STAGE OF EDUCATION FOR GIRLS COMPARISON BETWEEN 1956-57 AND 1968-69

Union Territory/State	*Literacy Rate*		*Primary (I-V)*		*Middle (VI-VIII)*	
	1961(P.C.)	*(1971)*	*1956-57*	*1968-69*	*1956-67*	*1968-69*
1. Andhra Pradesh	12.03	15.65	43.5 (910)	60.0 (1590)	6.8	13.9 (198)
2. Assam (y)	17.11	18.68	45.5 (305)	56.4 (622)	12.0 (39)	22.3 (128)
3. Bihar	6.90	8.79	14.4 (355)	27.2 (1045)	1.7 (18)	6.4 (133)
4. Gujarat	19.10	24.59		62.7 (1086)		24.7 (220)
5. Maharashtra	16.76	25.95	48.5 (1526)*	71.0 (2245)	9.7 (256)*	26.6 (442)
6. Punjab	17.41	25.75	36.5 (375)@	56.9 (530)	10.3 (57)@	31.1 (141)
7. Haryana	9.21	14.68		37.4 (240)		20.8 (65)
8. J & K	4.26	9.10	9.2 (26)	43.0 (105)	4.0 (6)	24.4 (30)
9. Kerala	38.90	53.90	99.8 (947)	115.5 (1517)	35.9 (194)	61.0 (429)
10. Madhya Pradesh	6.73	10.82	17.1 (278)	30.6 (833)	2.8 (32)	10.9 (158)
11. Karnataka	14.19	20.74	44.2 (591)	72.0 (1365)	8.9 (95)	15.6 (158)
12. Nagaland	11.34	19.21	<	71.4 (20)	<	31.3 (5)
13. Orissa	8.65	13.75	18.5 (177)	46.6 (636)	1.7 (4)	9.1 (67)
14. Rajasthan	5.84	8.26	9.5 (103)	22.2 (380)	2.4 (14)	8.0 (71)
15. Tamil Nadu	18.17	26.83	49.0 (959)	88.9 (2038)	12.3 (135)	32.5 (416)
16. Uttar Pradesh	7.02	10.20	14.4 (584)	65.7 (3727)	3.3 (71)	11.2 (335)
17. West Bengal	16.98	22.08	50.8 (795)	57.0 (1701)	48.8 (118)	22.6 (350)
18. Delhi	42.55	47.64	76.7 (83)	78.7 (188)	38.1 (25)	70.8 (85)
19. Himachal Pradesh	9.49	20.04	24.5 (15)	57.2 (131)	5.4 (1)	22.3 (25)
20. Manipur	15.93	19.22	48.0 (18)	87.0 (67)	8.6 (2)	22.0 (9)
21. Tripura	10.19	20.55	38.4 (18)	57.1 (60)	9.1 (20)	25.5 (13)

Note: Absolute numbers (in thousands) are given in brackets.
*Includes Gujarat @Includes Haryana (y)Includes Assam
(<) Includes Meghalaya and Arunachal Pradesh

While the enrolment ratios shown as percentages of enrolled girls to the female population in the relevant age group has been used as a common denominator for all States, the absolute number provide some idea of the magnitude of the achievement. It is clear from the tables that while all States have been making rapid progress in the education of girls, the rate of progress has been uneven between different States. The ranking order of States for each level of education show certain variations in the achievements of the same States at different level of education. While Bihar and Rajasthan have maintained uniformly the lowest performance at all levels, States like Andhra Pradesh, Assam, Maharashtra, Karnataka, Uttar Pradesh, Himachal Pradesh, Manipur and Tripura show a higher achievement at the Primary levels during this 12-year period. The only States where both primary and middle levels show equal or similarly high achievement are J&K, Kerala, Nagaland, Delhi and Tamil Nadu. The case of West Bengal is rather unique as it seems to have merely maintained its position at the primary level and lost ground at the middle level during this period. At the secondary level only Kerala, Tamil Nadu and Delhi registered very definite progress. At the university level, majority of the States registered a distinct improvement. Enrolment in vocational and technical courses at the lower level in a number of States, however, has remained static. Some of the exceptions to this rule are Assam, Maharashtra and Delhi. For professional and technical courses at the higher level, the increase is marginal. This is not conducive to the diversification of women's education at the higher levels, or to the employment of educated women.

A statewise study undertaken at the request of the Committee found a very significant correlation between the growth of girls' education and the female literacy rate. No such significant correlation could, however, be established among the girls' education and (a) per capita income of the State; (b) density of population; and (c) sex ratio.

A recent study of patterns of literacy has emphasized the importance of population composition in determining the literacy rate. For example, cities and regions with a high proportion of Muslims or Scheduled Castes and Tribes are marked by low literacy rates while those with relatively high percentage of Christians have a high literacy rate. While there is always a big gap in the literacy rates of urban and rural population, broadly speaking Southern States have always maintained a higher literacy rate. It is interesting to note that the literacy of Kerala's rural population is higher than the country's city population as a whole.

TABLE - 2.19

ENROLMENT RATIOS (PERCENTAGES) BY STAGE OF EDUCATION FOR GIRLS COMPARISON BETWEEN 1956-57 AND 1968-69

State/Union Territory	*Secondary and Higher Secondary (ix & xi)*		*Vocational and Special Courses*		*University and College General*		*Professional and Special Colleges*	
	1956-57	*1968-69*	*1956-57*	*1968-69*	*1956-57*	*1968-69*	*1956-57*	*1968-69*
1. Andhra Pradesh	2.2	6.8	0.08	0.04	0.04	0.09	0.007	0.03
2. Assam	3.9	13.6	0.08	0.21	0.04	0.17	0.001	0.01
3. Bihar	0.6	2.4	0.12	0.02	0.01	0.05	0.001	0.02
4. Gujarat	-	14.5	-	0.23		0.21		0.04
5. Maharashtra	4.0	13.5	0.46	13.47	0.09	0.22	0.016	0.10
6. Punjab	4.6	13.3	0.11	0.12	0.08	0.34	0.021	0.10
7. Haryana	-	7.4	-	0.07	-	0.18	-	0.14
8. J & K	2.2	8.5	-	0.01	-	0.26	-	0.03
9. Kerala	13.2	28.0	0.06	0.02	0.11	0.52	0.008	0.11
10. Madhya Pradesh	0.9	5.2	0.05	0.04	0.01	0.02	0.006	0.03
11. Karnataka	3.5	9.3	0.10	0.11	0.04	0.17	0.011	0.06
12. Nagaland		7.1		0.34				
13. Orissa	0.6	3.1	0.21	0.04	0.01	0.05	0.001	0.01
14. Rajasthan	1.0	3.6	0.07	0.05	0.02	0.07	0.002	0.03
15. Tamil Nadu	4.2	17.0	0.06	0.03	0.02	0.17	0.004	0.09
16. Uttar Pradesh	1.7	3.9	0.03	0.02	0.05	0.21	0.005	0.03
17. West Bengal	4.6	10.0	0.31	0.22	0.16	0.52	0.020	0.07
18. Delhi	15.9	46.1	0.61	0.79	0.33	1.18	0.132	0.17
19. Himachal Pradesh	2.4	9.2	0.12	0.06	0.01	0.12		0.06
20. Manipur	4.1	11.1	0.53	0.55	0.03	0.36	-	-
21. Tripura	9.0	13.6	0.77	0.56	0.03		-	0.03
India	3.0	9.1	0.14	1.30	0.05	0.19	0.008	0.06

Low Educational Development among Muslim Women: Apart from the lower rate of literacy among Muslim women, our survey on the Status of Women in Minority Communities has definitely revealed that the number of Muslim Women with no formal education continues to be very high even in those States which have otherwise progressed considerably in the development of women's education.

Slow progress of Education among Scheduled Castes and Scheduled Tribes: Tables 2.22 and 2.23 indicate the very low level of educational development of women among Scheduled Castes and Scheduled Tribes.

TABLE - 2.20

RANKING OF STATES FOR EACH LEVEL OF EDUCATION, ACCORDING TO RANGES OF ENROLMENT RATIO OF GIRLS. COMPARISON BETWEEN 1956-57 AND 1968-69

State/Union Territory	*Literacy*		*Primary*		*Middle*	
	1961	*1971*	*1956-57*	*1968-69*	*1956-57*	*1968-69*
1. Andhra Pradesh	2	2	2	3	1	1
2. Assam	2	2	2	3	1	2
3. Bihar	1	1	1	1	1	1
4. Gujarat	2	2	-	3	-	2
5. Maharashtra	2	3	2	3	1	2
6. Punjab	2	3	2	3	1	3
7. Haryana	1	2	-	2	-	2
8. J & K	1	1	1	2	1	2
9. Kerala	3	4	4	4	3	4
10. Madhya Pradesh	1	2	1	2	1	1
11. Karnataka	2	2	2	3	1	2
12. Nagaland	2	2	3	3	-	3
13. Orissa	1	2	1	2	1	1
14. Rajasthan	1	1	1	1	1	1
15. Tamil Nadu	2	3	2	4	1	3
16. Uttar Pradesh	1	2	1	3	1	1
17. West Bengal	2	2	3	3	4	2
18. Delhi	3	3	4	4	3	4
19. Himachal Pradesh	1	2	1	3	2	2
20. Manipur	2	2	2	4	1	2
21. Tripura	2	2	2	3	1	2

Note: Ranks (in ascending order) used for different ranges of enrolment and literacy rates.

Literacy Rates : Rank 1 for less than 10 p.c.
Rank 2 for 10 to less than 25 p.c.
Rank 3 for 25 to less than 50 p.c.
Rank 4 for 50 p.c. and above.

Enrolment Ratio in
Primary Classes : Rank 1 for less than 30 p.c.
Rank 2 for 30 to less than 50 p.c.
Rank 3 for 50 p.c. to less than 75 p.c.
Rank 4 for 75 p.c. and above.

Enrolment Ratio in
Middle Classes : Rank 1 for less than 15 p.c.
Rank 2 for 15 to less than 30 p.c.
Rank 3 for 30 p.c. to less than 45 p.c.
Rank 4 for 45 p.c. and above.

TABLE - 2.21

RANKING OF STATES FOR EACH LEVEL OF EDUCATION, ACCORDING TO RANGES OF ENROLMENT RATIO OF GIRLS COMPARISON BETWEEN 1956-67 AND 1968-69

State/Union Territory	*Secondary & Higher Secondary*		*Educational*		*University & College General*		*Professional Special Colleges*	
	1956-57	*1968-69*	*1956-57*	*1968-69*	*1956-57*	*1968-69*	*1956-57*	*1968-69*
	(1)		*(2)*		*(3)*		*(4)*	
Andhra Pradesh	1	1	1	1	1	1	1	2
Assam	1	2	1	2	1	2	1	1
Bihar	1	1	1	1	1	1	1	1
Gujarat	-	2	-	2	-	2	-	2
Maharashtra	1	2	3	4	1	2	1	4
Punjab	1	2	1	1	1	3	1	4
Haryana	-	1	-	1	-	2	-	4
J & K	1	2	-	1	-	2	1	3
Kerala	1	4	1	1	1	4	1	4
Madhya Pradesh	1	1	1	1	1	1	1	2
Karnataka	1	2	1	1	1	2	1	3
Nagaland	-	1	-	3	1	1	1	1
Orissa	1	1	2	1	1	1	1	1
Rajasthan	1	1	1	1	1	1	1	1
Tamil Nadu	1	3	1	1	1	2	1	4
Uttar Pradesh	1	1	1	1	1	2	1	2
West Bengal	2	2	3	2	2	3	1	3
Delhi	2	4	4	4	3	4	4	4
Himachal Pradesh	1	2	1	1	1	1	-	3
Manipur	1	2	4	4	1	2	-	-
Tripura	1	2	4	4	1	1	-	2

Note: Ranks (in ascending order) used for different ranges of enrolment and literacy rates.

Column 2 is for vocational and professional education—junior education—junior level, i.e., school standard.

Column 4 — similar courses of university standard.

(i) Literacy Rates :
Rank 1 for less than 10 p.c.
Rank 2 for 10 to less than 25 p.c.
Rank 3 for 25 to less than 50 p.c.
Rank 4 for 50 p.c. and above.

(ii) Enrolment Ratio in H.S. and Secondary classes.
Rank 1 for less than 7.5 p.c.
Rank 2 for 7.5 to less than 25 p.c.
Rank 3 for 25 to less than 50 p.c.
Rank 4 for 50 p.c. and above.

(iii) For University enrolments as p.c. of all female population. — Rank 1 for less than 15 p.c.; Rank 2 for 15 to less than 30 p.c.; Rank 3 for 30 p.c. to less than 50 p.c.; Rank 4 for 50 p.c. and above.

(iv) For Vocational (school standard) enrolment relative to female population. — Ranks denote same range as University

(v) Professional enrolments as p.c. of female population. — Rank 1 for less than .03; Rank 2 for .03 to less than .05; Rank 3 for .05 to less than .08; Rank 4 for .08 or above.

TABLE - 2.22
PERCENTAGE DISTRIBUTION OF LITERATES AND ILLITERATES AMONG MEMBERS OF SCHEDULED CASTES AND SCHEDULED TRIBES, INDIA 1961

Literates/Illiterates		*Scheduled Castes*			*Scheduled Tribes*		
		Total	*Rural*	*Urban*	*Total*	*Rural*	*Urban*
Literates	Persons	10.27	8.89	21.78	8.54	8.17	22.41
	Males	16.95	15.05	32.16	13.84	13.38	30.43
	Females	3.28	2.52	10.02	3.17	2.91	13.45
Illiterates	Persons	89.73	91.11	78.22	91.46	91.83	77.59
	Males	83.05	84.95	67.84	86.16	86.62	69.57
	Females	96.72	97.48	89.98	96.83	97.09	86.55

Source: Bose, Ashish, *Studies in India's Urbanization*, 1901-71, pp. 298-99.

TABLE - 2.23
DISTRIBUTION OF 1,000 SCHEDULED CASTES AND SCHEDULED TRIBES MALES AND FEMALES BY EDUCATIONAL LEVELS, INDIA 1961

Educational Level	*Scheduled Castes*				*Scheduled Tribes*			
	Males		*Females*		*Males*		*Females*	
	Rural	*Urban*	*Rural*	*Urban*	*Rural*	*Urban*	*Rural*	*Urban*
Illiterates	849	678	975	900	866	696	971	865
Literates	151	322	25	100	134	304	29	135
Literates without educational levels	113	206	20	67	99	166	23	78
Primary or Junior Basic	35	98	5	31	34	117	6	49
Matriculation or above	3	18	N	2	1	21	N	8
Total	1000	1000	1000	1000	1000	1000	1000	1000

Source: Ibid, pp. 298-99.

TABLE - 2.24
EDUCATIONAL IMBALANCE AT THE DISTRICT LEVEL LITERATES AS PER CENT OF TOTAL POPULATION

		Persons	*Males*	*Females*
1.	Andhra Pradesh	24.56		15.65
	Hyderabad	39.91		29.57
	Adilabad	14.14		6.48
2.	Uttar Pradesh	21.64		10.18
	Dehradun	45.06		33.85
	Basti	15.57		4.85
3.	Madhya Pradesh	22.12		10.84
	Indore	44.35		31.42
	Bastar*	9.64		4.09
	Rural	8.11	13.31	2.92
	Urban	49.21	59.55	36.98
4.	Orissa	26.12		13.75
	Cuttack	36.37		22.49
	Koraput*	10.57		4.71
5.	Rajasthan	18.79		8.26
	Ajmer	30.19		18.18
	Barmer	10.02		2.70
6.	Bihar	19.79		8.49
	Patna	29.77		15.04
	Champaran	14.06		5.44

* Predominantly inhabited by Scheduled Tribes.

The influence of these sociological factors on education makes it clear that the use of national or state averages in assessing educational progress are not always meaningful. Table 2.24 illustrates the wide gap that characterises literacy development of districts or regions within the States which we have identified as being particularly backward in their attention to the development of women's education.

In our opinion, any plan for educational development of worker which does not take these imbalances into account will contribute to the increase of inequalities between different section of the population. Removal of these imbalances will require special attention from public authorities based on careful identification of factors responsible for them. Special programmes will need to be designed for their removal if equality of educational opportunities is to be brought within the access of the majority of women in this country.

Co-Education

The imbalances just pointed out make it difficult to put forward a set pattern of recommendations. Besides the general problems of education, there are certain specific issues on which it is not feasible to insist upon a uniform pattern for the whole country. One such example is co-education. This issue has been examined by various Committees and Commissions.

In 1953, the Secondary Education Commission observed that there could be no hard and fast policy with regard to co-education as social attitudes differed very greatly in this respect. The Commission, therefore, recommended:

(i) opening of separate schools wherever possible that there could be no hard opportunities for physical, social and mental development of the girls;

(ii) girls whose parents had no objection should be free to use co-educational facilities in boys' schools. The Commission, however, prescribed specific conditions in the way of mixed staff, teaching of subjects, which appeal to girls such as home craft, music, drawing, etc., and separate facilities for co-curricular activities for such institutions.

In 1959, the National Committee on Women's Education recommended that co-education should be adopted as a general policy at the primary stage, but as transitional measure, separate schools may be provided in places where there was a strong public demand for them and enrolment of girls was large enough to justify separate schools. At the middle and secondary stages more co-educational schools should be started, subject to the condition of adequate attention being paid to special needs and requirements of girls. Separate secondary schools for girls should, however, be provided specially in rural areas. The Committee while recommending alternatives in areas where co-education was unacceptable, suggested efforts to remove difficulties and apprehensions against co-education by providing right type of staff, encouraging parental visits and the appointment of women teachers and women heads in co-educational institutions.

In 1962, the Committee on the Differentiation of Curricula for Boys and Girls admitted the division of academic opinion on co-education and recommended the following:

(i) Adoption of co-education as the general pattern at the elementary stage with a vigorous propaganda to overcome resistance to co-education. As a transitional measure, however, separate primary or middle schools might be provided in case of a large demand;

(ii) Full freedom to management and parents to establish co-educational or separate institutions at the secondary and collegiate stage;

(iii) Appointment of women teachers in all educational institutions at the secondary and university stage which are ordinarily meant for boys. Similarly some male teachers should also be appointed in secondary schools and colleges meant for girls, removing the existing ban on such appointments.

In the course of our investigation we found continued evidence of this divergence of views regarding co-education. According to our survey, as many as 57.56 per cent regard absence of separate schools as a reason for not sending girls to schools. Some persons consider that co-education may lead to immoral behaviour. In Punjab, we were told that Swami Dayanand Saraswati had prescribed a distance of at least 5 miles between boys' and girls' schools. Among those communities which observe *purdah* there is naturally a demand for separate schools. The Meos in Haryana and Rajasthan, the Maplahs in Kerala, a large number of Muslims in Bihar, Uttar Pradesh, etc., fall in this category. It is interesting to note, however, that there was no demand for separate schools in J&K, although the majority of the population of that State is Muslim. In certain areas we found the resistance to co-education to be higher among the Hindus than Muslims. For instance, in the village Bankheri in Madhya Pradesh, not a single girl from upper caste Hindu families was attending school even at the primary level, because there was no separate school for them, while in a village with a predominantly Muslim population in Bihar Sharif there was no objection to girls attending a co-educational school up to middle level. Another respect in which our findings have been somewhat different from findings of earlier Committees is regarding the variation in urban and rural attitudes to co-education. We have found the resistance to be more of an urban middle-class phenomenon. One of the reasons for this is increasing indiscipline and rowdyism in institutions for secondary and higher education. The underprivileged classes do not seem to have such objection to co-education. In Himachal Pradesh the rural population expressed surprise at our question. In their view, if boys and girls could work together in fields there could be no reason why they could not study in same schools.

The advocates of co-education support it not only from the point of view of economy and efficiency but some of them also claim that the performance of students is better in co-educational schools especially if the sex ratio is even. Our survey of official opinion shows a clear preference for co-education as indicated by Table 2.25. The significant point to be noted is that the support for co-education, particularly at the primary and middle levels, comes not only from the Directors of Public Instruction and Principals but from field staff working in rural areas such as Block Development Offices and Mukhya Sevikas. It should also be noted that the support from this last category is considerably reduced at the level of secondary education. During our tours we found that a large number of persons are opposed to co-education at the secondary stage because they feel that adolescent youth should be segregated.

TABLE - 2.25

VIEWS OF OFFICIALS REGARDING CO-EDUCATION AT DIFFERENT LEVELS

Level	*T.No. of Persons*	*Strongly in Favour*	*Generally in Favour*	*No Objection*	*Do not Like*	*Strongly Oppose*	*No Response*
Primary	917	519	174	175	9	4	36
	(100.0)	(56.6)	(19.0)	(19.1)	(1.0)	(0.4)	(3.9)
Middle	917	327	262	211	62	18	37
	(100.0)	(35.7)	(28.6)	(23.0)	(6.8)	(1.9)	(4.0)
Secondary	917	142	186	198	225	115	51
	(100.0)	(15.5)	(20.3)	(21.6)	(24.5)	(12.5)	(5.6)
University	917	155	170	238	174	114	66
	(100.0)	(16.9)	(18.5)	(26.0)	(19.0)	(12.4)	(7.2)
Polytechnic &	917	151	156	245	184	122	69
Vocational	(100.0)	(15.4)	(16.9)	(26.7)	(20.1)	(13.3)	(7.6)
Professional	917	174	181	258	130	96	78
& Technical	(100.0)	(19.0)	(19.7)	(28.1)	(14.2)	(10.5)	(8.5)

We have been told repeatedly that boys' schools are better equipped, have more choice of subjects and have better academic standards. In one boys' school in Aligarh district there were 30 girls studying even when there was a separate school for them in the same vicinity. The quality of teaching was poor in the girls' school and therefore, the parents preferred to send them to boys' school. According to the Bihar study "most responses underlined lack of required teaching facilities as the reason for women going to men-predominated educational institutions". In other States also similar opinions were voiced.

Karnataka is the only State in the whole of India where all schools at the primary level (I-IV) are separate for girls; but from class V onwards co-education is the norm. The official explanation for this policy was, that separate schools made it easier to enrol and retain girls for 4 years. Once parents got used to the idea, they agreed more readily to their daughters' continuing their studies further. The Committee is not in a position to assess the impact of this policy.

Contrary to the recommendations of various national Committees, some states, e.g., Bihar, have definitely adopted a policy against co-education to the extent of discouraging it.

In our opinion, the considerations of efficiency, economy as well as equal opportunity require the acceptance of co-education as a long-term policy. In view of the divergent social attitudes, however, we recommend:

(i) Co-education should be adopted as the general policy at the primary level;

(ii) At the middle and secondary stages separate schools may be provided in areas where there is a great demand for them. But the effort to pursue co-education as a general policy at these stages should continue side-by-side;

(iii) At the university level co-education should be the general policy and opening of new colleges exclusively for girls should be discouraged;

(iv) There should be no ban on admission of girls to boys' institutions;

(v) Wherever separate schools/colleges for girls are provided, it has to be ensured that they maintain required standards in regard to the quality of staff, provision of facilities, relevant courses and co-curricular activities;

(vi) Acceptance of the principle of mixed staff should be made a condition of recognition for mixed schools. There is a misgiving, however, that this provision may lead to exclusion of girls from some schools. Therefore, it is suggested that this measure may be reviewed a few years after it is implemented;

(vii) Wherever there are mixed schools, separate toilet facilities and retiring rooms for girls should be provided.

Curricula

The need for a separate curricula for girls has been a controversial issue since the nineteenth century and reflects the ambivalence regarding the purpose of women's education. It is argued that:

(i) society assigns different roles to men and women. Since women are expected to be good wives and mothers their education must be adopted to these roles;

(ii) the average school life of girls being shorter than that of boys the courses for girls must also be shorter;

(iii) the intellectual inferiority, lack of aptitude and physical weakness of girls call for simpler and easier courses of study;

(iv) the qualities to be inculcated in girls have to be different from those of boys so that they do not become bold and independent in spirit.

These arguments received official support and became a part of the Government's policy towards women's education. Starting with the Hunter Commission of 1882, most Government committees on education accepted the validity of these arguments. This position remained even after independence and resulted in certain subjects being regarded as specially suitable for girls. Home/Domestic Science, needle work and fine arts thus came to be regarded as exclusively girls' subjects in schools. Mathematics and science on the other hand were regarded as too difficult and unnecessary for girls and were, therefore, kept optional. Consequently, majority of girls' schools did not provide the facilities for teaching of science and mathematics.

The pace of socio-economic change, the new attitude towards women's roles in society which came with the freedom movement, and the outstanding success of some girls in subjects like mathematics and science were, however, offering serious challenges to these established views. The National Committee of Women's Education (1959) taking note of these changes, recommended common curricula for boys and girls, with no differentiation on the basis of sex. Following this, the Committee on the Differentiation of Curricula for Boys and Girls (1964), examined the whole problem comprehensively and rejected the traditional view that 'mere biological difference of sex created different physical, intellectual and psychological characteristics between men and women' which 'necessitated the provision of differentiated curricula for them'. In their opinion, the differences which men and women exhibit are the result of social conditioning, expressed through:

(i) the differential pattern of division of labour between the sexes;

(ii) the stereo-types of 'masculine' and 'feminine' personalities to which both men and women are expected to conform; and

(iii) the unequal social position accorded to the two sexes.

The Committee therefore recommended a common course, at all levels, and advised the inclusion of home science in the core curriculum for boys and girls up to the end of the middle stage to counteract the influences of traditional attitudes which regard certain tasks as 'manly' and others as 'womanly'. The Education Commission (1966) endorsed these recommendations.

Our investigation indicates that this new trend of thought is now widely accepted. According to our survey, 69.82 per cent of the respondents agree that girls should get the same type of education as boys.

In spite of this marked change, however, a demand for differential curricula comes from parents whose sole object in educating girls is to improve their prospects in the matrimonial market. These parents often discourage girls from taking up 'difficult' subjects. Sometimes 'difficult subjects' require coaching and the parents are not prepared to spend 'that extra' on the girls, while for the boys 'it has to be done'.

The number of girls taking up science and mathematics is steadily increasing. In our tours we found girls were very much interested in science subjects. In reply to our specific question, many of them expressed a desire for science to be made compulsory up to high school. Quite a few wanted to study subjects which would give them a larger perspective. In a school in Madhya Pradesh they wanted 'general knowledge' and 'news' to be part of the curriculum.

In spite of the recommendation of the Education Commission, many States still continue to prescribe different curricula for boys and girls at the school level. This has had an adverse effect particularly on the teaching of mathematics to girls. Many girls' schools still make no provision for the teaching of science subjects. This has resulted in a lack of adequate number of women teachers in these subjects. We found in some schools science being taught by teachers who had never studied science themselves.

Home Science has for long been emphasized as a subject most suited for girls, and a large majority of girls take up this course. We are not against the teaching of home science but we feel that the courses now current in this subject require major revision. In our opinion, the present pattern of uniformity in these courses neglects the environmental factors and availability of local resources. Introducing these dimensions would make them more relevant and realistic. In one school we visited, the lesson in progress was how to decorate a room. There were two styles of decoration - 'Desi' and 'Videshi'. On enquiring, the girls told us that in 'Videshi' style the room should have a sofa set, etc., but they were not taught how to decorate it in 'Desi' style.

This course if revised and developed with proper scientific foundations, would be suitable for both boys and girls and meet the needs of general as well as vocational education.

For example, cooking should include knowledge of nutrition, dietetics, canning and food preservation, etc.

We recommend:

(i) There should be a common course of general education for both sexes till the end of class X, all courses being open to boys and girls.

(ii) At the primary stage, simple needle craft, music and dancing should be taught to both sexes.

(iii) From the middle stage, differences may be permitted under work experience.

(iv) In classes XI-XII girls should have full opportunity to choose vocational and technical courses according to local conditions, needs and aptitudes.

(v) At the university stage there is a need to introduce more relevant and useful courses for all students.

Pre-Primary Schools

Attempts to reduce inequalities in educational opportunities must begin early if they are to have any impact. A child who has attended a pre-primary school is better adjusted to the school environment. It has been found that adequate attention at this stage can help to reduce the problem of wastage and stagnation in the first two years of primary school. It positively helps the children to overcome their environmental disadvantages. It is the best time for socialization and inculcating egalitarian values in the children as they are unaware of differences of caste, class, creed or sex and are unhampered by social inhibitions or taboos.

We were particularly impressed by the achievement in this respect of the 'balwadis' in the rural areas. The children in these institutions come from all classes of the rural population and mix freely in an atmosphere of happy cooperation. As there is no resistance to sending girls to these institutions, they also help to get parents accustomed to the idea of continuing the schooling of girls. We feel that these institutions can make a real contribution to the changing of social attitudes in the rural areas.

Apart from the benefit that these institutions can bring to the very young, they serve another useful function, namely, relieving the mothers of small children for other work, and increasing the chances of schooling of older girls by releasing them from the responsibility of looking after the siblings.

We therefore recommend:

(i) The provision of three years pre-school education for all children by making a special effort to increase the number of 'balwadis' in the rural areas and in urban slums.

(ii) In order to enable them to fulfil the social functions discussed above, an effort should be made to locate them as near as possible to the primary and middle schools of the locality.

Universalization of Education for the Age group 6-14

Primary

The problems of girls' education at this stage are mainly of accessibility of schools, enrolment and retention. There are still many areas where new primary schools need to be established. Many of the unserved villages are small and scattered, while some villages have more than one school, a position which will have to be rationalized in the interest of economy and efficiency. Though complex and difficult the magnitude of the problem is not large and it can be solved by planned and determined efforts.

We recommend:

(i) Provision of primary schools within walking distance from the home of every child within the next 5 years.

(ii) Establishment of ashram or residential schools to serve clusters of villages scattered in difficult terrains. Where this is not immediately possible, peripatetic schools may be provided for the time being.

(iii) Provision of mobile schools for children of nomadic tribes, migrant labour and construction workers.

(iv) Sustained propaganda by all types of persons, preferably women — officials and non-officials, social and political workers, to bring every girl into schools in class I preferably at the age of 6. They should visit local schools and involve parents and community leaders in order to promote the schooling of girls, particularly in backward areas.

(v) Provision of incentives to prevent drop-outs. Since poverty is the major cause of drop-outs the most effective incentive, in our opinion, is the provision of mid-day meals. The rate of children passing the primary level has definitely gone up in States which have introduced mid-day meals. In Kerala, which has the highest literacy rate among women, this provision is one of the major factors for the enrolment and retention of children in schools today. In reply to our questionnaire, the majority has given highest priority to this incentive. The other important incentives which require to be provided to needy children are free school uniforms, scholarships or stipends and free supply of books and other study material. For girls particularly the lack of adequate clothing is a great deterrent to attending schools. For schools which do not prescribe any uniform some provision of clothing is necessary.

(vi) Special incentives for areas where enrolment of girls is low. This will need to be worked out according to local conditions. We suggest special awards or recognition to the community, teachers, students, etc.

(vii) At least 50 per cent of teachers at this stage should be women.

(viii) Provision of at least two teachers in all schools, and conversion of the existing single-teacher ones as early as possible.

(ix) Developing a system of part-time education for girls who cannot attend school on a full time basis. This system should provide education to girls at a time convenient to them.

(x) Adoption of the multiple entry system for girls who could not attend school earlier or had to leave before becoming functionally literate.

(xi) Provision of additional space in schools so that girls can bring their younger brothers and sisters to be looked after, either by girls themselves in turn, or by some local women.

Middle

Recommendations made for the primary stage are applicable to middle schools as well. There is a great paucity of educational facilities at this level. We would like to reiterate opening of schools and greater flexibility in admission procedure, to help girls to complete their schooling.

Sex Education: During our tours we tried to elicit opinion on the question of imparting sex education to girls. We asked teachers in particular to give us their views on the issue, both as teachers and mothers of young daughters. While the large majority agreed on the necessity of such instruction, most of them doubted their own ability to handle it. They also felt that such instruction would be totally impracticable in co-educational schools. We feel that the matter needs to be carefully planned by experts.

We recommend:

(i) Introduction of sex education from middle school.

(ii) Appointment of an expert group by the Ministry of Education to prepare graded teaching material on the subject. The group should include some experts on mass media, to advise on the use of films and other mass media for this purpose.

(iii) This material may be used for both formal and non-formal education.

Secondary

The gap between boys and girls is the highest at the secondary stage. At the same time, secondary education is becoming increasingly the minimum qualification for most employment, both in the tertiary and secondary sector, as well as for most professional training. Since very few girls manage to complete secondary school, this insistence debars them from most vocational training.

We recommend:

(i) Free education for all girls up to the end of the secondary stage.

(ii) Improving the quality of teaching and provision of facilities for important subjects like science, mathematics and commerce.

(iii) Introduction of job-oriented work-experience, keeping in view the needs, the resources and the employment potential of the region, e.g., courses leading to training as ANM (Auxiliary Nurse Midwife), typing and commercial practice, programmes oriented to industry and simple technology, agriculture and animal husbandry.

General Recommendations

(i) Provision of mixed staff in all mixed schools. This should be made a condition of recognition.

(ii) Adequate provision of common-rooms and separate toilet facilities for girls in all schools.

(iii) Adequate arrangements for co-curricular activities for girls in all schools.

(iv) Provision of more need-cum-merit scholarships and hostel facilities for girls.

Higher Education

The problems at the level of higher education are general and require reform of the system to make it more relevant and responsive to the needs of society. The progress of women in this sector with all its limitations has been relatively satisfactory in comparison with the position in school education and we have no special recommendations to make.

It is, however, necessary to discuss one issue which is very often raised in this context. It is argued that a large proportion of the expenditure incurred on the higher education of girls is wasted because many of them get married and do not use the knowledge and the skills they acquire for social purposes. This argument is also used to make out a case for curtailing the opportunities now open to women in higher education. We do not agree with this view. We believe that the spread of higher education among women, whether general or professional, is still restricted, and that, for the needs of a modern society, there is need to expand it considerably. We also believe that an educated woman does become a better citizen and that the benefit of her education goes to enrich the life of her family. If her talents and skills are not fully utilized today in work outside the home, the responsibility is of the society which does not provide adequate opportunities for such women to be of greater social use. The proper policy would be to see that their talents are fully utilized for social and national development.

We therefore recommend:

(i) Development of more employment opportunities, particularly of a part-time nature, to enable women to participate more in productive activities.

(ii) Development of employment information and guidance services for women entering higher education. Many of them suffer from lack of information regarding job opportunities and regret their choice of subjects when faced by difficulties in obtaining employment.

Non-formal Education

The greatest problem in women's education in India today is how to provide some basic education to the overwhelming majority who have remained outside the reach of the formal system, because of their age and social responsibilities as well as the literacy gap. The large majority of them are illiterate and semi-literate. Out of every 100 women in the 15-25 age group, about 7 are in some educational institution, about 18 are drop-outs from the system and 75 are illiterate. If national plans for development have to make any headway, then it is imperative to increase the social effectiveness of this most significant group of young women, even if we cannot do so for the still older group. Our review has indicated the impossibility of educating them through any kind of formal institutionalized process. Apart from the prohibitive cost that such an attempt would involve, a formal system, by its very nature and pattern of organization is limited to cater to the educational needs of only those who enter it formally and are able to stay in it for a considerable length of time. It is essentially designed for young, full-time students who are not called upon to shoulder any other major responsibility of life during their period of study.

The Government of India's efforts in the field of adult literacy and adult education since independence have been largely based on a policy of encouraging voluntary agencies to undertake this task with supporting funds and guidance from the Government. The declared objectives of these programmes were:

(i) Familiarising the masses with the democratic process;
(ii) Activating large-scale co-operation in the building up of a welfare state;
(iii) Imparting rudimentary literacy skills as a means for self-emancipation, self-fulfilment and social justice.

These objectives, however, laudable, are extremely difficult to translate into concrete terms which would be within the grasp of both the agents and recipients of such education.

The Fourth Plan introduced a programme of functional literacy built round farmers' training in selected districts where high yielding varieties of crops were being cultivated. According to the estimates of the Ministry of Education, about 3 lakh persons received this training during the Fourth Plan, "out of whom women may be estimated at approximately 30%". This programme will be continued in the Fifth Plan, the target being

1.3 million persons. The Ministry 'hopes' that women will constitute 40 to 50 per cent of this group. It is also proposed to extend this programme to dry farming, small-scale farming, family planning, etc. Apart from this a programme of functional literacy for adult women is being formulated by the Department of Social Welfare. The curriculum will include training in vocational and occupational skills in areas like kitchen, gardening, food cultivation, poultry keeping, animal husbandry and household arts like sewing, knitting, etc., along with home management, child care and civic education. A similar programme for non-student youth (age group 6-14 and 15-25) draws a sharp distinction between men and women — emphasizing family life education, health, nutrition, child care and craft and self-employment for the latter.

In our opinion, these are fields which can no longer be limited to women. Changes in family life, food habits, the control of the family, all require joint efforts of men and women and continuing this kind of artificial division between men and women may defeat the purpose of these programmes. As for vocational and occupational skills, the needs of women are perhaps greater than those of men. While we do not deny the value of crafts, women's need for vocational training cannot be limited to them. The skills will differ according to the industrial and market potentials of regions and it is imperative to relate the training to local needs, resources and employment possibilities, instead of adopting an artificial sex selective approach.

We fear, however, that such ad hoc approaches, through a multiplicity of programmes being implemented by various governmental agencies, will lead to overlapping, lack of coordination, and ultimately to wastage of resources on administrative machinery. The problem, though of great magnitude, is an integrated one, and cannot be solved by these short-term programmes. While they may bring education to a few thousands, all the time lakhs are being added to the ranks of illiterates and drop-outs. What is needed is a continuous process, not short-term intensive courses as undertaken under existing programmes of adult education.

A formal system, designed for the young, can use certain

compulsive, corrective and didactic methods which would be inapplicable to a non-formal system where the majority of students would be adults, with experience of problems of life and little time to spare for being educated. Such a system would, therefore, need to have certain definite characteristics, different from a formal system. In our opinion:

(a) It must be useful in such a way that the usefulness is immediately perceived by the recipients;

(b) It must be related to specific areas of experience familiar to the students, since educational material totally alien to their world of experience would pose enormous obstacles to understanding and interest;

(c) It should aim to develop skills to acquire information and to apply it to real problems, and to understand events and happenings in the immediate environment.

The basic requirement for such a system, is a reduction of the psychological gap between those who teach and those who learn. A feeling of identity of interests and common experience are vital for such a system to overcome obstacles of low motivation and apathy. It follows that the system should be a part of the community, involving a large proportion of its members both as teachers and learners. In our opinion it is imperative to use all available educational resources in the community for this purpose, rather than import educational 'agents' from outside. The school teacher, the doctor, the ANM (Auxiliary Nurse Midwife), an agricultural extension worker and the successful farmer, the mechanic, the welfare worker, the local political representatives, and the handful of educated persons who either live in or come to the village periodically, all should be able to contribute to this programme.

Any attempt to professionalize the system will, in our opinion, defeat the purpose. The entry of professionals is likely to lead to development of (the limiting, selective and) a rigid approach, with fixed curricula and classroom procedures which generally result in increasing distance and distinction between those who teach and those who learn. This has happened frequently in adult education programmes, when they develop into 'course'. Besides, the prohibitive cost that such professionalization would involve, would inevitably limit its operation to a few selected centres. The teachers in a non-formal system must have other skills of direct relevance to the problems of the community. Without this kind of community involvement such programmes are likely to lack stability and continuity.

Contents of the System

While it is necessary to guard any fixed or uniform curricula, certain broad areas could be identified. The object of the system should be to provide access to information and use of information for better participation in social life. Literacy would certainly have to form the core of the package, but the experience of various literacy programmes in India and abroad indicate that it is necessary to make it instrumental or 'functional' rather than the end object. It has also been suggested that in the first phase of this programme the main emphasis should be on reading and basic arithmetical skills.

The system that we have in mind is a continuous programme of learning useful things, in which members of the entire community can participate in their spare time and where the barrier that now divides the educated from the uneducated become irrelevant. Though primarily meant for adolescents and adults, the system should not excuse the young, particularly all those who for economic or social reasons have been denied any formal education. Some of the latter may even use this as a stepping stone to enter the formal system if our recommendation regarding multiple entry is accepted.

The system will need a community group to organize and sponsor it. The panchayats and the women's panchayats that we recommend, would appear to be the ideal bodies for this purpose, Government's role should be limited to providing technical guidance and advice, and enabling government functionaries at the local level to participate in the programme, apart from supportive assistance in the form of literature and reading material. The system can make an impact only if the access to information is available through reading material and equipment. Development of basic libraries, in villages and the slum areas in towns, is an imperative necessity for this purpose. We therefore recommend concentration of governmental effort on providing this infrastructure suggested in the discussion on the problem of formal education.

Equality of Sexes as a Major Value to be included through the Educational Process

The deep foundations of the inequality of the sexes are built in the minds of men and women through a socialization process which continues to be extremely powerful. Right from their earlier years, boys and girls are brought up to know that they are different from each other and this differentiation is strengthened in every way possible — through language forms, modes of behaviour of labour, etc. They begin to learn very early what is proper or not proper for boys and girls and all attempts at deviation are noticed, discouraged and sometimes punished. The sissy and the tomboy are equal objects of derision. There is nothing wrong in this if it were merely a question of distinction. But it soon gets inextricably tied up with the traditional concepts of the roles of men and women and their mutual relationships which are based on inequality. The process of indoctrination affects the development of individual personalities.

The only institution which can counteract the effect of this process is the educational system. If education is to promote equality for women, it must make a deliberate, planned and sustained effort so that the new value of equality of the sexes, can replace the traditional value system of inequality. The educational system today has not even attempted to undertake this responsibility. In fact, the schools reflect and strengthen the traditional prejudices of inequality through their curricula, the classification of subjects on the basis of sex and the unwritten code of contact enforced on their pupils.

We received criticisms of school textbooks in this respect in many places. In Manipur and Andhra Pradesh in particular, a number of women were highly critical of the inclusion of stories of Sita and Savitri, as ideals of womanhood, since they tend to perpetuate the traditional values regarding the subordinate and dependent role of women. This result in the development of social attitudes among even many educated persons, men and women, who accept women's dependent and unequal status as a natural order of society.

Such a system of values is contradictory to the goals set before this nation by the Constitution. The concomitant of equality is responsibility and unless this is admitted by men and women equally, the desired transformation of our society will receive a severe setback. This is one area where a major change is needed in the context and organization of education. Educators must admit their responsibility and bring about this much needed change in the values of the younger generation.

Three

The Perspective Plan

Education is the most important instrument for human resource development. Education of women, therefore, occupies top priority amongst various measures taken to improve the status of women in India. In recent years, the focus of planning has shifted from equipping women for their traditional roles of house-wives and mothers to recognizing their worth as producers, making a major contribution to family and national income. Efforts have been made over the past three decades of planned development to enrol more girls in schools and encourage them to stay in schools, to contribute their education as long as possible, and to provide non-formal educational opportunities for women. The fulfilment of the Constitutional directives in respect of providing free and compulsory education up to the age of 14 years has been included as one of the components of the 'Minimum Needs Programme' and given overriding priority.

Education in India is constrained by the socio-economic conditions of the people, their attitudes, values and culture. During the pre-British era, education was linked to the socio-religious institutions, reinforcing the patriarchal social structure. During the British period, education became a tool of colonial power, enabling a small minority to have access to education, and all the benefits it entailed. The social reformers of the nineteenth century raised the demand for women's transformation but to make them more capable of fulfilling their traditional roles. Since Independence, the policy makers have argued for universal education and for making education as a tool for bringing about social equality.

In spite of concerted efforts to improve the enrolment of girls and provide adult education for women, their educational status is still far from satisfactory. Female enrolment in educational institutions is low as when compared with males and drop-out rates are high. There are also regional and inter-group disparities.

The factors which do not permit the closing of the existing gap between the education of men and women are many. While undertaking a review of the educational system at the time of formulation of the National Policy on Education 1986, it was noted that the system is caught in a state of ambivalence, aiming at creating an equal society while at the same time not disturbing the class, caste and gender relationships. Issues in women's education are, therefore, not issues only of educational sector, but they extend to issues of environment, employment, production processes. Indeed, the entire gamut of social and economic policy has a bearing on women's education. The need for educating girls is not considered worthwhile. In urban areas, by and large, there is a greater acceptance of its need than in rural areas. Some other factors responsible for low enrolment are:

(i) The requirement for older girls to stay at home to take care of siblings when mothers are away at work;
(ii) Need for girls to work in order to help in augmenting the family income;
(iii) Early marriage of girls;
(iv) Social customs that hinder female mobility after puberty;
(v) Lack of relevance of school curriculum; and
(vi) Lack of facilities in the form of school buildings, hostels and women teachers, etc.

Strategy Towards Women's Education in the Five-Year Plan

Women's education has assumed special significance in the context of the country's planned development. This is because women constitute nearly half the nation's population representing a valuable human resource and play an important role in the development of the community and the national economy. Education enables women to acquire basic skills and abilities, and fosters a value system which is conducive to raising their status in society. Recognizing this fact, great emphasis has been laid on women's education in the five-year plans. The First Five-Year Plan advocated the need for adopting special measures for solving the problems of women's education. It held that women "must have the same opportunities as men for taking all kinds of work and this presupposes that they get equal facilities so that their entry into the professions and public services is in no way prejudiced". It further added that "at the secondary and even at the university stage it should have a vocational or occupational basis, as far as possible, so that those who complete such stages may be in a position, if necessary, to immediately take up some vocation or other". Accordingly the educational facilities for girls continued to expand in the subsequent plans. The major schemes undertaken encompassed elementary education, secondary education, university education, postgraduate education and research, technical education, scholarships, social/adult education and physical education. The Second Plan continued the emphasis on overall expansion of educational facilities. The Report of the National Committee on Women's Education (1959) made a strong impact on the Third Five-Year Plan. It launched important schemes like condensed school courses for adult women, Bal Sevika training and child care programmes. Subsequent plans supported these measures and also continued incentives such as free text-books and scholarships for girls. This trend continued in the Fourth and Fifth Five-Year Plans.

Although there was a large-scale expansion of facilities for education up to the Fourth Plan, vast disparities existed in the relative utilization of available facilities by boys and girls at various stages of education. Hence, the major thrust in the Fifth Plan was to offer equality of opportunities as part of the overall plan of ensuring social justice and improving the quality of education imparted. To promote enrolment and retention in schools in backward areas and among underprivileged sections of the population, in addition to the incentives like free distribution of textbooks, mid-day meals, etc., girls were to be given uniform and attendance scholarships. In spite of these schemes, it was noticed that insufficient numbers of women teachers resulted in low enrolment of girls. To remove this bottleneck, scholarships were given to local girls to complete their education and training leading to a teaching career. Besides, condensed and correspondence courses were organized for the less educated women. Emphasis was also laid on the need for orientation of the curriculum to meet the special needs of girls.

A landmark in the Sixth Plan was the inclusion of women's education as one of the major programmes under Women and Development which was an outcome of the publication of the report of the Committee on the Status of Women in India. The programmes for universalization of elementary education were specially directed towards higher enrolment and retention of girls in schools. It was envisaged to promote Balwadi-cum-creches attached to the schools to enable girls responsible for sibling care at home to attend schools. Women teachers, where necessary, were to be appointed in rural areas to encourage girls' education. Science teaching in girl schools and colleges had to be strengthened to achieve greater participation of women in science and technology. Streamlining the admission policies to promote greater enrolment of women in engineering, electronics, agriculture, veterinary, fishery and forestry courses was stressed. For boosting the education of women belonging to backward classes, the number of girls' hostels were to be increased. Instead of adding more separate women's polytechnics, which were developed as multi-purpose institutions for imparting training in arts, crafts, etc., co-educational institutions were encouraged as far as possible. The adult education programme too received a fillip.

The Seventh Plan envisages restructuring of the educational programmes and modification of school curricula to eliminate gender bias. Enrolment of girls in elementary, secondary and higher education courses, formal as well as non-formal, has been accorded high priority. At the elementary stage, education has been made free for girls. Sustained efforts are to be made through various schemes and measures to reach 100 per cent coverage in elementary education. Financial assistance schemes to voluntary agencies to run early childhood education (pre-school centres) as adjuncts of primary/middle schools are to be expanded, particularly to help evolve innovative models suited to specific learner groups or areas. Efforts are to be made to enrol and retain girls in schools, especially in rural areas, and also to enrol children belonging to Scheduled Castes, Scheduled Tribes and other weaker sections. Teacher training programmes are to receive continued priority with a view to increase the availability of trained women teachers, and thereby to enhance girls' enrolment and retention in schools.

Incentives by way of distribution of uniforms, free textbooks and attendance scholarships to needy girls are to be continued. Non-formal elementary education is to be expanded to benefit girls in the age group of 6-14 years. Talented girls are to be encouraged to pursue higher education. It is also proposed to expand the 'Open Learning System', including correspondence courses for them. In order to promote technical and vocational education for girls, more women's polytechnics are to be set up and programmes for vocationalization of education are to be expanded.

To expedite education among the girls of the Scheduled Castes and Scheduled Tribes, additional facilities will continue to be provided under the "Development of Backward Classes" sector. Girls above the matriculation stage will get higher scholarships/ stipends than boy students. Financial assistance is envisaged for construction of hostel buildings for girls at the district level and for purchase of equipment, furniture utensils, books and periodicals in these hostels.

Under the National Sports Policy, participation of women and girls in sports and games is to be encouraged. Stress is to be laid on the identification of sports talent among women, and provision made for sports scholarships, coaching and nourishment support for promising girls with a view to improve the standards of their performance in competitive games. Besides, the schemes for encouraging traditional folk, tribal and hill arts and cultural activities are to be expanded and strengthened.

Situational Analysis

Notwithstanding the planned objectives and endeavours, actual progress in upgrading the educational status of women has been slow. The literacy level among women has risen from 7.9 per cent in 1951 to 24.3 per cent in 1981 (excluding Assam). Among males, the corresponding rise was from 24.9 to 46.3 per cent. Thus the gap in percentage literacy points between male and female literacy increased from 17 in 1951 to 22 in 1981 (Annexure I). In absolute terms too, the number of illiterate women has increased during the period, from 158.7 million to 241.7 million (excluding Assam). Women comprised 57 per cent of the illiterate population in 1981, and girls formed 70 per cent of non-enrolled children in the school age group.

There are disturbing regional variations in the levels of literacy in the country. (Annexure II gives women's literacy rate for State and Union Territory). The literacy rate for women varies from 65.7 per cent in Kerala, as per 1981 census, to 11.4 per cent for Rajasthan. The gap between male and female literacy rates in percentage points is only 9.5 in Kerala, but 24.9 in Rajasthan. States like Madhya Pradesh, Uttar Pradesh and Bihar are also lagging behind in girl's education. Certain ecological constraints like difficult terrain, variety of dialects as in Arunachal Pradesh, migratory habits due to inclement weather as in parts of Jammu & Kashmir, etc. have also been instrumental in perpetuating low levels of literacy in such areas for the population as a whole and particularly for women.

Elementary Education

High priority has been accorded to elementary education in the National Development Plans to fulfil the requirements under Article 45 of the Constitution for universal, free and compulsory elementary education for children upto the age of 14 years. Progressive rise in the enrolment ratio, i.e., the percentage of children enrolled to their total population in the age group during the various Plan periods is given in Table 3.1.

By the end of the Sixth Plan, it was apparent that in order to achieve universal elementary education, an additional enrolment of 255.3 lakh is required of which the girls constitute 140.7 lakh, i.e., a little more than 55 per cent. Besides, there is a sharp fall in the number enrolled at the middle level, viz., from nearly 332 lakh to 91 lakh indicating a large dropout rate, wastage and stagnation. The enrolment ratio falls from 76.7 to 36.3. The retention of girls in schools from classes I to VIII, therefore is a task requiring urgent attention.

Among Scheduled Tribes particularly, the enrolment of girls is far below that of boys. At the primary stage, the enrolment of Scheduled Tribes boys is almost double the enrolment of girls, and the difference increases at higher stage (Annexure III). Girls belonging to Scheduled Castes communities are also lagging behind boys. The ratio of Scheduled Castes boys to girls in the elementary classes is 2:1. In the VI to VIII classes, 61.9 per cent of girls in the general population are enrolled, whereas among Scheduled Castes this proportion is only 29.9 per cent (Annexure III). The reasons for Scheduled Castes and Scheduled Tribes girls lagging behind the boys are mainly rooted in socio-economic conditions and environmental constraints such as inaccessibility of schools in tribal areas. Irrelevance of formal education curriculum to the immediate environment is also responsible for low initial enrolment and subsequent drop-out rates. Among the urban and rural poor, the compulsion on girls to assist in household chores including care of younger siblings, and on children of both sexes to work for their own survival and contribute economically to the household income, forces them to remain outside the education system.

TABLE - 3.1
ENROLMENT RATIO - ELEMENTARY CLASSES - 1984-85

Year	*Classes I-V*		*Classes VI-VIII*		*Classes I-VIII*	
	Total	*Girls*	*Total*	*Girls*	*Total*	*Girls*
1	2	3	4	5	6	7
1950-51	42.6	24.61	12.9	4.5	32.4	17.4
	(191.55)	(53.85)	(31.20)	(5.30)	(222.75)	(59.15)
1955-56	52.9	32.4	16.5	6.6	42.5	22.5
	(251.67)	(76.39)	(42.93)	(8.67)	(294.60)	(85.06)
1960-61	62.4	41.4	22.5	11.3	48.7	30.9
	(349.94)	(114.01)	(67.04)	(16.30)	(416.98)	(130.31)
1968-69	78.1	59.6	33.5	19.4	82.5	46.5
	(543.68)	(202.11)	(125.36)	(35.47)	(669.04)	(237.58)
1973-74	77.0	59.9	32.8	21.0	61.6	46.5
	(612.55)	(231.09)	(139.50)	(42.97)	(752.05)	(274.06)
1979-80	83.6	65.9	40.2	27.7	67.2	52.0
	(709.43)	(271.81)	(194.83)	(65.28)	(904.26)	(337.09)
1984-85	94.1	76.7	50.6	36.3	78.3	61.9
	(839.32)	(331.93)	(261.53)	(90.68)	(1100.84)	(422.61)
Projected Population 1984-85 (lakhs)	891.38	432.71	516.61	249.93	1407.99	682.64

Figures in Parentheses indicate actual enrolments in lakhs.
Source: Five-Year Plan Document.

According to the Fourth Educational Survey (1978), in the plains 95 per cent of the rural population have access to a primary school within one kilometer of their habitation (having a population of 300 persons or more). Middle schools are available to 78.8 per cent of rural people within three kilometres from their habitation. But commuting to distant schools does pose a problem for girls. There are very few separate schools for girls. The parents, particularly in rural areas, are reluctant to send their daughters to co-educational schools. Moreover, in most schools, the teachers are male. Despite considerable emphasis in the plans, the proportion of women teachers continues to be low. Provision for accommodation for women workers including teachers is far from satisfactory.

A large number of primary and middle schools, in rural areas especially, lack facilities such as a proper building, adequate number of teaching rooms, drinking water and toilets for girls. More than 85 per cent primary and 70 per cent middle schools in rural areas do not have these facilities, according to the Fourth All India Educational Survey (1978). Hostel facilities for girls continue to be meagre.

Secondary Education

There is a progressive rise in the rate of enrolment in secondary education of girls during the various Plan periods as seen below:

Period	*(Figures in Lakhs)*
1950-51	1.61 (16)
1965-66	11.72 (24)
1970-71	17.08 (37)
1980-81	30.98 (43)
1984-85	49.37 (44)

(Figures in brackets show enrolment of girls per 100 boys)
Source: Ministry of Human Resource Development.

The enrolment ratio of girls in the age group 15-18 years for secondary classes is 14.3 per cent as against 29.3 per cent for boys. Secondary education continues to be more or less confined to urban areas, and is affordable and accessible largely to the higher castes and the upper and middle economic strata. Although a large number of secondary schools have come up in rural areas, their enrolment particularly, in respect of girls is low. The main constraints in improving secondary and higher level education among girls have been a lack of availability of trained lady teachers, dearth of separate institutions for girls and lack of hostel facilities.

The 10+2+3 system of education has been introduced with the aim of establishing a uniform pattern of education all over the country in terms of its structure, curriculum and mobility across the States. This system has laid a common foundation for higher education without differentiation between boys and girls. Both girls and boys under the new system will learn the rudiments of science and mathematics, social sciences and humanities up to matriculation and thus gain a holistic base education which will equip them to play an active and meaningful role in the employment market.

Higher Education

In the higher educational courses, girls constitute 24 to 50 per cent of the students enrolled depending upon the type of courses. The most popular course with girls has been teachers training where they already constitute nearly fifty per cent of those enrolled. The number of girls in science courses had risen to 41 per 100 boys in 1984-85. In engineering and technology courses, however, the enrolment of girls is only 6 for 100 boys. This proportion has to be enhanced through suitable incentives in the forms of scholarships and other facilities for girls studying for these courses.

Girls enrolled for higher education, particularly those in science and technical courses, are mainly from the higher economic strata. There is a need to introduce positive measure to improve the enrolment to girls in higher education courses in rural areas and among backward groups like SCs and STs.

Non-formal Education

The concept of adult education has found support in several plan programmes. However, until the Sixth Plan, no special emphasis was given to women's education. In the Sixth Five-Year Plan, adult education was included as a part of the 'Minimum Needs Programme' and the goal of reaching 100 per cent literacy by 1990 was set under the New Twenty-Point Programme. Adult education centres exclusively for women were set up, which provided education in subjects like health, nutrition and family planning. An effort was made to build up an awareness about these subjects among women through discussions, talks and distribution of relevant literature.

Under the Adult Education Programme, apart from increasing adult literacy, the content of education was to be modified to incorporate new value systems regarding the role of women in the family and community. The Seventh Plan also envisages, among other schemes, the preparation of district level plans with local community participation both for activating and implementing the literacy programme, and the creation of special mechanisms to monitor the progress of implementation at the State level. The Integrated Rural Development Programme (IRDP), National Rural Employment Programme (NREP), Training of Rural Youth in Self-Employment (TRYSEM), and other such programmes, are also to have a component of functional literacy for women beneficiaries. The programme of Functional Literacy for Adult Women (a component of the ICDS programme) was unfortunately abandoned, though the concept of utilizing *Anganwadi* workers, who belonged to the villages and were in contact with young mothers, could have been an effective mechanism for imparting non-formal education. The scheme has since been revised to focus on issues of immediate relevance to women but has yet to be introduced.

The scheme of 'condensed courses of education and vocational training' for adult women was started in 1958 under the aegis of the Central Social Welfare Board, and was suitably expanded over the years to vocational training in areas with high employment potential. Measures are to be taken to enhance the competence of the teaching staff/training institutions involved in this programme.

The various programmes, however, have not yet been able to make any significant impact on literacy levels of the Indian population, particularly on women. According to a World Bank Report, in 2000 A.D. there will be 500 million illiterates in India, constituting 54 per cent of the world's population of illiterates. As per the Seventh Plan, the total number of adult illiterates is about 900 lakh, of whom 580 lakh are women. Although it is encouraging to note that the proportion of women in the adult education centres has gone above 50 per cent (52.34 per cent in 1984-85), women still constitute about 57 per cent of the illiterate population. Among these, literacy levels of SC and ST women are still worse. Even those treated as literates, have very low levels of literacy, scant opportunities for continuing education and use of literacy skills. Therefore, they often relapse into illiteracy.

National Policy on education-Initiatives for Women

The National Policy on Education (NPE)- 1986 is a landmark in the approach to women's education. It has attempted for the first time to address itself to the basic issues of women's equality. In the section titled "Education for Women's Equality," the policy states:

> Education will be used as an agent of basic change in the status of women. In order to neutralize the accumulated distortions of the past, there will be a well-conceived edge in favour of women. The National Education System will play a positive, interventionist role in the empowerment of women. It will foster the development of new values through redesigned curricula, textbooks, training and orientation of teachers, decision makers and administrators.

It gives overriding priority to the removal of women's illiteracy and obstacles inhibiting their access to and retention in elementary education. Emphasis has been laid on women's participation in vocational, technical and professional education at different levels as also to promote women's participation in non-traditional occupations and existing and emergent technologies.

The Programme of Action for Implementation of NPE (POA) spells out the meaning of women's empowerment:

> Women become empowered through collective reflection and decision making. The parameters of empowerment are :
>
> (a) Building a positive self-image and self-confidence.
> (b) Developing ability to think critically.
> (c) Building up group cohesion and fostering decision making and action.
> (d) Ensuring equal participation in the process of bringing about social change.
> (e) Encouraging group action in order to bring about change in the society.

(f) Providing the wherewithal for economic independence.

The programme entails the following:

(i) A phased time bound programme of elementary education for girls, particularly up to primary stage by 1990 and up to the elementary stage by 1995.

(ii) A phased time bound programme of adult education for women in the age group 15-35 by 1995.

(iii) Increased women's access to vocational, technical, professional education and existing and emergent technologies; and

(iv) Review and reorganization of educational activities to ensure that they make a substantial contribution towards women's equality, and creation of appropriate cells/units therefore.

A number of measures have been suggested to achieve the states objectives of the National Policy on Education. The Action Plan enunciates that every educational institution should take up by 1995 active programmes for the development of women. All teachers and non-formal education/adult education instructors should be trained as agents of women's development. Special programmes should be developed by research institutions to promote general awareness and positive self-image amongst women through programmes like discussions, street plays, wall papers, puppet shows, etc. Preference in recruitment of teachers up to school level should be for women.

National Literacy Mission (NLM) which aims at eradication of illiteracy in 15-35 age group by 1995 concretizes what is envisaged in NPE as regards literacy and adult education. The Mission document emphasizes the importance of imbibing the values of national integration, conservation of environment, women's equality, observance of small family norm, etc., and goes on to say that "the focus of NLM would be on rural areas, particularly women and persons belonging to the Scheduled Castes and Scheduled Tribes."

For universalization of elementary and adult education, the present programme of non-formal centres for girls needs to be extended to all educationally backward pockets of the country. Increased assistance should be given to voluntary organizations to run non-formal education centres for girls. In rural areas, special support services should be provided to relieve the girls from sibling care and other household work like fetching water, fuel, etc. Skill development linked to employment opportunities in the villages is required to be given priority so that there is an incentive on the part of the parents to educate girls. It is necessary to develop adult education programmes for women linked with upgradation of their skills and income generating activities. Skill development for girls should be a continuous process of learning and should be supported by programmes administered by other agencies such as Polytechnics, Industrial Training Institutes (ITIs), Women's Centres in Agricultural and Home Science Colleges, etc. Continuing Education Centres should be set up in a phased manner to organize vocational training, provide opportunities for retention of literacy skills and application of this learning for improving their living conditions. Their are 104 ITIs functioning exclusively for women and 97 wings in general ITIs reserved for women. These would need to be revamped during 1988-90 in terms of diversification of trades and courses, keeping in view the job potential, and facilities for vocational counselling, imparting information about credit, banking, entrepreneurial development and women's access to technical education, etc.

Women's studies programmes would also have four dimensions, viz., teaching, research, training and extension. Women's issues would be incorporated in courses under various disciplines. Research would be encouraged on identified areas/subjects. Seminars/workshops would be organized on the need for women's studies, and for dissemination of information and interaction. Educational institutions would be encouraged to take up programmes like adult education, awareness building, legal literacy, information and training support for socio-economic programmes of women's development, instructional programmes through media, etc., which directly benefit the community and bring about the empowerment of women.

All the foregoing endeavours will be planned, coordinated, monitored and evaluated continuously both at the national and state levels. The Women's Cell in the National Council for Educational Research and Training would be revived and strengthened. National Institute of Educational Planning and Administration and Directorate of Adult Education would have cells to plan and administer women's training programmes. The Women's cell in the University Grants Commission would be strengthened to monitor the implementation of various programmes at the higher education level. It is proposed that women's cells should be set up in all the States.

Perspective for Women's Education up to 2000 A.D.

The programmes for women's education will have to be implemented as a priority so that women attain a comparable level of education by 2000 A.D. The strategy to be adopted for raising literacy levels and education among women has to keep in view the vast cultural, geographical and ecological variations as also the problems relating to poverty and ignorance. The cultural and geographical variations call for decentralization of educational planning. Within the national perspective planning, implementation and monitoring of educational programmes has to be done at district and block levels, keeping in view the socio-economic and geographic parameters of the area. The vocational and occupational components have to be designed in accordance with the availability of resources and job opportunities in the regions. Voluntary organizations and women's groups active in the area should be involved in the task.

In view of the social and cultural handicaps that have operated against women's education and taking account of the multiple roles that women are required to play, the need for adopting set of objectives specific to women's education is imperative. The objectives to be achieved by 2000 A.D. in regard to women's education are:

(i) Elimination of illiteracy, universalization of elementary education and minimization of the dropout and stagnation rate in the age group 6-14 years, to negligible proportions.

(ii) Ensuring opportunities to all women for access to appropriate level, nature and quality of education and also the wherewithal for success comparable with men.

(iii) Substantial vocationalization and diversification of secondary education so as to provide a wide scope for employment and economic independence of women.

(iv) Making education an effective means for women's equality by (a) Addressing ourselves to the constraints that prevent women from participating in the educational process; (b) Eliminating the existing sexist bias in the system; (c) Making necessary intervention in the content and processes of education to inculcate positive and egalitarian attitudes, and (d) Ensuring that teachers' perceive this as one of their essential roles.

(v) Providing non-formal and part-time courses to women to enable them to acquire knowledge and skills for their social, cultural and economic advancement.

(vi) Impetus to enrol in various professional degree courses so as to increase their number in medicine, teaching, engineering and other fields substantially.

(vii) Creating a new system of accountability, particularly in respect of the basic educational services, to the local community, *inter alia*, by active involvement of women.

In brief, it is reiterated that the goals and strategies spelt out in the National Policy on Education, POA and the National Literacy Mission will ensure a much larger access for women to education.

High priority has to be accorded to creating awareness, through the various communication media, of the need for women's education and their active participation in economic and political development of the nation.

The curricula for school as well as university education have to be reviewed and revised so as to remove sex bias, inculcate among the masses a recognition of equality between men and women, and make women aware of their own potentials as well as provide them necessary opportunities to develop their capabilities in every field. Greater accessibility of educational facilities to girls is to be achieved by reducing the distance of schools from village habitations, and expanding non-formal elementary education, adult education, and the open school system. Appointment of lady teachers in schools would help draw more girls to schools and instil confidence among their parents. Towards this end, provision of quarters for lady teachers would be essential. Efforts should be directed at training local women as teachers.

Provision of creche facilities and Balwadis near the elementary and secondary schools for girls would enable the girls to attend schools and ensure care of younger siblings. Incentives like mid-day meals, better rates of scholarships, freeships, etc., would go a long way in preventing dropout.

Above all, better health facilities, smaller families, and relief from drudgery through improved technology for household chores, are essential prerequisites for better enrolment of girls at school and higher educational institutions. Inputs from other sectors are, therefore, important. Greater coordination of health, employment, welfare and education interventions will have an effect on the status of women and girls.

According to Educational Statistics for 1984-85 published by the Ministry of Human Resource Development, the enrolment of girls at primary level, which covers the age group 6-11 years, is 331.9 lakh. Surveys and field research have pointed out that there is 25 per cent inflation in the enrolment figures, and 22 per cent enrolment is outside the age group. Thus the effective enrolment gets reduced by about 47 per cent. Accordingly, the coverage for 1984-85 for the 6-11 years age group may be estimated as 176 lakh. The population projected for the age group is 422.7 lakh. This means that only 40.7 per cent of the girls in the age group 6-11 are enrolled in schools. On a similar basis, the enrolment of 11-14 years age group gets reduced to 48.1 lakh (from 90.7 lakh) which is only 19.2 per cent of the population of 249.9 lakh estimated for the age group. The population projections for the girls in the age group 6-11 years and 11-14 years for 1989-90 are 462 lakh and 267 lakh respectively. In order to have full coverage, the additional enrolment required would be 286 lakh for 6-11 age group and 219 lakh for 11-14 years age group, the total being nearly 5 crore. The task appears to be stupendous. Along with enrolment, there is the problem of very high dropout rates. Stemming from highly inflated enrolment rates and subsequent dropouts in the 6-11 years age group, enrolment of 11-14 years age group girls, even at primary level, may not be possible even by 1995.

In view of the social and cultural handicaps that have operated against women's education, the need for adopting a set of objectives specific to women's education is imperative. These would need to encompass the elimination of illiteracy and measures for retention of girls in schools, substantial vocationalization and diversification to enhance economic opportunities for women, improvement in the quality of education in terms of the values it promotes and inculcates, and finally the provision of access to professional courses for women. Such measures would be necessary as also efforts to remove the inherent prejudices working against women's education.

Recommendations

1. Awareness needs to be generated among the masses regarding the necessity of educating girls so as to prepare them to effectively contribute to the socio-economic development of the country, to strengthen their role in society and to realize their own capacities. The media and various forms of communication have to be geared to this end.
2. A fruitful rapport has to be established between the community at large and the teachers and other education personnel. As per the Programme of Action under National Policy on Education-1986, every educational institution should actively participate in bringing about such awareness.
3. Involvement of local leaders, voluntary agencies and women's groups is also necessary. Mahila Mandals need to be revitalized and reoriented to provide an effective forum for the purpose. One measure to achieve this could be to assign the responsibility to Mahila Mandals for ensuring that all children in a community attend school. An incentive scheme should be introduced to motivate panchayats to ensure 100 per cent enrolment of girls in their villages.
4. Early childhood care and education introduces children into the school system gradually and smoothly. When children get used to attending schools, it ensures in some measure retention of children, including girls, at elementary stages also. Hence there is needed to have a comprehensive and effective programme of early childhood care and education linked to an integrated package of learning for women. The most comprehensive example of this is the Integrated Child Development Services Programme which needs to be universalized.

5. For improving enrolment and minimizing drop-outs and wastage in case of girl students, it would be helpful if learning is made more attractive by providing adequate teaching materials in schools.
6. The number of teachers should also be increased so that the interaction between the teacher and the taught, which is so essential for good education also increases. This would help in the retention of girls in schools and would be more effective if teachers from the area are employed. In single teacher schools, the teacher must be a woman. In Orissa all jobs of primary teachers have been reserved for women.
7. School curricula should be imaginatively developed to stimulate creativity largely through play rather than overburdening children with formal or rote learning. Regional language should normally be the medium of instruction.
8. School timings should be flexible and fixed to suit local conditions and the needs of the working girls and must be available within the walking distance of the child. A substantial increase is required in the number of schools for girls.
9. In addition to incentives like free textbooks, free supply of uniforms, award of attendance scholarships and mid-day meals, facilities such as proper school building, safe drinking water, and toilet, etc., need to be provided to encourage school enrolment and retention of girls especially girls from educationally deprived social groups and from hilly, tribal, desert and remote areas and urban slums.
10. Local talent must be developed in order to meet the need for recruiting women teachers at the primary and elementary levels especially in rural and tribal areas. In this endeavour national agencies like CAPART and CSWB, voluntary agencies, Mahila Mandals and local self-government agencies can make a significant contribution. They can also play a useful watchdog function to ensure that educational and other programmes are run efficiently and effectively.
11. There should be a reservation of 50 per cent posts for women teachers in elementary schools. Women teachers working in the rural areas should be provided suitable accommodation.

12. Multi-entry system for girls who cannot attend schools continuously should be adopted.
13. Wherever necessary, schools meant exclusively for girls may be set up. The recommended distance of 3 kilometres for locating a middle school is a handicap for many girls. To ensure participation of girls in middle schools, it is necessary to provide hostel facilities.
14. The Savitribai Phule Foster Parent Scheme of Maharashtra could be adopted in other States/Union Territories to help girls of poorer families to at least complete primary school. Under the scheme, well to do persons and organizations are persuaded to adopt one or more out of school girls and contribute in cash or kind or both @ Rs. 25 per month for her education. The money can be spent on uniforms, stationery or anything else, needed by the girls or also partly used to alleviate the economic distress of the parents. The Zila Parishad, Block Education Officer and headmasters play a pivotal role in implementing the scheme, which is purely voluntary and if district level officers are appointed for coordination of programmes for women, they could also actively take it up.
15. Condensed courses of education at elementary and middle school levels for girls must be started in all the rural areas and for weaker sections of the urban community.
16. Many girls in the 11-14 years age group would first have to be brought into the primary stage through non-formal education. By devising alternative education approaches non-formal schooling and through like intelligent use of technology, the pace of middle school education can be accelerated. If retention up to 75 per cent is achieved up to class V, universal elementary education may be possible in some parts of the country by 2000 A.D. Other backward areas would have to be given much more attention in, professional as well as financial terms to enable them even to universalize primary education for girls by 1995. The National Literacy Mission will need to address these issues on a priority basis.
17. Special efforts are necessary for bringing tribal children particularly, girls into the school system. Tribal dialects, extreme poverty, problems of commuting, rigidity of formal

education and its irrelevance to the tribal culture and the tribal's distrust of the ways of the mainstream society, must be borne in mind in formulating strategies.

18. The educational forecasts, may look more achievable if the system is opened up for flexible non-formal education which 'the below average states' should be persuaded to adopt in a large measure. The existing educational infrastructure particularly, in tribal and rural areas should be made effective and responsible.
19. Non-formal education is an alternative to the formal system which has the potentiality of becoming the major programme of education for girls who cannot attend school during normal school hours due to various reasons. The Central Government is already implementing a centrally sponsored scheme under which grants to the extent of 90 per cent are provided towards maintenance of non-formal education centres exclusively for girls in nine educationally backward states. This programme should be strengthened further and extended to other states where education of girls is lagging behind. It should at least cover all the pockets of low enrolments of girls and areas of high dropout rate. Besides literacy, it must also provide relevant information on skill development and inculcation of positive self-image among girls.
20. Secondary education for girls should entail:
    (i) A ten-year course in general education learning and diversified higher secondary education which may be either terminal or lead to further professional preparation; and (ii) Diversified courses after Grade VIII in technical subjects, viz., agricultural technology, health services, food production activities such as , dairy and poultry and non-traditional areas need to be untroubled. A legal literacy component is also recommended at this stage.
21. Diversified courses leading to occupational preparation should be of parallel duration to the general secondary courses. In addition, there should be a variety of short and long term, whole time, part-time and apprentice courses. The trend of thinking is now to place emphasis on the last.

Keeping in view the rapid modernization and advancement in technology for agriculture, there is an urgent need for skilled artisanship for promoting productive activities on the one hand, and a variety of learning programmes for adjustment of the rural society to socio-economic change on the other. Efforts should be made to ensure that girls have every opportunity to enter into apprenticeship in areas that are non-conventional, and incentives be provided for the same. Further, at least 30 per cent seats should be reserved for girls in apprenticeship training courses on a non-transferable basis.

22. General and vocational training courses should be combined so that prospects of a career immediately on completion of schooling may attract girls from weaker sections. While designing the vocational courses, available occupational opportunities as well as the need to overcome market stereotypes should be kept in view.
23. Since secondary education has remained almost beyond the reach of weaker sections, liberal incentives and other facilities to release the girls from household chores appear to be essential. It would also help to locate the institutions in the areas of their habitation.
24. Multiple entry system should be introduced in the secondary classes. Part-time education facilities should also be made available.
25. Condensed courses should be organized in cooperation with local vocational training institutions to cover all rural areas and areas inhabited by weaker sections in urban areas. Such courses may be organized for small groups of girls, and combined with job training. Efforts should be made to cover atleast 215 lakh women in the age group 15-30 years under the condensed courses programme wherever possible the condensed courses of the CSWB should be expanded and strengthened. New programmes that are to be initiated must avoid duplication in the areas where the CSWB's programmes exist.
26. Correspondence courses and self-study programmes can be especially useful for girls desirous of continuing education but are unable to do so because of circumstances. Apart from

imparting elementary education and knowledge about farming techniques, the curriculum for non-student girls should include courses of training in occupational skills. Similar programmes should also be designed for girls in the urban areas.

27. The open school system should be expanded extending the facility to all the girls in rural and backward areas.
28. Science education for girls has been neglected so far. Secondary schools for girls must be helped to build good science programmes over the Eighth Five-Year Plan. Special scholarships for girls opting for science courses need to be instituted at the secondary and higher education levels.
29. Special scholarship may also be offered to rural women, who opt for teachers' training, especially those who complete the condensed courses at the secondary stage.
30. There is a need to open more colleges and polytechnics for girls, especially in rural areas.
31. Incentives like scholarships, freeships, etc., should be provided to enable girls from rural areas to pursue higher education for girls belonging to weaker sections. In addition to freeships and scholarships bursaries should also be provided to meet their requirements for food and lodging.
32. Girls should be encouraged to enter professional courses. Reservation of seats for girls in such courses may be considered to level out the existing bias in access to certain professional streams.
33. Vocational counselling and guidance service be organized exclusively in a more meaningful way to help girls in colleges and universities opt for suitable courses relevant to their talents and interests, and free of traditional bias.
34. Vocational and technical education for women, both formal and non-formal, should be a major feature of the programmes of rural universities. The women's wings of the universities could undertake large-scale extension programmes in order to activate girls and women in the surrounding areas to take advantage of educational and occupational facilities of various types, particularly those leading to meaningful employment, essential for reducing women's marginalization.

35. In order to increase the representation of rural girls in higher education courses, 30 per cent seats, may be reserved for girls to begin with.
36. All agencies involved with preparation of curricula prescription of textbooks and organization of educational processes will have to evince awareness towards women's issues. University/College Departments of Women's Studies, appropriate voluntary agencies, women's groups, etc., should be involved in giving a new perspective to the various issues of content and processes of education. Women's universities and women's centres in colleges need to take an active role in women's development and in influencing the attitudes of future generations.
37. Facilities for part-time self-study and correspondence courses should be provided on a large-scale to enable girls who are not in a position to join higher educational institutions on a regular basis, to continue their studies.
38. In addition to courses leading to degree/diploma, short courses in specific subjects through summer school sessions, and ad hoc programmes like seminars, workshops, etc., should be organized for working women with a view to upgrading their knowledge and skills, not necessarily leading to degrees.
39. Integrated learning programmes for women are recommended which will not only lay emphasis on literacy but on empowering women through awareness building on social issues, bringing about attitudinal change, promoting skill training for employment, providing information on health care, nutrition and hygiene as well as on legal rights. Such programmes are beginning and must continue to be designed and structured so as to be relevant for the vast majority of rural women. The revised scheme linked to ICDS known as the 'Women's Integrated Learning for Life', should be introduced as an integral part of the non-formal education system.
40. Entrepreneurship development programmes should be organized separately for education of women in the age group 18-30 years, with a minimum of matriculation level of education. The objective of such training should be to:

(i) Make them aware of the various opportunities for self-employment; (ii) Motivate them to take up self-employment; (iii) Impart needed skills and training; (iv) Promote motivation for achievement among them; and (v) Create access to resources such as capital credit, etc.

41. A large number of girls cannot participate in whole day education programmes. Provision of non-formal and part-time programmes, with flexible school hours and sensitivity to the agricultural cycle are, of particular importance. In addition to the primary and upper primary stages, distance learning opportunities need to be provided at secondary and higher secondary levels.

42. Adult education will have to be composed of three inter-related stands aimed at:
    (i) Continuous flow of new information especially to rural and tribal areas, particularly to inculcate positive attitudes towards women;
    (ii) Continuous training of the people in the use of modern tools and methods of production; and
    (iii) Acquisition of permanent reading and computation skills.

    Following from the above, three types of programmes may be offered to the learner:
    (a) Information and literacy.
    (b) Information and training in new technology and literacy.
    (c) Information and training in new technology with or without literacy. Continuous information flows relating to human affairs, gender relations and the use of science and technology for betterment of life would be the common factor in all the three programmes.

43. The growing availability of communication media should be directed towards keeping up information flows and portraying positive images of women in non-conventional roles. Audio-visual materials, combined with non-formal training arrangements, could impart to various, population groups the kind of instruction they need in the use of new technologies. Involvement of mass media in motivating women to attend literacy classes is most essential.

44. Rapid strides in the development of technologies and tools for the reduction in women's drudgery and easy access to work places, water and fuel supply, child care, health services and population control can contribute significantly to the success of learning programmes for women. Women's literacy programmes would succeed better if they centre around women's concerns and also provide opportunities of recreation and sharing of experiences.
45. District plans should be prepared keeping in view literacy requirements of the learners and identifying agencies which can take up such programmes in districts.
46. All women working in industries or employed elsewhere should be made literate by the employers by allotting time from the working hours for their education. Place of teaching, teachers and teaching material should be arranged by them. Necessary legislation to this effect may be enacted.
47. At least 50 per cent seats in pre-service courses in all teachers training institutions should be reserved for women. Spatial planning to ensure that women from rural areas are selected as teachers is essential.
48. Provision of composite teacher training courses for women who have had insufficient education to improve their educational qualifications along with their training, should be made.
49. The existing Integrated Rural Development Programme, National Rural Employment Programme, Development of Women and Children in Rural Areas, Training of Youth in Self-Employment Programme, Integrated Child Development Programme, etc., should have a component of literacy for their women beneficiaries. Training should be provided to the functionaries of various development departments by the Directorate of Education in the States.
50. The State Resources Centres should produce suitable learning material for women on a priority basis. Literature for neoliterates should be suitably devised by experts, keeping in view the needs of different groups of learners.
51. Decentralization is the key to the successful application of the strategies outlined above. In this decentralized approach,

the village cluster or the block level is seen as most appropriate for the delivery of programmes. It is, therefore, necessary that the block is allocated a flexible budget so as to make funds available to village clusters/villages for innovative educational activities and for equalization of educational opportunity.

52. An overall coordination of health, welfare and educational inputs would be most desirable. This would entail (a) Convergent policies in these sectors; (b) Coordination of delivery mechanisms; and (c) Pooling of allocations.

53. The strategies spelt out in the National Policy of Education, 1986, the Programme of Action for its implementation and the National Literacy Mission and the successful achievement of the goals, imposed in these documents, would be important for improvement in the status of women.

Four

Empowerment of Women

Political status of women can be defined as the degree of equality and freedom enjoyed by women in the shaping and sharing of power and in the value given by society to this role of women.

The Indian Constitution guarantees political equality through the institution of adult franchise and Article 15 which prohibits discrimination *inter alia* on grounds of sex. It should be kept in mind that this recognition of political equality of women was a radical departure not only from the socio-cultural norms prevailing in traditional India but also in the context of the political evolution of even most advanced countries at that date. With the exception of the socialist countries, no other State in the world had accepted women's equality as a matter of course.

The United States and the United Kingdom granted franchise to women only after World War I, after decades of struggle by their women. Most other countries, Eastern or Western, conceded it only after World War II. Japan granted franchise to women in 1946, China in 1949. The exceptions were Thailand and the Philippines which granted a limited franchise, similar to the Indian case, in 1932 and 1933 respectively. Amongst the West European countries, France granted franchise to women in 1945, Switzerland in 1971.

In the case of India, the two major forces which acted as a catalyst in the achievement of political equality of women were the national movement and the leadership of Gandhi, who declared himself to be "uncompromising in the matter of women's rights." According to Gandhi in *Young India*, 17.10.1929:

> Women must have votes and an equal legal status. But the problem does not end there. It only commences at the point where women begin to affect the political deliberations of the nation.

The Pre-Gandhian Period

The nineteenth century reform movement and the spread of education among the women had definitely initiated the process of improving the status of women. However, this process was essentially limited to improving the position of women within the traditional family structure. Prevalent social attitudes, particularly among the upper and middle-classes, continued to regard domestic life as women's sole occupation.

Nevertheless there was a minority of women who voluntarily participated in both social welfare and revolutionary movements. They were active in the cause of women's education, welfare of the weaker sections in society and relief to distressed persons during emergencies like floods, droughts, famines, etc. A still smaller group became involved in the revolutionary movement, actively participating as couriers, distributing literature, looking after various institutions and risking police repression, imprisonment, and even capital punishment.

In both these cases, the women received a certain degree of support from their families in such activities, either overt or covert. Most of them came from the affluent or middle-class families in urban areas. The social attitude to this first awakening was one of reserved acceptance, extending sometimes to admiration and pride in the heroism displayed by some of these women. But it by no means amounted to accepting this as a norm for women's role and behaviour in society.

The nineteenth century reformers professed concern for the low status of women, but their efforts were concentrated towards improving women's position within the family, for the purpose of strengthening the family as the basic unit of social organization. Raising the status of women was seen only as granting her the right to property, re-marriage after widowhood, abolition of child marriage and the right to education.

A characteristic of this movement was its elitist approach. Most of the demands were relevant only for a limited section of women, i.e., the upper and middle-classes. They did not represent the problem affecting the majority of women. The social change envisaged was a limited one of transformation within the system, rather than that of the system.

The turn of the nineteenth century witnessed some results of the dissemination of education to women, though restricted, and the impact of the ideas of the reformers in the changes taking place in the status of women. This was manifested in the emergence of women's organizations, when women entered public life in larger numbers than before. This period saw the birth of organizations such as The Women's Indian Association (this was later merged in the All India Women's Conference), the National Council for Women and The All India Women's Conference. It also opened a new chapter in the women's movement for equality. A demand for women's franchise was initiated in 1917 when a deputation of Indian women led by Sarojini Naidu, presented to the British Parliament a demand for the enfranchisement of women on the basis of equality with men.

The constitutional reforms of 1919 left the matter to the discretion of the elected legislatures in the provinces and finally the Reforms Act of 1921 enfranchised a very small fraction of the Indian population including women. This right to vote, however, was subject to certain reservations: women could vote only if they possessed qualifications of wifehood, property and education. These qualifications, apart from making the women's right dependent on her marital status, in fact restricted it to an infinitesimal minority of women.

The gap between the radical nature of the demand and actual achievement was a characteristic of the period till independence. It represented not only the reluctance of the foreign rulers to accept the democratic aspirations of the people, but also their own political view regarding the limited role of women in Indian society. They could not believe that Indian society would ever regard women as equal partners of men. Nor could they expect women to act independently of the men, as a separate political force. Therefore, women did not feature in the framework of representation of classes, communities, and interests, which was offered by the colonial authorities as the solution of the Indian question.

The Gandhian Era

A transformation of the attitude to women was precipitated by the Gandhian view regarding women's role in the social revolution and reconstruction:

Woman is the companion of man gifted with equal mental

> capacities. She has the right to participate in the minutest details of the activities of man, and she has the same right of freedom and liberty as he... By sheer force of a vicious custom, even the most ignorant and worthless men have been enjoying a superiority over women which they do not deserve and ought not to have. Gandhi, *Young India*, 26.2.1918.
>
> Since resistance in satyagraha is offered through self-suffering. It is a weapon pre-eminently open to women..... She can become the leader in satyagraha which does not require the learning that books give but does require the stout heart that comes from suffering and faith. Gandhi, *Young India*, 24.2.1940.

Responding to his call, women of different communities and all walks of life came out to join the struggle — as political campaigners, joining protest marches and demonstrations, as constructive workers, participating in and often taking charge of the village reconstruction programmes, as workers in the cause of social and economic justice working for the removal of untouchability and other forms of social oppression. The highly educated and the not so well educated joined hands to spread literacy and develop self-reliance among the people. Women who had spent their lives behind *purdah* came out to fight orthodoxy, superstition and communal separatism.

Social legitimation for such activity was not forthcoming at first but the women joined the men to fight in the movement. Events proved that without the cooperation of women the freedom struggle would not have been so successful. Under Mahatma Gandhi's direction the civil disobedience movement and the salt *satyagraha* saw women in the forefront. The breaking of the forest laws, boycott of foreign cloth and liquor shops resulted in women suffering police repression, incarceration in prisons and other indignities. Scores of women were in the vanguard of the movement. According to Nehru in *Discovvery of India*:

> Our women came to the forefront and took charge of the struggle. Women had always been there of course but now there was an avalanche of them which took not only the British Government but their own men-folk by surprise. There were these women, women of the upper or middle cases,

> leading sheltered lives in their homes, peasant women, working class women, right women — pouring out in their tens of thousands in defiance of government orders and police *lathis*. It was not only the display of courage and daring but what was even more surprising was the organizational power they showed.

This kind of participation had a direct impact on the attitudes of women also. A meeting of representative women's organizations in 1930 drafted a memorandum demanding immediate acceptance of adult franchise without sex discrimination. It was turned down by the Government, but in 1931 the Karachi Session of the Indian National Congress took the historic decision, committing itself to political equality of women, regardless of their status and qualifications.

The Government of India Act of 1935 increased the number of enfranchised Indians, the proportional suffrage rights of women and relaxed some of the previous qualifications. All women over 21 could vote provided they fulfilled the conditions of property and education.

Independence brought the promise of actual liberation and equality. The Constitution pledged the nation to achieving a just society, based on the principles of equality and dignity of the individual, and proclaimed the right to political and legal equality as fundamental rights of all Indians. The guarantee against discrimination in employment and offices under the State opened the avenues to offices of power and dignity.

It has been argued that political equality is meaningless in a country where the mass of the population suffers from poverty, continuous threat of starvation, illiteracy, lack of health, and inequality of class, status and power. It is more so in the case of women who suffer from another dimension of inequality, namely the weight of traditional attitudes that regard them as physically, intellectually and socially inferior to men. It is, however, clear from Mahatma Gandhi's statement that the equal and political rights of women were only to be a starting point to enable the society to transform itself by ending all exploitation, a process in which women would be the prime movers.

Indicators of Political Equality and Role of Women

Looked at from this angle, political rights and status appear as only instrumental for achieving general equality of status and opportunities and social, economic and political justice. It, therefore, becomes important to examine the efficiency of this instrument in the practical operation of the political process. We have used the following indicators for this examination:

Indicators of Participation in the Political Process

The readiness and willingness of the people to participate in the political process is a basic requirement for a democracy. The role of women in this field can be measured by the turn out of women voters and number of women candidates in each election. Table 6.1 gives the percentage turnout of voters in Lok Sabha 1962-71, statewise andd sexwise.

Indicators of Political Attitudes

Since attitudes play a major role in determining political behaviour, the level of awareness, commitment and involvement of women participating in politics, particularly their autonomy and independence in political action and behaviour, are important measures of their political status.

Impact of Women in the Political Process

If political rights are only an instrument to achieve other goals, then this is the crucial measure of women's political status. Yet this is the most difficult to measure. Quantitative data is of little use because they may not indicate the actual reality in the political process. We have tried to measure this by looking at the women's view of their own roles and efficacy in the political process, and society's attitude to these new roles of women. This is indicated by the success of women candidates at various, elections, the efficiency of women's pressure groups, the nature of the leadership and women elites in parties and Government, and the effectiveness of campaigns for women's mobilization particularly on issues that directly concern them.

In the course of our examination we have tried to separate certain myths from the actual state of affairs, by indicating the gaps that exist between popular notions and opinions and empirical realities, between what the law provides and the policy demands on the one hand and what society actually permits on the other. The evidence for our examination has been collected by various means, from published research on Indian political behaviour, some first-hand studies sponsored by the Committee, comments of political workers and parties, and the views of the large number of women belonging to different socio-economic categories, whom the Committee met during the tours.

Indicators of Participation

In a democratic system participation in politics has to be viewed at the levels of acquisition and exercise of power and rights of a citizen. The study of general elections at these two levels offers certain quantitative measures of participation of citizens both as voters and as candidates. Unfortunately the statistics for the first two general elections do not throw light on the number of women candidates or voters. Our comparison, therefore, has to be limited to the last three general elections, viz., those of 1962, 1967 and 1971. Table 6.1 indicates the percentage turn out of men and women voters in the last three general elections to the Lok Sabha by States.

The overall picture of women participation is given in Table 6.2. It will be seen that the difference between percentage turnout of men and women voters has been decreasing. Between 1962 and 1967 the percentage of women who exercised their franchise increased nearly by 9 per cent but in 1971 it decreased by 6.33 per cent. This decrease is, however, nearly equal to the fall in the total voting percentage in that year. Since the difference between men and women voters does not show any substantial increase, it may be inferred that there was no significant change in the trend, which is visible when we compare the figures of 1962 and 1971. During the nine years period, while the total voters' turn out increased by only 0.95 per cent increase in the percentage of women voters was 2.52 per cent.

A comparison of the turn out in different States shows that the States of Orissa, Bihar, Madhya Pradesh, Himachal Pradesh, Rajasthan and Uttar Pradesh registered a low turn out of total

TABLE - 4.1
PERCENTAGE TURN OUT OF VOTERS IN GENERAL ELECTIONS — LOK SABHA 1962-71— STATEWISE AND SEXWISE

Sl. No.	Name of State/ Union Territory	1962			1967			1971		
		By Men Voters to Men Electors	By Women Voters to Women Electors	Total Voters to Total Electors	By Men Voters to Men Electors	By Women Voters to Women Electors	By Total Voters to Total Electors	By Men Voters to Men Electors	By Women Voters to Women Electors	By Total Voters to Total Electors
	1	2	3	4	5	6	7	8	9	10
1.	Andhra Pradesh	69.03	60.34	64.72	72.08	65.26	68.67	64.39	54.71	59.57
2.	Assam	51.50	37.23	45.09	66.50	50.83	59.28	58.37	41.57	50.69
3.	Bihar	55.39	32.86	44.88	61.28	40.74	51.53	60.00	37.01	49.10
4.	Gujarat	63.39	52.02	57.96	69.19	58.17	63.76	60.61	50.19	55.59
5.	Haryana	-	-	-	75.41	69.44	72.62	67.78	60.48	64.34
6.	Jammu & Kashmir	-	-	-	57.25	52.08	55.16	67.61	46.59	58.12
7.	Kerala	74.10	67.08	70.55	77.13	74.20	75.64	65.77	63.30	64.53
8.	Madhya Pradesh	60.36	28.90	44.79	64.35	42.48	53.47	58.24	37.59	48.00
9.	Maharashtra	66.02	54.29	60.43	68.82	60.49	64.75	63.54	56.12	59.94
10.	Mysore	65.18	53.07	59.30	67.36	58.34	62.95	61.73	52.71	57.42
11.	Nagaland	-	-	-	-	-	-	56.82	50.37	53.77
12.	Orissa	33.07	13.21	23.56	53.56	33.05	43.70	51.85	33.74	43.20
13.	Punjab	65.90	58.13	62.37	73.44	68.43	71.14	63.36	55.87	59.89

14. Rajasthan	62.63	41.35	52.44	64.96	51.02	58.27	60.07	47.50	54.04
15. Tamil Nadu	73.07	64.55	68.77	79.23	73.94	76.56	74.48	69.17	71.82
16. Uttar Pradesh	59.42	39.76	50.35	59.27	48.96	54.51	52.23	38.84	46.10
17. West Bengal	61.98	47.62	55.75	70.88	60.15	66.03	64.79	58.74	62.16
18. Himachal Pradesh	43.68	22.04	33.60	57.97	44.05	51.20	48.44	33.38	41.18
19. Manipur	66.27	64.44	65.34	68.73	65.80	67.23	53.37	43.55	48.35
20. Meghalaya	-	-	-	-	-	-	-	-	-
21. Tripura	73.33	61.77	67.95	76.45	72.98	74.84	65.00	55.91	60.84
22. Andaman & Nicobar	-	-	-	79.22	76.77	78.45	69.72	72.33	70.55
23. Chandigarh	-	-	-	65.42	65.28	65.36	62.79	73.11	62.92
24. Dadra & Nagar Haveli	-	-	-	80.05	76.55	78.29	71.46	68.06	69.78
25. Goa, Daman & Diu	-	-	-	69.35	67.42	68.37	57.01	54.91	55.92
26. Laccadive Minicoy & Amindivi Islands	-	-	-	78.27	86.16	82.02	(Uncontested)		
27. Delhi.	65.82	71.71	68.29	68.91	70.25	69.49	66.81	63.29	65.18
28. Pondicherry	-	-	-	76.01	73.72	74.85	71.93	68.28	70.10
29. Mizoram	-	-	-	-	-	-	-	-	-
Total	62.05	46.63	54.76	66.73	55.48	61.33	61.00	49.15	55.35

Source: Report on the Fifth General Election in India, 1971-72.

voters. The turn out of women voters in these States was still lower, resulting in a high difference between men and women. Assam and Jammu & Kashmir also come under this category. These States, as has been indicated in the previous chapters, are generally known for the educational and social backwardness of their women. All the demographic indicators, viz., sex ratio, literacy rate, life expectancy, etc., point to a low status of women in these States. This is reflected in the low participation.

TABLE - 4.2
TURN OUT OF WOMEN VOTERS LOK SABHA ELECTIONS

Year	*Total Voting Percentage*	*Percentage Turnout of Female Voters*	*Difference between Percentage turn out of Male & Female Voters.*
1962	54.76	46.63	15.42
1967	61.33	55.48	11.25
1971	55.35	49.15	11.85

It has generally been found that there is a close relationship between literacy and political awareness. The States and Union Territories which have registered the maximum mobilization of women voters generally have a high female literacy rate. It should, however, be noted that it is impossible to establish a similar correlation between education or economic development and exercise of franchise by women. One great difficulty about the Indian political scene is that it is impossible to generalize about the interrelationship between any factor and political behaviour. Patterns of political behaviour from different regions show different relationships, influenced as they are by interrelated factors like the social status of women, their economic position, the cultural norms and the overall regional outlook towards women's participation in the wider society. Table 4.3 shows the percentage participation of women voter turn out in the states of Orissa, Himachal, Bihar, M.P. and J&K.

According to Table 4.4 the number of women participating as candidates at different elections, however shows a much greater difference. For the Lok Sabha, their highest number, reached in 1971, was 17 per cent of the total seats. As compared to the total number of candidates, women have never exceeded 4 per cent.

TABLE - 4.3
MINIMUM MOBILIZATION

	1		2		3		4	
1962								
Total	Orissa	(23.00)	Himachal	53.00	M.P.	44.79	Bihar	44.88
Women	Orissa	(13.25)	Himachal	22.04	M.P.	28.90	Bihar	32.00
Diffe-rence	M.P.	(32)	Bihar	23	Raj.	21	Orissa & UP	(20)
	1		2		3		4	
1967								
Total	Orissa	(43.70)	Himachal	51.20	Bihar	51.53	M.P.	53.47
Women	Orissa	33.05	Bihar	40.74	M.P.	42.48	Himachal	44.05
Diffe-rence	M.P.	(22)	Bihar	(21)	Orissa	(20)	Assam	(16)
	1		2		3		4	
1971								
Total	Himachal	(41.18)	Orissa	43.20	M.P.	48.00	Bihar	49.10
Women	Himachal	(33.38)	Orissa	33.74	Bihar	37.01	M.P.	37.59
Diffe-rence	Bihar	(23)	M.P. & J.K.	(21)	Orissa	(18)	Assam	(17)

Note: States have been arranged in ascending order, for total turn out, turn out of women votes, and difference between men and women voters. Higher difference indicates lower mobilisation of women.

TABLE - 4.4
WOMEN CONTESTANTS FOR THE LOK SABHA

Year of General Election	*Total Seats Contested*	*Number of Women Contestants*	*Percentage*	*Number of Women Elected*	*Percentage of Winners*
1	2	3	4	5	6
1962	491	65	13	33	50.6
1967	515	66	13	28	42.4
1971	518	86	17	21	25.9

The Statewise number of these contestants has been generally in accordance with the total number of seats allocated to the States. The maximum number was in UP, except in 1971, when Bihar, the next biggest State in terms of Lok Sabha seats, took the lead by one candidate. The record of Madhya Pradesh is also high except in 1971, when it dropped. This indicates that there is no correlation between the general level of women's participation, (which is consistently low in UP, and Bihar), and the selection of women candidates, which is mostly done by the parties. Punjab, where women's participation rate has outstripped that of men in the urban areas, has an extremely poor number of candidates. Kerala and Maharashtra show increase in the number of candidates over the years, and West Bengal a sudden one in 1971, but the most visible trend is the stagnation or even decline in the number in most States. Karnataka, though not backward in any sense, did not put up a single woman candidate in three of the general elections, and only one in the other two. Jammu & Kashmir, Nagaland and most of the Union Territories never put a single woman candidate. (Table 4.5)

Women in Manipur, Andhra Pradesh, Tamil Nadu, Karnataka and Orissa were particularly vocal in criticizing the political parties for sponsoring so few women. In their view the small number of candidates represented not the aspiration of women, but the indifference of political parties in giving them nominations.

The factors that determine the number of women candidates from different regions are obviously not related to the level of poll participation, literacy or economic and social position of women in a region. On the other hand, the States where women's position is relatively low have a record of higher number of candidates. On the whole, we have to note that the number of women seeking elections either for the Lok Sabha or for the State Assemblies, has been in no way comparable to their proportion in the population.

Apart from the election figures, our discussion with different groups of women in all the States points towards certain general conclusions. At the level of participation, women have improved their response to the political rights conferred by the Constitution. Keeping other things equal, overall development such as literacy, increased mass communication, etc., may help to draw a larger number of women into the political mainstream. The present participation of women in the political process, however, presents sharp contrasts. The overall statistics indicates that women, participation though improving, is still so small as to be discouraging, particularly when compared with that of men. Though there has been a substantial number of new women entrants, during our tours we were informed by many women that there has been a large number of drop-outs from active participation. When these are from families with long political traditions, they indicate a certain process of disillusionment. This is also corroborated by some of the State studies mentioned earlier.

TABLE - 4.5

STATEWISE DISTRIBUTION OF WOMEN CONTESTANTS FOR LOK SABHA IN DIFFERENT GENERAL ELECTIONS

States/UT	*No. of Women Contestants*			*No. of Women Elected*		
	'62	'67	'71	'62	'67	'71
1	2	3	4	5	6	7
Andhra Pradesh	7	4	7	4	3	2
Assam	3	1	3	2	N	1
Bihar	8	12	18	6	4	1
Gujarat	5	1	1	2	1	N
Haryana	-	1	N	-	N	N
J & K	-	N	N	-	N	N
Kerala	1	3	4	N	1	1
M.P.	11	11	8	7	5	3
Tamil Nadu	4	5	2	1	1	1
Maharashtra	2	4	5	1	1	N
Karnataka	1	N	1	1	N	1
Orissa	N	1	2	N	N	N
Punjab	N	3	1	N	2	N
Rajasthan	6	2	4	1	1	2
U.P.	14	13	17	6	7	6
West Bengal	2	3	9	2	2	1
Nagaland	-	N	N	-	N	N
Union Territories						
Andaman etc.	-	N	N	-	N	N
Chandigarh	-	N	N	-	N	N
Dadra etc.	-	N	N	-	N	N
Delhi	N	1	3	N	N	2
Goa, Daman, etc.	-	1	1	-	N	N
Himachal Pradesh	1	N	N	N	N	N
Laccadive etc.	-	N	N	-	N	N
Manipur	N	N	N	N	N	N
Pondicherry	-	N	N	-	N	N
Tripura	N	N	N	N	N	N
Grand Total	65	66	86	33	28	21

Note: The States and Union Territories as in the IV General Election have been followed in this table. Himachal Pradesh, Manipur and Tripura became States afterwards.

Muslims and tribal women show a lower level of participation both as voters and candidates, though there are exceptions to this. Our survey on Muslim women indicates that a large number of the women interviewed had voted in the previous election. We also met tribal women in Tripura, Meghalaya and Baster (MP), who, though not formally educated, have a keen interest in politics and participate regularly.

Women of Scheduled Castes and other intermediary groups reveal a higher participation rate. In West Bengal, women from these groups were more aware and participated relatively better than the tribal women. Studies in Gujarat and Maharashtra have also corroborated this fact. We met a number of women from these communities in villages in different states, whose determination to participate in elections was quite obvious.

In terms of voting participation, the rural-urban difference seems to be narrowing down, though the belief in the lower participation of rural women continues to be widespread. During the general elections of 1972, the Committee appointed some observers. The results of their investigation, as well as those of their studies indicate that urbanization *per se* does not have much influence on women's participation. On the other hand, the argument that domestic duties prevent them from participation is more commonly voiced by women in urban areas, particularly by the middle-classes.

In many of the villages visited by us, we came across women who have been exercising their franchise, and were fully conscious of the power that this right gave them. A group of Scheduled Caste women whom we met in a village in Madhya Pradesh had not only voted in the last elections but were very much conscious of the power conferred on them by the franchise. They were emphatic that they would hereafter vote only for such candidates who will continue to take interest in their welfare even after the election. In a village in UP, Scheduled Caste and Muslim women were very vocal, not only about their franchise, but also about the secrecy of the ballot.

There is a general consensus that the political parties have neglected their task of politically educating and mobilizing women adequately. They have also tended to ignore the claims of women in nominating candidates for elections. This criticism was voiced even by successful women legislators.

Majority of the women candidates come from relatively well-to-do families, with a sprinkling of members of old princely houses. Only one party has occasionally backed women candidates from Scheduled Castes or Tribes and Muslims. Majority of the women candidates are educated, though their levels vary. About 70 per cent to 80 per cent of the women Members of Parliament are, however, relatively better educated.

In terms of political socialization or background, the smaller group among the candidates come from families with fairly long traditions of political participation. They are, therefore, highly articulate, have a sharp perspective of politics, and have continued in the struggle for power through several successive elections. The larger group consists of new entrants. Some of them had no previous political experience but entered the political arena for the first time through elections.

The greatest deterrent to women's active participation as candidates is the increasing expense of elections. Women were emphatic that families were still not prepared to finance the elections of their women from family funds, though they would do so for the men. Since most women have no economic resources of their own, their aspirations could only be fulfilled if they were fully backed by a political party. Because of this factor, the majority of women candidates today are those who can command some independent means.

The other factors which deter many women from active participation in politics are the threats of violence and character assassinations which have increased recently. This was mentioned to us by many legislators and political workers. Some of them have a long record of political activism, but still hesitate to face candidature at elections.

Indicators of Political Attitudes

It must be kept in mind that these three indices used to assess political roles are largely heuristic devices, which usually overlap in describing the empirical situation. Attitudes have a bearing on participation and impact, while attitudes in turn depend to a great extent on impact and levels of participation.

Relative differences in the political attitudes of men and women have been studied by various scholars and form a feature of most of our political literature since independence. Certain broad trends can be discerned, the most important of which are mentioned below. The point which emerges in the very beginning of our analysis is that there is no single homogeneous pattern. Levels of political awareness vary from region to region, from class to class and from community to community, and are conditioned greatly by the political culture of the area, the approach of the political parties to the women and the quality of local leadership.

It is generally held that political awareness varies with the levels of modernization in a given area, with concomitant factors such as literacy rates, education and exposure to urbanization and mass media. This correlation however seems more apparent than real, as proved by studies in different regions.

We have already pointed out the distinction in the influence of literacy and education on awareness and participation. While the former is generally found to be an important determinant for both awareness and participation, education does not command a similar influence. While a correlation can be established between education and awareness, this does not always extend to participation. We have also noted that similarly, urbanization alone cannot be identified with high political awareness or participation. In terms of urban rural variables, there is no significant difference in political awareness.

On an average, working women including professionals, indicate a higher degree of awareness, but this is not necessarily reflected in their participation. There is a uniform finding from different regions regarding the complaint of urban middle-class women that they find their family responsibilities a handicap to political participation.

There is no positive relationship between higher socio-economic status and the degree of awareness. We may cite a few illustrations from Prof Sirsikar's study: In Gujarat, the high income group women are less aware and participate less in the political process; in Maharashtra, the higher the socio-economic status, other factors being equal, lesser is the proportion of women who participate. This is further borne out by the apathy of professionals with high socio-economic status. By and large, politics constitutes a peripheral interest for women from this strata, though a significant number of women legislators come from an affluent background.

Most studies on political behaviour have so far held that women are considerably influenced by their husbands and family wishes in political matters. During the course of our tours, however, we received ample evidence that this pattern is beginning to change and many women now exercise considerable autonomy in using their right of franchise. They emphasize their ability to do so because of the secrecy of the ballot. Many women told us that though their husbands still try to influence their judgement "they can't find out whom we have really voted for." In rural areas the influence of village elders plays an important role in determining political choice which also influence the women's behaviour. However, it would not be correct to describe this as a universal rural.

In spite of such changes, it is still evident that there is a difference in the level of political information and perception regarding implications of the right of franchise, etc., between men and women, both quantitatively and qualitatively. Most scholars have attributed this to the lack of interest shown by political parties, in improving the political knowledge of women. Some have also levelled this charge against the women's organizations and pressure groups. A study of urban voters in Rajasthan provides an illustration — 44.5 per cent of the women did not have any clear cut idea about their criterion for voting: 19.5 per cent considered the personality of the candidates, 22.3 per cent caste and family as a factor, while only 8.3 per cent and 5.5 per cent considered the party and the issues respectively.

All the State profiles indicate one common trend — that women are concerned with problems that affect their day to day lives. The issues are price-rise, non-availability of essential commodities, hoarding and black marketing, adulteration, unemployment and poverty. On several occasions during the last few years, women have organized protests against these problems.

There are indications of growing trends of disillusionment with the political process among women. This may be partly attributed to their reactions against the prevalence of corruption and inefficiency in political circles but a great deal of such attitudes is on account of their feelings of ineffectiveness in solving problems which affect their lives. According to a study conducted in West Bengal, about 25 per cent of the respondents stated that having votes has not helped women and even men. About 8 per cent stated that they would not vote on principle since it did not help in any way. Another study done in Rajasthan in 1971 showed that 42 per cent of the women interviewed including housewives and working women, supported revolution for social progress as opposed to the 'ritual' of elections. The majority of respondents in this study felt that the problems of the country needing solution in order of priority were as follows: (1) employment and poverty; (2) rising prices; (3) corruption; and (4) law and order.

The freedom movement and the period immediately succeeding independence brought the involvement and commitment of women in the political process. However, the institutionalization of this process resulted in difference in perception of goals and methods of achievement. The absence of a movement in the period after independence explains the low involvement of women in the political process. Such involvement is however always visible during national emergencies.

It was repeatedly brought to our notice that the unity between political, economic and social issues that characterized the freedom movement was one of the causes for women's high degree of participation. The divorce between social problems that affect women directly, and the political process, has been one of the major causes of women's lower participation in politics in recent years.

Indicators of Impact of Women on the Political Process

While the percentage of political participation and the number of women contestants have shown a gradual increase, their record of success at elections, however, presents a very different picture. The number and percentage of successful women candidates for the Lok Sabha has been declining steadily from 33 (50.6 per cent) in 1962 to 21 (25.9 per cent) in 1971. The variations in the number of contestants and those elected are uneasily accountable. The sharp decline in successful candidates in 1971 has been attributed to the sudden increase in the number of independent women candidates which increased from 10 in 1967 to 31 in 1971, only one of whom was elected, thus bringing the percentage of successful contestants down to 25.9 per cent. This however, does not explain why the parties nominations should have been so new. Table 6.6 indicates the party affiliations of contestants and successful candidates for the Lok Sabha since 1962.

TABLE - 4.6

FEMALE CONTESTANTS AND THEIR POLITICAL PARTIES. (FIGURES BELOW THE LINE INDICATE SUCCESSFUL CONTESTANTS)

Year of the Election	*Cong.*	*Swat.*	*BJS.*	*CPI*	*CPM*	*PSP*	*SSP*	*Ind.*	*Others*	*Total*
1	*2*	*3*	*4*	*5*	*6*	*7*	*8*	*9*	*10*	*11*
	33	9	3	3	-	1	3	8	5	65
1962	-	-	-	-		-	-	-	-	-
	28	4	N	1		N	N	N	N	33
	36	3	3	3	1	1	2	10	7	66
1967	-	-	-	-	-	-	-	-	-	-
	21	3	1	N	1	N	N	2	N	28
	21(14)*	3	3	3	2	1	1	31	7	86
1971	-	-	-	-	-	-	-	-	-	-
	15 (N)	1	2	1	1	N	N	1	N	21

* Figures in brackets indicate "Congress (O)"

N=Nil

Cong=Congress, Swat=Swatantara, BJS=Bharatiya Jana Sangh, CPI=Communist Party of India, CPM=Communist Party (Marxist), PSP=Praja Socialist Party, SSP=Samyukta Socialist Party, Ind.=Independent.

A statewise comparison of successful women candidates for the Lok Sabha shows that the number of successful candidates has been greater in UP, Bihar, Madhya Pradesh and Andhra Pradesh where the number of contestants has also been greater. Orissa, Haryana, Goa, Daman and Diu and Manipur are the only areas where women contested but were never returned. Percentage-wise Karnataka was the most successful. It set up only one candidate in 1962 and 1971 and elected the same. Bihar, UP, Madhya Pradesh, Tamil Nadu and West Bengal were the only States which sent women to the Lok Sabha in every election. In terms of the overall performance, however, Andhra Pradesh and Assam may also be considered satisfactory.

Analyzing the first general elections Smt. Laxmi N. Menon had inferred that the number of women candidates was in inverse proportion to the percentage of literacy among them. This hypothesis is confirmed when tested against the figures of subsequent elections in Madhya Pradesh, Bihar and UP. But Orissa, Jammu & Kashmir and Rajasthan do not substantiate this hypothesis. On the other hand, Kerala, West Bengal, Maharashtra and Tamil Nadu do not support the reverse of this view, i.e., the number of women contestants does not decline relatively with a higher literacy rate. We may infer, therefore, that literacy is not one of the facts that determine the number of women contestants or their success. The backing of the party which sponsors them, the personality of the contestants, including their family background, and the campaign strategy adopted, play a much more important role in determining the success or failure of women candidates.

Since 1952 a total number of 212 women members have served in the Indian Parliament, 129 in the Lok Sabha and 83 in the Rajya Sabha. Delhi, Himachal Pradesh, Orissa, Rajasthan and Tamil Nadu have sent more women representatives to the Rajya Sabha than to the Lok Sabha. Jammu & Kashmir has not had a single woman representative either in the Lok Sabha or the Rajya Sabha.

State Legislatures

Women representatives in the State Legislatures also present a varied pattern. The most significant trend, however, is either a decline or stagnation in the percentage of successful contestants. In the First General Elections (1952), Gujarat elected four out of five women candidates to the Gujarat Assembly. In 1862 the number increased to 15 out of 24 but it dropped to 8 out of 17 in 1967 and 8 out of 21 in 1972. In the case of Karnataka, except for 1957 and 1962 the ratio of female to male representatives has been extremely low, the number of successful candidates dropping to 7 in 1967 and increasing marginally to 11 in 1972. In Maharashtra the number of successful candidates improved from 5 in 1952 to 14 in 1957 but has been declining ever since. The Rajasthan Assembly, which had 24 women between 1957 and 1962 contained only 6 in 1967-68. The West Bengal Assembly had 14 women in 1962, but has only 6 now.

Political Parties and Women

The election manifestos of the parties indicate that practically all of them agree that women constitute a backward section of the society to whom special privileges should be granted to bring them on a par with men. The parties also agree that the existing gap between men and women should be reduced to the minimum possible.

Indian National Congress

The India National Congress is pledged to implement the principles of the Constitution. The recent manifestos of the party have emphasized development of education and employment opportunities for women.

The Congress has consistently maintained its position as the party sponsoring the largest number of women candidates both at Parliamentary and State Assembly elections. The number of women contestants sponsored by the Congress, however, has remained much below its stipulated target of 15 per cent of the total candidates. This percentage was initially decided by the party in 1957 and has been repeatedly reiterated since then but to no effect.

While the Congress has covered the largest area in sponsoring women as representatives and enjoys the distinction of having the largest number of successful women candidates in its ranks, women's position in the party hierarchy is not particularly impressive. This is significant in view of the undisputed leadership of the party by a woman. While the Working Committee, (the highest body in the party) contains 3 women out of a total of 21, and 2 out of 4 General Secretaries are women. There is considerable evidence that but for the pressure from the Working Committee, many States would continue to exclude women from the various Committees of the party at different levels. Two State Committees have women presidents. Some of the State Committees had no women members for ten years or more. Their representation in District Committees and most local units remained poor. The following examples will illustrate this fact:

The Assam Pradesh Congress Committee did not have a woman member till 1972. The State Executive Committee had 2 women members in 1959 and none from then till 1970. Between 14

District Committees, the number of women has not exceeded 5. The Maharashtra Pradesh Congress Committee has only 19 women out of a total membership of 442 while its State Executive has only 3 out of 54. In the West Bengal, women form about 18 per cent of the primary members of the Congress. There are 2 women in the State Executive of 30 members and only a few in District Committees. The new Constitution of the party provides that 50 per cent of the nominated members on all Committees (who constitute 15 per cent) will be women.

The Congress Mahila Front had been active in mobilizing women in support of the party. In recent years it has been voicing the demand of women workers within the party. In some States it is becoming very critical of the neglect of women's demands by the official leadership. There is a general feeling among women political workers that they do not have enough opportunities to develop or demonstrate their organising ability. Exclusion from the decision making bodies within the party is responsible for considerable resentment among women political workers.

Communist Party of India

The Communist Party of India believes that in the capitalist system complete equality of women is impossible. Only a socialist system can liberate women fully by ending all types of exploitation. Women have a role to play in bringing about the social revolution which cannot be achieved if they remain in a backward condition. According to its election manifesto the party stands for equality of women in every sphere of national life. The party demands equal pay for equal work, removal of all restrictions on employment of married women, extension of maternity benefits to all employed women and enforcement of the social laws that have been enacted to improve their status. The party appreciates the need for adequate financial allocation and extra facilities for women's education. It promises to achieve removal of all disabilities to secure women's equality with men in inheritance of property, marriage and divorce laws, entrance to education institutions, professions and services.

Out of the total membership of 2½ lakh of the party, women are estimated to form about 5 per cent. Four women are members of the National Council which contains a total of 110 members.

The State units of the party, however, show variance in the pattern of women's representation.

In their discussion with us the representative of the party observed that the fundamental rights of equality and protection of women guaranteed by the Constitution have not been achieved in reality because of the social situation. Some special amenities and incentives have to be provided to enable women to enjoy these rights, since rights without opportunities were meaningless.

The greatest cause of women's inability to enjoy these rights was their economic dependence and poverty. Attempts to implement the equal pay for equal work principle by industrial tribunals have invariably ended in retrenchment of women workers. Poverty also prevented them from enjoying the protection of the social laws enacted to improve their status. The answer to this handicap lay in fuller participation of women in the process of social production which should not be limited to small scale and cottage industries only. They suggested specific protection against retrenchment of women and drew the attention of the Committee to a trade union demand for 20 per cent reservation of jobs for women in industry. In their opinion, this could be insisted upon in selected industries like textiles where the number of women workers has been declining. Free legal aid, particularly for women in adverse economic circumstances should also be provided to enable them to utilize the rights provided under the social laws.

Regarding education, while the party supported co-education as the ultimate objects, they noted the possible necessity of secondary schools for women. Hostel accommodation and generous provision on stipends was also essential to improve women's education.

Communist Party of India (M)

The party believes that genuine equality between the sexes is impossible in a capitalist order, and can only be realized in the process of a socialist transformation of society. The party declares itself as opposed to any kind of discrimination against women. It is critical of the poor progress in the field of women's welfare since independence and demands greater facilities for women's education, removal of social disabilities, equal rights in matters of marriage, admission to professions and other services and equal pay for equal work. This party also holds that the nation cannot progress if its women remain in their present condition of illiteracy, limited opportunities for development and as victims of obscurantist customs and prejudices.

Women constitute about 1 per cent of the party's membership. The Central Committee has one woman out of a total membership of 31. The State Council in West Bengal has 6 women members out of a total 70. In the State Executive there are three women including one from the State Secretariat. A majority of the district and local council contain one or two women members with exception of the Calcutta District Council which has 6 women out of a total membership of 65.

In their discussion with the Committee the representatives of the party emphasized the need for economic independence of women without which there could not be real equality between men and women in any sphere of life—social, political, legal or even family life. In the absence of economic independence, women were as good as private property of men. In this context, they felt that the growing problem of rural unemployment was posing an increasing threat to the security and status of women in the rural areas. With the increase in landlessness and the decay of village industries, new avenues for employment of the vast masses of rural women were imperative. In the absence of land, basic economic security and literacy, rural women have been unable to enjoy their constitutional and legal rights to an even greater extent than their counterparts in the urban areas. This extreme poverty was also the real cause for the low enrolment of rights in schools in these areas. Their suggestions to the Committee included the following:

(i) Mass employment and mass education including education of women about their emancipation.
(ii) Free education of girls at all levels.
(iii) Inclusion of principle of equal pay for equal work in the fundamental rights and removal of existing disabilities in the law of inheritance, marriage and divorce and admissions to profession and service.
(iv) Equal shares of land and job facilities for peasant women

and maternity benefits, and common kitchens for all working women.

(v) Implementation of constitutional and legal rights and propaganda against orthodoxy and conservative attitudes towards women.

Bhartiya Jana Sangh

This party stands for advancement of women and is keen to take special steps to remove social and educational disabilities, to enable them to discharge their responsibilities to the family, society and nation, without any fundamental change in the traditionally established principles of social organisation. The party promises to enlarge and make more substantial the property rights of women, granting them absolute rights as members of their husband's family.

The Central Executive of the Bhartiya Jana Sangh contains five women members, one of whom is the Vice-president. The All-India Council has 83 women members. The President of the Kerala State Committee and the Vice-President of seven State Committees are women. Two States have a woman Joint Secretary. Apart from the member of the State Executives, district Committees elect one woman to State Councils. This Constitutional provision is normally adhered to by 60% of the districts. The Constitutional requirement of a minimum of two women members in district committee is normally only in 50% cases. In the local committees, however, this minimum of two cannot be met by even 20% of the committees, because it is difficult to find active women workers at the village level.

In their discussion with us, representatives of the party emphasized the need to increase the consciousness and political participation of women without which the Constitutional guarantees would remain unimplemented. Their suggestion included the spread of civic and political education to foster a sense of national pride and political awareness to students, housewives and working women also who needed to be taught their civic and political rights and duties. It was their view that legislation could not improve the status of women, when society including women themselves continued to foster a sense of male superiority at all stages. In spite of outstanding performance of some women in politics, science, etc., most women are conservative, backward and wholly dependent on men. Governmental and non-governmental efforts must combine to develop not 'independence' but 'individuality' of women so that they can cooperate in family, social and national life. Illiteracy and unemployment were the causes of their low position.

They were highly critical of the present trend in advertising and films which used the female figures in very bad taste. They felt that there should be some restriction or control on the mass media as these trends were leading to immorality and degeneration, particularly amongst the youth of the country. The problem of security, particularly for working women was becoming more acute, and it was necessary to provide more hostels for working women.

Regarding social laws, they said that women who protest against polygamy receive no protection and hence were afraid to do so in public. In cases of divorce, courts should examine the reasons for a woman seeking a divorce and not go by the 'matrimonial wrong' theory.

Their suggestions included:

(i) free education for girls up to the end of secondary stage,
(ii) night schools for working women,
(iii) vocational training in village school,
(iv) compulsory home science classes in every schools,
(v) expansion of condensed course and
(vi) development of mobile libraries.

To promote employment they suggested:

(i) reservation of some jobs for women in different spheres and
(ii) legislation on equal pay for equal work,
(iii) relaxation of conditions for employment of women, particularly rural areas.

Indian National Congress (Organization)

This party is also pledged to uphold and implement the Constitutional guarantees and directive principles of State policy that have a bearing on women's status. Out of a total membership of 28 in the Working Committee, two are women, one of them is the General Secretary.

In her discussion with the Committee, the representative of the party observed that the reason for decline in the representation of women in the legislative bodies lay in the slackening of the momentum of women's mobilization achieved during the freedom struggle. Political conflicts now-a-days were only on economic issues and parties had not succeeded in drawing out women even though unemployment was worse among them. The development programmes for women in rural areas had no definite objective and had not been successful.

While women had developed an interest in voting, their political interest was still extremely undeveloped, the main reason for this being their economic backwardness. Interest in social welfare work had declined among political workers and the few who are still willing to continue such work suffered from lack of direction. The general decline in political interest of women was visible in the lack of applications for nominations and in participation in various organisational activities of the party. As a result, the 20% quota reserved by the party for women could not be filled in the last elections. There was considerable competition in obtaining nominations at different levels which deterred most women. The other two difficulties which prevented women from political work was their lack of economic resources and difficulties in leaving their families.

Socialist Party

The Social Party believes that women still suffer under a variety of social inequalities and demands special opportunities for women to enable them to enjoy their Constitutional rights.

In her discussion with the Committee, the representative of the party emphasized the ignorance and indifference of women regarding the rights guaranteed under the Constitution though they had developed considerable enthusiasm in casting their votes. The average Indian woman is still a secondary citizen whose status is subverted by the traditional confinement within the home, illiteracy, declining employment opportunities and the male attitude to women as objects of enjoyment. Molestation and atrocities on women have been increasing but there has not been adequate public protest against such acts either from society or from the Government.

In order to rescue women from their ignorance, backwardness and unemployment, a determined effort needs to be made by Government, social workers and social institutions to educate both men and women to release them from the bondage of outmoded traditions and superstitions. The representative drew attention to the Charter of Women, which has been adopted in 1969 by the Samajvadi Mahila Sabha, Maharashtra, the Women's front of the Socialist party. The major demands are as follows :

> Free education at all levels, vocational and technical education at secondary level, provision of part-time jobs, establishment of vocational guidance bureau, security arrangement and amenities for women working on night shifts and village level workers, Uniform Civil Code, social mobilization against the dowry system and greater scope for women in electoral contests and party organisation.

Positions in Government

Though only a very few women were able to reach the highest level of power and authority, those who did so were recognized for their administrative and capacity to manage their affairs. Since 1952 there have been 13 women ministers in the Union Government - 6 of them were Deputy Ministers, 5 became Ministers of State, 1 attained Cabinet rank and 1 was Prime Minister. There was one Vice-Chairman of Rajya Sabha and several in the panel of Chairmen of both houses of parliament. Besides this, many others have been members of various standing and ad hoc committees. About 16 of the women parliamentarians had previous experience of holding political offices in the States, either in the pre-independence ministries formed in 1937 or in the post-independence period. At the State level two women have held the office of Governor, two of Chief Minister, one of Speaker and one as Deputy Speaker since independence. Though only few have held cabinet rank, women have held office in most of the States. Compared to their overall number in the legislatures, the number holding offices was not low.

Role of Women Elites in the Political Process

One of the common characteristics of the women leaders in the political process during the period immediately after independence was their experience of participation in the freedom movement. The women members of the Constituent Assembly which also functioned as the Central Legislative Council in the first 5 years after independence were mostly veterans of the freedom struggle. Most of them had worked in the movement for women's welfare and development. They were the spokesmen of the women's cause in the Legislative Body and played an important role in mobilizing public opinion in support of the social legislations that changed the legal status of women within the first few years after independence. Some of them also played their part in shaping the policies and programmes of women's development that were taken up by the Government of India.

While most of the women leaders who had attained a national stature during the freedom struggle were to be found in the circles of the Central Government or legislatures, in the States a new generation of women entered the political process. The accounts from the States emphasize that experience of social work, particularly among women, while it is still considered a qualification for candidates seeking representation in local bodies, has ceased to be an important qualification for women representatives in the legislatures. As pointed out by some of the political workers interviewed by the Committee, political conflicts these days, particularly at the State level seldom reflect social differences.

The issues are primarily economic which are used by various political parties to seek power in the State Government structure. The women who have been involved in this process mostly come from the economic and political elite of the States and their entry into the political process, particularly representation, depends more on their support within the party rather than on the electorate. Their electorate campaigns are conducted by party workers among whom women form a minority. Only some women candidates have attained their position through active political and organisational work among the masses.

Women candidates and legislators have rightly seen their

roles as representatives of the people. Both in Parliament and in State legislatures they have been more concerned with problems of a general nature dealing with issues of national and State importance. In the earlier years, while women participated in such general discussions, on questions relating to women, their championship of women's causes cut across party lines and evoked concerted articulation. In recent years, however, women legislators have not shown such concern or interest in problems that affect women specifically. During a recent debate in the Rajya Sabha on a private resolution on equal pay for equal work for women, not even one-third of the women members attended the discussion and only a few spoke. This lack of interest has led to criticism by women outside the circle of active politicians that the women political elite today are not much concerned with the problems affecting large masses of women in the country.

An analysis of debates and discussions in the legislative bodies indicate the very meagre attention given by these institutions to women's problems. It would appear that the political elite of the country, of both sexes, had come to believe that the problem of women had practically been solved with the measures — legal and administrative — adopted in the first few years after independence. The very articulate debates on women's problems that took place in the earlier period, in which women members invariably played a major role has not been repeated in the later years.

The reason for this lack of concern among the political elite to the problems of women is the absence of an active women's movement. While the number of political organizations seeking to mobilize women is now much higher than in the earlier period, their identification with different political parties prevents most of them from arousing women's consciousness for the solution of problems which are specific to women.

We have already pointed out the significant gap between the degree of politicization and participation of women and its reflection in the representation of women in the legislative bodies. States which have a larger group of women representatives both in the State Assemblies and in Parliament are also States where the level of politicization among the masses of women is low. States where political mobilization of women seems to have developed more have very few women members in the legislature. It would appear, therefore, that the institutionalization of political activities has resulted in a failure on the part of women to exert adequate pressure on political institutions for solution of the problems that affect their lives.

A number of women who have entered the power structure have reached it mainly through certain ascriptive channels. This, coupled with their small numbers in the legislatures as well as decision-making bodies within the parties explains their inhibition and failure to voice the problems of women in these institutions. The reasons for this gap have to be sought in the nature of campaigns to mobilize women, and in the functioning of the particular women's pressure groups.

Five

Effectiveness of Campaigns to Mobilize Women

Mobilisation by Political Parties

It has been observed during all elections that political parties used women both as instruments of campaign and objects (women's welfare) set forth for achievement. The hand-bills, poster and public meetings emphasize the specific promises for women in the parties' manifestoes. Some local problems are also used in the propaganda. For instance, during the 1971 parliamentary elections, women of Bombay were promised copious water supply from municipal taps and abolition of prostitution.

In larger cities all the parties try to engage a number of active women workers for campaigning among women. During the 1962 elections, in one constituency in Bombay the Congress had 400 such workers, the PSP 200, the Jana Sangh 400 and the Samyukta Maharashtra Samiti 100. Housewives in urban areas were generally approached during the leisure hours of the afternoon.

Rural women, and women in smaller towns, however, generally do not get similar attention from the parties who often content themselves by approaching the heads of families or village elders. During the 1971 Parliamentary elections, villagers complained of the campaign methods of all parties. In their opinion, vehicles passing through villages, shouting party slogans or approaching only prominent persons in villages, ignored the need of explaining matters to the villagers, particularly the women. In their opinion this would be much better achieved by village meetings which the women could also attend or by house to house approach by politically committed workers. Studies on the efficacy of mass media generally agree that interpersonal contact and public meetings are more effective with women than other mass media.

The inadequate number of women party workers have sometimes led to the use of paid canvassers. This experiment has, however, not yielded very happy results, particularly in rural areas. Villagers are generally opposed to women from outside coming in for canvassing except when they are known to be politically committed workers. One study of the 1962 elections in UP noted the very critical reactions of the local community to paid women canvassers brought from outside. Their employed status was the subject of many adverse comments in private discussions.

Most parties accept the religiosity of women and make use of religious festivals to approach them by organizing religious functions. Even secular parties have indulged in this practice. It has generally been found that women attend such functions in larger numbers than men.

In spite of such occasional attempts, however, the common theme emphasized in practically all studies is that instead of approaching women voters individually or in a group, by and large all political parties and candidates attach greater importance to winning the support of the male active heads of families in the belief that their wishes would prevail with the women as well.

It is clear from the experience of all the general elections, that though the women constitute nearly 50 per cent of the electorate they are unaware of their strength nor has this source been adequately tapped by any political party. There has not been any bargaining on the part of organised women with the political parties for their support, except in Jammu where the Istri Sabha put forward a demand for reservation of 6 seats as the price of support from its members. The political parties' failure to adequately mobilize women's support indicates that they have not yet appreciated this as a source of power. In the opinion of some scholars, if a political party organizes this half of the nation its chances of winning the elections would improve considerably.

Mobilization by Non-Political Organizations

The most important of these organizations are those which focus their activities exclusively on the welfare and liberation of women and are run by women themselves.

All India Women's Conference

This was founded in 1926. Recognized as a forum for voicing the problem and grievances of women, it has non-political, primarily social objectives. From its inception it has stood for equal social, political and economic rights for women. The most notable feature of such activities was its campaign for reform of marriage and inheritance laws and mobilization of support for the Hindu Code Bill, Most of the women members of the Constituent Assembly who fought for, this measure in the central Legislature in the early 50's were leaders of the All India Women's Conference.

Since independence, however, the Conference has been focusing its attention primarily on the welfare and relief of women and children. The specific pressures and programmes started by the organization for this purpose include enforcement of the anti-polygamy and divorce laws, development of institutional facilities for working and destitute women, liberalizing the abortion law, family planning and equal pay for equal work. The conference is mainly a deliberative body using resolutions as its main method of pressurizing the government.

National Council of Women in India

Founded in 1925 it had objectives very similar to that of the AIWC. In the post-independence period it has concerned itself mainly with education, medical care and family planning. Its activities and membership are confined mainly to urban areas.

Bharatiya Grameen Mahila Sangh

Established in 1955, the Sangh aims to work among and improve the conditions of rural women, to vocalize their aspirations through appropriate channels which could act as pressure groups on the government and other public authorities, for the removal of women's disabilities and to promote local leadership among rural women through constructive programmes. Its secondary objective is to assist in planned rural development, deal with agriculture, cottage industries, rural housing, etc. The Sangh has been active in organising various training programmes for farm women, for women in border areas, and in organising *Mahila Mandals* in villages.

National Federation of Indian Women

Established in 1954, this federation has a different set of objectives. It aims at raising political and social awareness of women to fight for social justice and a social transformation, which alone can release them from their present restricted position in society. Their constructive programmes include mainly literacy but they have been active in mobilizing women's protest against all types of injustice and social evils. They have been emphatic in condemning ill-treatment and exploitation of Harijan women and women workers. The recent protests by women in different parts of the country against rising prices, hoarding, adulteration and corruption were organized as a result of an appeal from the National Federation of Indian Women.

From the discussions that representatives of these organizations had with the Committee, it appears that while their broad objective and activities show certain similarities, there are certain differences in their concentration and orientation. Though the leadership of all these organisations come mainly from the urban educated middle-class, the membership of the National Federation is composed largely of women from the less affluent sections of society, particularly working women. The hard core of its workers come from this group.

All of them admitted that they had not been fully successful in reaching the message of their new rights conferred by the Constitution and the Social laws to all women in the country. They also admitted that lack of consciousness among women had been a major cause for non-implementation of these laws.

Stri Shakti Jagaran

This is a new movement to mobilize women to fight for a just place for women in society, using Gandhian ideals and techniques. Launched by the Mahila Sarvodaya Sammelan in 1973, the movement believes that the status of women can be raised by women alone. It appeals to all women to abandon *purdah*, untouchability to caste or class distinctions, dowry and ostentatious expenditure during marriages, discrimination between boys and girls and to resist corruption in all spheres, both within and outside family.

Apart from these bodies there are many professional or other specific women's organisations working in different parts of the country. A large number of them are engaged in some type of welfare work among women and children. The Federation of University Women's Associations has been studying problems of women and is currently engaged in exploring opportunities for part-time employment. The All-India Medical Women's Conference also has been discussing problems of women doctors, and issues arising from the present emphasis on family planning and nutrition. Though some of these organisations, like the Trained Nurses' Association, the Women Lawyers' Association, etc., are more in the nature of trade unions, some of them also take up some welfare or constructive work among women. They have not, however, undertaken any campaign to mobilize women in general.

Though the trade union movement in India is not a new one, it did not involve women in any substantial numbers till later. Since most trade unions in India are associated with some political party they are normally one of the most powerful agencies for political mobilization. In the case of women, however, this part of their activity has been rather secondary. While women leaders in the trade union movement have played major role in bringing about changes in the labour laws to provide protection for women both inside and outside the legislatures, most trade unions admit that they have not made much efforts in mobilizing women to assert their legal and Constitutional rights. One of our studies found that participation in trade union activities had no direct relationship with women's political awareness.

Whenever these organizations have acted in concert, to defend the rights of women, their influence as pressures groups has however been fairly effective. We have already noted their role in the enactment of the social laws. For example, the reform of Hindu laws, the proposed amendment of the income tax law, to club the incomes of husband and wife for purposes of assessment, was protested against by most women's economic forums. It is generally believed that this protest was responsible for the abandonment of the idea.

Conclusions

Our findings indicate that women's participation in the political process has shown a steady increase, both in elections and in their readiness to express their views on issues directly concerning their day-to-day life. But their ability to produce an impact on the political process has been negligible because of the inadequate attention paid to their political education and mobilization by both political parties and women's organizations. The structures of the parties make them male dominated and in spite of outstanding exception, most partymen are not free from the general prejudices and attitudes of the society. They have tended to see the women voters and citizens as appendages of the males and have depended on the heads of families to provide block-votes and support for their parties and candidates.

The entire exercise of our Committee has indicated that in certain important areas and for certain sections of the female population there has been some regression from the normative attitudes developed during the freedom movement. Large sections of women have suffered a decline of economic status. Every legal measure designed to translate the Constitutional norm of equality or special protection into actual practice has had to face tremendous resistance from the legislative and other elites. Even after the promulgation of these laws, the protection enjoyed by the large masses of women from exploitation and injustice is negligible. As an example we would like to mention the cases of persecution of Harijan women that have increased in recent years. Among women themselves the leadership and the attitudes of the elites, social or political, have become diffused and diverse with sharp contradiction in their regard and concern for the inequalities that affect the status of women in every sphere.

We are, therefore, forced to observe that all the indicators of participation, attitudes and impact come up with the same results — the resolution in social and political status of women for which Constitutional equality was to be only the instrument, still remains a very distant objective. While there is no doubt that the position of some groups of women have changed for the better by opening to them positions of power and dignity, the large masses of women continue to lack spokesmen who understand their special problems and are committed to their cause, finding place in the representative bodies of the State.

From this point of view, though women do not numerically

constitute a minority, they are beginning to acquire the features of a minority community by the three recognized dimensions of inequality: Inequality of class (economic situation), status (social position) and political power. If this trend is allowed to continue the large masses of women in India may well emerge as the only surviving minority continuously exposed to injustice.

The chasm between the values of a new social order proclaimed by the Constitution and the realities of contemporary Indian society as far as women's rights are concerned remains as great as at the time of independence. The right to political equality has not enabled women to play their roles as partners and constituents in the political process, because we have forgotten Gandhiji's warning not to treat political rights as an end in itself but only as a means.

Instead, these rights have helped to build an illusion of equality and power which is frequently used as an argument to resist special protective and acceleratory measures to enable women to achieve their just and equal position in society. It is surprising that in spite of the special powers provided by Article 15 (3) of the Constitution almost no efforts have been made to redress the unequal status of women in different spheres. We have frequently heard the view that the greatest indicator of the status of women in this country is that it had been ruled by a woman for many years. We are compelled to disagree with this view, because in our opinion this is not an indicator of the real status of women in this country.

Though at the public level there are a number of women who recognize and advocate the desirability of giving equal opportunities to women in economic and political spheres, the norms and attitudes regarding a woman's role in society remains traditional. In this sense, the new rights prove to be only concessional. Thus it is clear that despite certain legal and even institutional changes, the final legitimation for a successful reorganization of society lies in a revolution in norms and attitudes in the minds of the people. The recommendations that we make are out of a desire to make the political rights of women more functional as required by the needs of a democratic system.

The Question of Reservation of Seats for Women in Legislative Bodies

Women Groups' View

Before we take up our recommendation we have to record our views on a suggestion to which we have given considerable thought. In the course of our tours we received a demand from groups of women in some States for a system of reservation for women in the legislative bodies in the States and in Parliament. We summarize their arguments below:

(a) The difficulties being experienced by women in obtaining adequate representation and spokesmen of their cause in these bodies, and the declining trend in the number of women legislations is the result of the reluctance of political parties to sponsor women candidates. The parties reflect the established value of a male dominated society, which would be difficult to alter without certain structural changes in the socio-political set-up. The parties would continue to pay lip service to the cause of women's progress and the policy of 'tokenism' by having a few women in the legislative and executive wings of government whose minority and dependent status offer serious obstacles of their acting as spokesmen for women's rights and opportunities.

(b) If this process continues over a period of time more and more women, losing faith in the political process to change their condition in life, may opt out of the political system and become either passive partners or rebels. In the present context in India the greater majority would undoubtedly follow the first path because most of them have not shaken off the feelings of subjugation and inferiority generated by centuries of subordination.

(c) A system of reservation of a proportion of seats for women in these bodies would provide an impetus to both the women as well as to the political parties to give a fairer deal to nearly half the population in the various units of government. If women enter these bodies in larger number the present inhibitions that result from their minority position in these institutions may disappear faster and give them greater freedom to articulate their views.

(d) A system of reservation may also increase the women legislators' sense of responsibility and concern for the problems affecting women, thus ensuring the presence of a body of spokesmen of the women's cause in the representative bodies of the States. Such a system would also help to increase the degree of political mobilization of women both in the electorate and within the parties.

The Scholars View

Support for reservation also came from a group of scholars who undertook an examination of women's role in the political process at the Committee's request. We summarize views below:

(a) The process of Indian women coming into their own 'politically' has been slow and halting because Indian political culture is apolitical, and force of tradition has been particularly against participation of women in politics. Improving the political status of women is an integral aspect of the overall problem of socio-economic change and 'broadening the political elite structure'. At a later stage of development changes in the socio-economic order may buttress changes in the political status of women but "it has to be the other way round in present day India".

(b) The failure of Indian society to "look upon women's participation with sympathy and understanding" is an exceedingly retarding factor in political socialization of both men and women. 30 per cent reservation of seats in the legislative bodies for women will alter the very character of our legislature and will compel the political parties to change their strategies and tactics and induce them to give women their due. Reservation of seats for women cannot lead to their becoming `isolated pockets in the nation', because "women are not marginal to society as a minority group might be". It could, instead lead to an increase in women's participation and motivate them to shoulder their political responsibilities.

If "access to policy making powers and facilities is a component of social status" then the presence of more women in the legislatures will help to direct the rate and type of changes in the position of women. Only a system of reservations, increasing the number of women representatives will help to broaden the base of women's representation in the legislative bodies.

Such a transitional measure to break through the existing structure of inequalities will not be retrogression "from the doctrine of equality of sexes and the principle of democratic representation" and may serve the long term objectives of equality and democracy in a better manner than the present system where inequalities get intensified. As compared to the situation before independence when with a system of reservation, women constituted 3.3 per cent of the membership of the central legislator, the average proportion of women in parliament since 1952 without reservation has been marginal. The existing limitations on the role being played by this minority of women legislators may increase if their number declines further with the continuation of the already recognized trend in this direction.

We however received a strong opposition to the suggestion from representatives of political parties and most women legislators. They felt that any system of special representation would be a retrograde step from the equality conferred by the Constitution. There was also some resistance to women being equated with the socially backward communities as all women do not suffer from the same disabilities as these underprivileged groups. The representatives of some parties however did not have any strong objection to reservation of seats for women in local bodies for which certain precedents were already existing.

Reasons for not Recommending Women in State Assemblies

Though we have to record that the problem of under representation of women in the representative bodies of the State both quantitatively and qualitatively is a real one, after considering the matter very seriously we find ourselves unable to recommend a system of reservation to the State Assemblies and Parliament. Our reason for rejecting the suggestion are summarized below:

(a) The women's cause in India has always been championed by all progressive elements, men as well as women. A climate favourable for the betterment of women's status can best be created by their joint efforts.

(b) So far women have served as representatives of the people. Separate constituencies for women would narrow their outlook.

(c) There is a fallacy in the entire argument for separate representation for women. Women's interests as such cannot be isolated from economic, social and political interests of groups, strata and classes in the society. In point of fact the problems connected with status of women are linked with formulation, articulation and modalities of the realizations of the interests.

(d) Such a system of special representation may precipitate similar demands from various other interests and communities and threaten national integration.

(e) Experience has shown that the privilege of reservation once granted, is difficult to withdraw. This would amount to perpetuation of unequal status.

(f) Women have been competing as equals with men since 1952. They must continue to do so and stand on their own merits and intensify their political and social life. A departure from this equality now will be a retrograde step.

(g) The minority argument cannot be applied to women. Women are not a community, they are a category. Though they have some real problems of their own, they share with men the problems of their groups, locality and community. Women are not concentrated in certain areas confined to particular fields of activity. Under these circumstances, there can be no rational basis for reservation for women.

We do not think it would be proper for us to suggest such a major change in our political structure on the basis of the rather insubstantial evidence that we have received.

Even though we did not accept the suggestion for reservation for women in Parliament of the State Legislature, we find that in order to provide greater opportunities to women to actively participate in the decision-making process, it is imperative to recognize the true nature of the social inequalities and disabilities that hamper them. This can best be achieved by providing them with special opportunities for participation in the representative structures of local Government. The necessity to associate women representatives in local self-governing bodies is already accepted in this country and provision for reservation on seats for women through either election, co-option or nomination in these bodies exist in most of the state legislations that govern the constitution of these bodies.

It has been our experience, however, that this association, with the exception of a few areas is mostly regarded as a form of 'tokenism.' We feel that the time has come now to move out of this token provision for women's representation to a more meaningful association of women in the structure of local administration.

A second reason for this is the general apathy and indifference of these local bodies of women's development and change of status which has been reported to us by women's organizations and welfare and extension workers, particularly in rural areas. It may be noted that a large number of Mahila Mandals have been organized in both rural and urban areas through the initiative of welfare organizations like the Central Social Welfare Board and its state agencies, Ministry of Agriculture and Community Development and voluntary bodies like the Bharatiya Grameen Mahila Sangh. The status of these bodies is purely voluntary. Some of their members have acquired both experience and interest in developmental activities, but they are not representatives and their constitution does not result in associating or involving large majority of women in these activities. Nor do these bodies receive much recognition from the statutory local self-governing institutions. We received complaints of neglect and lack of funds for women's programmes from women workers throughout the country. This was confirmed by specialists working in the field of Community Development and Panchayati Raj.

We therefore recommend the establishment of Statutory Women's Panchayats at the village level to ensure greater participation by women in the political process. These bodies are not meant to be parallel organizations to the Gram Panchayats but should form an integral part of the Panchayati Raj structure, with autonomy and resources of their own for the management and administration of welfare and development programmes for women and children. We recommend them as a transitional measure to break through the traditional attitudes in rural society which inhibit most women from articulating their problems or participating actively in the existing local bodies. An exclusively women's body would eliminate this difficulty and provide opportunity to more women to gain experience and confidence in managing their own affairs. Their enhanced legal status, we believe, will have a direct impact on the general status of women in rural society and their increasing experience and responsibility may be expected to improve women's keenness and capacity for greater participation in the political process. Lastly, the existence of such statutory bodies would help to ensure better co-ordination of various Government services and programmes for women at the level of implementation. Like the Panchayats, these bodies could be directly elected by the women of the village and should have the right to send their representatives to the Panchayat Samitis and/or Zila Parishads. To ensure a viable relationship between the existing Gram Panchayats and the proposed women's Panchayats, the Chairman and Secretary of both these bodies should be ex-officio members of the other.

At the level of municipalities the principle of reservation of seats for women is already prevalent in certain states. We therefore recommend that this should be adopted by all states as a traditional measure.

We also recommend the constitution of permanent committees in municipalities to initiate and supervise programmes for women's development.

We recommend that political parties should adopt a definite policy regarding the percentage of women candidates to be sponsored by them for elections to Parliament and State Assemblies. While they may initially start with 15 per cent, this should be gradually increased so that in time to come the representation of women in the Legislative Bodies has some relationship to their position in the total population of the country or the State.

We further recommend the inclusion of women in all important committees, commissions or allegations that are appointed to examine socio-economic problems.

Ending Male Monopoly

Veena Nayyar on Reservation for Women

There can be no empowerment without power. Gender gaps in development, amply supported by statistics and empirical evidence, are largely due to the absence of women from decision-making bodies. Women remain outsiders in deciding the directions of development, resulting in unjustifiable disparities. Policy making is about answering the needs of the people. What is difficult to understand is why do the other half feel that they know our needs better? What earthly justification is there for assuming that women cannot speak for themselves? Nor is there any divine injunction imparting exclusive abilities to men. It is precisely this hijacking that accounts for inadequacy, ineffectiveness and failure of many a national policy. Participatory policy-framing right from planning to enactment in legislative bodies is the democratic answer. There is no way out but partnership and interdependence between men and women in the political structures and processes.

A conceptual shift must occur where the emphasis is no longer just on women's issues but also on applying a gender perspective to all national issues. The focus in framing policies should be on how women are affected by all national problems and how they themselves can bring about solutions. This paradigm shift is possible only through women sitting at the tables of power with men. As it stands, no politician denies this framework nor its democratic logic. The problem is that what they accept in principle they violate in practice. Actions have a habit of speaking louder than words. Women have not by accident been kept as outsiders. The gatekeepers of power have ensured this imbalance. Never mind that the nation has paid a huge price by making women the most wasted national asset. Never mind that the nation has not taken full account of the interests and needs of its people. Never mind that the nation has not been denied the benefit of different values, insights and styles of governance suited to a fairer and more balanced world for all.

Women's participation in political leadership is mandated by the Constitution. Rightly fearing that the 'domination syndrome' may prevail, if 'little men' prevail, the Constitution makers had wisely provided for Article 15 to achieve participation and party in governance and to make true the preamble: Liberty, equality and fraternity. With it a balanced representation was enshrined in the constitutional vision as a fundamental right. Those who oppose 33 per cent representations for women wilfully negate the Constitution. While all oaths are taken in the name of implementing the Constitution, yet in practice their only concern has been to perpetuate themselves in power defeating the 'letter and spirit of the Constitution'. That, of course, is a matter of their political morality but it has had negative implication for women and the country.

The methodology used for sabotaging the spirit of the Constitution has been one of the brazen practice of a *de facto* reservation for men. And no Act of Parliament was required for that. With declining value-based politics, the statistics in 11 parliaments indicate an average of ninety-five per cent representation by men. But for our Constitution Parliament may have been declared as a 'men only' institution! Yet you hear a few MPs even take the high moral ground claiming that merit brought them to Parliament. Women need to understand this political manoeuvring and claim their political spaces by fighting the deliberate doing-down of women. It begins with denial of opportunity, i.e., the denial of tickets to run the electoral races. In the first election in 1952 women had 4.2 per cent representation and in 1996 7.2 per cent in the Lok Sabha. And then we have the slide-back from the 1991 figure of 7.07 per cent to 7.02 per cent.

What makes it democratically unsustainable and morally unacceptable is that women have been denied tickets even when electoral track records clearly prevail that women candidates have by far been the winners over the male candidates. For decades the myth that women are losers was perpetuated by vested interests until in 1996 Women's Political Watch uncovered the untruth in their research of about 9,000 candidates of the 1991 elections. This research brought to light the reality that women are the electoral winners whenever they are fielded. In any other true democracy winnability would be the deciding factor. Yet what we witness is fifty years of blatant exclusion of women and tons of empty rhetoric. Clearly, there is no other option but to bring the democratic balance through a bill akin to the 81st Amendment. Reservation is the only route now.

With the 81st Amendment what women are seeking is not reservation but dereservation, i.e., male representation be scaled down to 67 per cent from 95 per cent (1952-96 Lok Sabha average). It is only when women will acquire an 'effective voice' and become a legislative force will agendas for women in terms of education, health, shelter, access and control of resources and ability to set targets for their empowerment can be implemented. The few who, understandably, fear the return to the rightful owners reclining their legislative place have put forward desperate arguments to delay the inevitable, to confuse the issue, to deprive women longer, and to stay put to conduct business as usual. Taking a cue from the colonial political master these panic-stricken representatives follow the policy of 'divide and rule'.

They do this by raising the issue of caste. They forgot about OBCs when it came to the 73rd Amendment because it concerned only governance at the village level and there was no conflict of personal interest between them and the women at that level. The hypocrisy of their concern for OBCs is further exposed where we note that it is in fact in the villages that caste discrimination is most entrenched. Why were the interests of OBCs not a factor then? Is anyone to believe that their hearts actually bleed for OBCs?

The last Parliament had close to 200 OBC male MPs. Why are OBC women not there if OBC women's representation is their real concern? These very OBC advocates made no attempt to promote OBC women even as late as the 1996 elections. How then can even the OBC women believe these less than honest advocates? Their talk of quotas within the quota is a blatant attempt to divide the women. What is worse is their transparent motivation to perpetuate themselves by playing divisive politics with women.

Motivated by self-interest they take another untenable position that reservation for women will benefit only urban women. It seems they need to be reminded that the rural women, with the 73rd amendment, got reservation first. What all women seek is representation at all levels of governance. In any case, what is wrong with reservation benefiting urban women? In any case a vast majority of male representatives line in urban areas and sport urban cultures.

While the country celebrates 50 years of independence yet its governance cannot even claim one per cent increase in women's literacy for every year of independence while male literacy stands at over 64 per cent. As women, we must understand that future is not given to us, it is what we do or what we fail to do which is important. We have two options — either to let governance be as it is and criticize from the fence or we get involved and work for changes.

We must be prepared to commit ourselves politically and organize ourselves as a political force both as an informed, organized vote bloc, and as elected representatives. Women's power is in women's 300 million votes. Every party, every MP's political destiny is in our hands. Not one can be elected without our support. Let us use this vote power by voting for women's interests only. The change will come when we mobilize ourselves right from the village, block, district, State and national level, and acquire our collective strength. (*Hindustan Times*, March 11, 1998).

Political Empowerment of Women a Necessity

A reiteration on political empowerment of women could not have come at a better time than on the occasion of International Women's Day, and by none other than Ms Usha Narayanan, the First Lady of India.

In her public debut as the First Lady, Ms Narayanan, chief guest at a meeting organized by the United Nations Information Centre on Friday, delivered the keynote address on "Women's Rights are Human Rights."

Regretting that political representation of women in legislatures had not increased in spite of promises by all political parties to give them one-third reservation in Parliament and in state legislatures, she felt that if human rights in all its aspects were to be practically realized, political empowerment was essential.

A former national president of Karuna (an all-India organization for the welfare of women and children,) Ms Narayanan is closely associated with the women's movement in the country. "It cannot be conceived as a war of sexes, but a struggle in which the domination of man has to be challenged in every field, and the cooperation of man has to be felicitated in every field," she emphasised. Despite a snag which disrupted the sound system, Ms Narayanan remained composed and continued with her speech.

This year also marks the 50th anniversary of the Universal Declaration of Human Rights. The guest speakers on the topic included Mr Starcevic, director, UN Information Centre, Ms Indira Jaisingh, a Supreme Court advocate, Ms Kamala Mankekar.

In his address, Mr Stacevic called for achieving a global partnership for human rights. Governments and civil society must build new forms of solidarity for the promotion and protection of the rights of both women and men. Now and in the years to come, he said, quoting from UN Secretary General Kofi Annan's message on Women's Day.

Women Empowerment: Redefining Agenda

Jinee Lokaneeta

The concept of Women Empowerment has predominantly become a focus on political participation. The latter in turn in the context of the debate on the 81st Constitutional Amendment Bill regarding reservation for women in Parliament, has become a restricted discourse on the role of women in formal representative institutions of decision-making whether it is a Panchayati Raj institution or Parliament. In the process, empowerment of women emerges as an extremely limited concept. The fact that empowerment should imply a power to participate in the decision making in all spheres of society, with no separation of the public and prenote and in all social, political, economic and cultural processes in society is completely obfuscated. This study seeks to argue that the State has appropriated the discourse of women's empowerment in order to nullify the emancipatory potential of the concept and reduced it to signify a demand for political participation defined only in terms of reservations into given set of political institutions. Hence the arena of political participation itself is in practice clearly demarcated by the State. It is further argued that the political parties with no political commitment towards struggle on women's rights not only fail to transcend the State agenda but further collaborate with the State in order to keep the patriarchal processes intact. Finally, the role of the women's movement in the sphere of political participation is analysed as a necessary step to redefine the agenda of women's empowerment.

State Appropriation of Empowerment

The State response to any articulation of demands by apprised sections of society has been in the form of appropriation of their agenda and compartmentalising it within the mainstream patriarchal, upper caste/class discourse. Hence, even while using the average of "empowerment" or "rights" the attempt is to limit the scope of those terms such that they are unable to challenge the dominant structures and processes in society. Their politics of struggle against unequal power relations is sought to be replaced by a limited concept of "empowerment" which may be restricted to say even a demand for reservations. The fact that empowerment should imply a struggle at various levels of society against the structural basis of oppression is completely obliterated in the process.

The concept of women's empowerment has been a victim of this very appropriation by the State. Not only has it reduced its scope by focusing it only on political participation but it has infact made political participation almost synonymous with a demand for women's reservations. The fact that political participation may mean a democratization of various political processes and groups in society and could be linked with the various struggles for women's empowerment, is obviously ignored by the State. The politics of struggle of the women's movement is sought to be undermined not only in terms of reducing its scope but the state is also attempting to take away the agency of the struggling women by acting as the providers of the empowerment.

Political Parties and Women's Empowerment

The right of political participation came as a result of the struggle of women within the national movement, the fact that despite 50 years of independence women still remain a marginalized force in representative institutions which is one parameter of political participation is reflective of not only the patriarchal nature of the state but the political parties of today. Reservations then become one form of increasing political participation in the sphere of representative institutions. All political parties have committed themselves to reservations for women in their imposed struggle for gender equality. But the hollowness of their commitment is clearly exposed as well as the fact that they have never allowed women to participate in decision making within their own party structures. This is true for all parties whether it is CPI, CPM or JD, Congress (I) or BJP. One look at the figures show that the percentage of participation in party decision making committees has ranged from 0 and 7 in CPM politburo and central committee to not more than 11 per cent or 12 per cent in Congress waving committee and BJP election committee respectively (Manishi, Sept. 19, 1996). It is also significant to note that despite the higher success rate of women in winning elections the percentage of women candidates fielded by each party has been extremely low. The CSDS Data Unit figures show that in the 1996 Lok Sabha elections, the Congress fielded only 9 per cent women while BJP and UF fielded 5 per cent women candidate each. It is therefore not very surprising that the highest percentage of women representation in the Lok Sabha has only been 8.1 per cent (1984) which came down to 7.2 per cent in 1996.

This dismal scenario in the sphere of political participation in political parties and representative institutions clearly reflects that the continuing patriarchal values on the part of all political parties have not directed there challenge towards their own parties. Infact they too have uncritically accepted their party's theoretical commitment to women's political participation despite the party's inability in increasing women's participation within its structures of decision making. The women of these parties seem content in restricting their struggle to the parliamentary arena and equating political participation with reservations for women.

Role of the Autonomous Women's Movement

In India, the autonomous women's movement emerged as a critique to the mainstream left parties and other progressive movements which had failed to articulate the specificity of the women's oppression. It was also under the influence of these autonomous women's groups that the political parties and women's movements became a heterogeneous movement. Here I am referring to the autonomous women's movement as distinct from the women's wing of parties set up separately to mobilize and organize women. If the discourse on political participation and reservations has been appropriated and distorted by the State and the political parties the role of the women's movements acquires special significance.

The autonomous movements have been organizing national conferences, on the issues concerning the women's movement at different points of time. Hence, since the 1980's when the issue of rape was taken up in the context of the Anti Rape Campaign and communalism in 1993 it had different themes in accordance with the issues concerning women and other oppressed sections. The issues have been always reflective of the turbulence in society. But interestingly the issue of political participation has never been accorded much importance in the themes of the conference. Infact the issue of reservations has never been addressed even to place it within a broader context of political participation. Some autonomous groups feel that reservation would not lead to any substantial change in the political processes. A numerical increase of women in the representative institutions may not necessarily lead to a progressive nation of women's rights since women are not a homogeneous category divided by castes, class, religion as well as differing ideologies.

Although one shares these apprehensions regarding reservations one also feels that it is only by interacting with the formal and informal political institutions, that the women's movement can constantly reiterate the limited scope of reservations and broaden the agenda to link it up with other forms of political participation. Even while becoming the nature of the State and its strategy of appropriation it is only the women's movement which can subvert a limited tool by linking it up with its agenda of women's empowerment in spheres. Since it has a close relationship with mass movements of other oppressed sections, it can challenge political groups, parties movements to fulfil their commitment to gender equality. The nation of political participation can be given a new direction by linking it up with the simultaneous struggles in other spheres of society. The women's movement has to reiterate the agency of women even in the sphere of political participation and intervene in the processes of democracy and representative institution despite its mistrust of the state.

Six

Political Participation and Decision Making

The theme of political participation of women has raised a major dilemma. On the one hand, it is the fundamental right of every citizen to contribute to the decision-making process. It is in fact the citizen's duty as well and is based on the presumption that each member has adequate means and conditions to achieve a full realization of his or her personality as an entity in society. On the other hand, from a feminist perspective, an analysis of women's participation in political process has questionedd the narrow definition of political participation as accepted by the mainstream of political scientists and policy makers. The New Delhi Document on Women in Development (1985) recognized that despite the rapid growth of informal political activity by women, their role in the formal political structure had virtually remained unchanged. This recognition has resulted in a serious debate on the concepts and indicators for political participation.

As a consequence of the debate appropriate indicators of political participation and fresh strategies have to be evolved, not only for formal political activities but also for full involvement and participation in non-formal mass action. It is surprising to note that there had hardly been any mention of this subject in the National Plan of Action for Women drawn up in 1976. Perhaps for the Government of India and the U.N. at that time, the issues of health, education and employment had a higher priority than political participation. However, subsequent national documents prepared at the time of the Nairobi Conference of 1985, the Non-Aligned Meet of the same year and the Forward Looking Strategies after Nairobi Conference, have recognized the importance of this theme and raised issues related to the nature of political participation of women, the problems faced therein and the strategies to be evolved.

It is necessary to attempt a definition of political participation which is broader than the one covering women's participation only in the electoral and administrative processes. It includes the gamut of voluntary activities with a bearing on the political processes, including voting, support of political groups, communication with legislators, dissemination of political views and opinions among the electorate, and other related activities. Besides social relationships, there are spheres of power-relationships which are generated and institutionalized by being used to encourage, control or move people's behaviour, attitudes and beliefs in specified directions. Political participation can be considered to include an involvement in any form of organized activity that affects, or seeks to affect, these power relationships. It refers broadly also to the "activities by those not formally empowered to make decisions, these activities being mainly intended to influence the attitudes and behaviour of those who have powers for decision making". In fact, protests and demonstrations against those in power also form part of political participation. Women's participation has covered a range of activities including movements, protests and support meetings on all issues connected with labour, dowry, rape, domestic violence, price-rise, food adulteration and deforestation, as also movements for the promotion of peace.

An analysis of the above terms, with particular reference to the participation of women, indicates that there has only been a limited application, mainly because of various dubious considerations of social, economic and political variables. Broad-based political participation of women is severely limited due to a nexus of traditional factors, these are the domination of Indian politics by considerations of caste, class, religion, feudal and family status, etc., all of which are parochial essentially patriarchal forces that work in favour of men against women. Consequently, women are still left on the periphery of the political process, and political participation remains elusive to most of them, in spite of their voting and election, and also capture of some seats of power and influence. As amply brought out by various scholars, the most crucial problem in any attempt to measure women's political participation simply by studying official or organizational membership and voting, is the finding that much of the Third World politics occurs outside conventional political institutions. Hence, political participation seeks also to reorganize the lives of members of human society, and ensure that the participation by women is not underestimated by being branded 'non-political' and women's concerns treated as 'social' in nature.

Gender equality is a prerequisite for effective participation of women in strengthening the institutional structure of democracy. Women have been marginalized because of several socio-economic constraints. The number of women in leadership position at the local, village, district and national level is still not commensurate with the numbers in society.

Review of Political Participation of Women: 1977-87

In India, limited adult franchise was granted to women in 1937. Since then, women have been participating in political processes, as voters, as candidates contesting the elections, involved in deliberations both in the State Assemblies and Parliament and also through holding public office at different levels and in the judiciary where women perform watchdog roles in the protection of sanctioned rights.

The decade under review coincides with the International Women's Decade. Hence, an assessment of the role of women's awareness, priorities, thrusts, etc., as a result of the forces generated during the women's decade can also be made.

Women as Voters

Voting is the basic activity by which the citizens get assimilated in the political process. Table 6.1 shows the comparative participation of men and women in three elections, viz., 1977, 1980 and 1984.

TABLE - 6.1

VOTER/WOMEN PARTICIPATION IN ELECTIONS: 1977, 1980 AND 1984

Year	*Total Voting Percentage*	*Per cent Turnout of New Voters*	*Per cent Turnout of Women Voters*
1977	60.49	65.63	54.96
1980	56.92	62.15	51.22
1984	63.61	68.17	58.60

Women's participation in formal elections is to a great extent dependent on the mobilization efforts of the political parties, general awareness among the community of the importance of exercising franchise, and the overall political culture. No serious effort appear to have been made to mobilize women as a political pressure group by any political party. Caste, personality and families of candidates appear to be more important to voters than party ideology or affiliations. Factors like education, religion, class and tradition also seem to affect women's participation.

One great difficulty with the Indian political scene is that it is impossible to generalize about the interrelationship between any single factor and political behaviour. Patterns of political behaviour from different regions show different relationships, influenced as they are by interrelated factors like the social status of women, their economic position, the cultural norms, and above all, the regional outlook towards women's participation in the wider society. Then again, there are some situations which are conspicuous by obvious contradictions. Kerala, which has a record of rapid growth in women's political mobilization and women's literacy, also has a record of electing very few women members to the legislature. In contrast, Uttar Pradesh, with its general low profile of women's political participation, has persistently elected a large number of women to the legislature.

Voting as an indication of political participation for women in India, has its own strengths and weaknesses. Voting has a tremendous impact for equalizing and mobilizing women. Yet, it has to be noted that voting requires the least initiative and internal motivation. Very often the woman citizen treats the day of voting as a welcome break from her dull and tiring routine and does not appear to have a notion of why she should vote for a particular candidate.

Women as Candidates

The number of women contestants in parliamentary elections has not increased significantly over the years. Political parties seem uniformly reluctant to field women candidates. The high cost of electioneering is another deterrent to most women candidates. Because of these factors there is an increasing tendency among women to contest elections as independent candidates. In spite of this, the present Parliament has the largest number of women members ever since independence (Table 6.2).

The proportion of seats won by women to the Lok Sabha stands in 1988 at 46 seats out of a house of 537 seats. The Rajya Sabha has 28 women in a house of 245 seats. There has been a greater representation of women in the Rajya Sabha by nomination.

The pattern is not very different at the State level. The all India total stands at 44 women elected out of 241 women contestants, as against 1486 men out of 8415 male contestants (Table 6.9). For instance, in Orissa in 1980, for the House of 147 members, 10 contestants were women of whom only 5 were elected. In 1980 in Tamil Nadu, 5 out of 17 women candidates won. An in-depth study of women at grassroots level politics reflects a similar trend. Interviews with 143 women members of Panchayat Samitis and Zila Parishads in Maharashtra reveal that the women of upper castes, wives of big landowners and politically influential persons, tend to predominate in the positions reserved for women in local bodies. However the redeeming factor is that women in rural area are capable of progressive thinking and have the potential for valuable social participation if a conscious effort is made to secure their involvement.

Women in Office

Despite the general depressed picture of women's role in Indian democracy, there has been a rise in the number of women in key positions of power. For many years, India had a woman Prime Minister at the helm of affairs. There are women Ministers both in the centre as well as in the states. In the administrative machinery also, there is an increased representation of women. In the Indian Administrative Service, there are currently 339 women out of a total of 4548. There are six women Vice-Chancellors in the country. The All India Services employ 994 women out of a total of 16,987 officers (5.8 per cent), the Indian Forest Service has only 10 women officers (0.6 per cent), and the IPS 21 women officers (0.9 per cent). Stereotyping of jobs still exists and women in positions of power have not been able to influence macro level policy decisions on women. (Table 6.4).

TABLE - 6.2

WOMEN CANDIDATES PUT UP BY POLITICAL PARTIES FOR ELECTIONS TO THE LOK SABHA

Year	Congress-I		Congress		C.P.I.		C.P.I.(M)		Swatantra		Janta		Independents		Others				
	No. of Conte-stants	No. of Succe-ssful Candi dates	No. of Conte-stants	No. of Succe-ssful Candi dates	No. of Conte-stants	No. of Succe-ssful Candi dates	No. of Conte-stants	No. of Succe-ssful Candi dates	No. of Conte-stants	No. of Succe-ssful Candi dates	No. of Conte-stants	No. of Succe-ssful Candi dates	No. of Conte-stants	No. of Succe-ssful Candi dates	No. of Conte-stants	No. of Succe-ssful Candi dates	No. of Conte-stants	No. of Succe-ssful Candi dates	Per cent
1957	-	-	26	23	4	2	-	-	-	-	-	-	7	-	5	2	42	27	5.4
1962	-	-	33	27	2	2	-	-	9	5	-	-	8	-	13	-	65	34	6.7
1967	-	-	33	23	3	-	1	1	2	2	-	-	10	3	13	2	62	31	5.9
1971	21	15	14	-	3	1	2	1	2	1	-	-	29	1	11	3	82	22	4.2
1972	22	6	-	-	3	1	2	2	-	-	15	8	24	-	4	2	70	19	3.4
1980	32	20	10	-	2	1	3	2	-	-	20	2	60	-	15	3	142	28	5.1
1984	39	36	-	-	2	1	3	1	-	-	4	-	96	1	20	3	140	42	8.1

Note: Blank columns indicate either the party was not in existence or data was not available.

TABLE - 6.3

NO. OF CANDIDATES CONSTITUTION ELECTED TO THE STATE LEGISLATIVE ASSEMBLIES BY SEX IN STATES / U T FROM 1978-83

Sl. No.	State/Union Territory	1978				1979-80				1982-83			
		Contested		Elected		Contested		Elected		Contested		Elected	
		M	F	M	F	M	F	M	F	M	F	M	F
(1)	(2)	(3)	(4)	(5)	(6)	(7)	(8)	(9)	(10)	(11)	(12)	(13)	(14)
1.	Andhra Pradesh	1491	47	284	10	-	-	-	-	1647	73	282	12
2.	Assam	917	21	125	1	-	-	-	-	448	3	108	1
3.	Bihar	-	-	-	-	2925	77	312	12	-	-	-	-
4.	Gujarat	-	-	-	-	950	24	178	5	-	-	-	-
5.	Haryana	-	-	-	-	-	-	-	-	1068	27	83	7
6.	Himachal Pradesh	-	-	-	-	-	-	-	-	432	9	65	3
7.	Jammu & Kashmir	-	-	-	-	-	-	-	-	505	7	75	-
8.	Karnataka	1137	28	215	9	-	-	-	-	1327	38	222	2
9.	Kerala	-	-	-	-	589	13	135	5	682	17	136	4
10.	Madhya Pradesh	-	-	-	-	1950	50	302	18	-	-	-	-
11.	Maharashtra	1777	42	280	8	1488	49	269	19	-	-	-	-
12.	Manipur	-	-	-	-	394	7	60	-	-	-	-	-
13.	Meghalaya	255	7	59	1	-	-	-	-	309	8	60	-
14.	Nagaland	-	-	-	-	-	-	-	-	244	1	60	-
15.	Orissa	-	-	-	-	720	10	142	5	-	-	-	-

16. Punjab	-	-	-	-	703	19	111	6	-	-	-	-
17. Rajasthan	-	-	-	-	1375	31	190	10	-	-	-	-
18. Sikkim	-	-	-	-	233	11	32	-	-	-	-	-
19. Tamil Nadu	-	-	-	-	1012	17	229	5	-	-	-	-
20. Tripura	-	-	-	-	-	-	-	-	119	11	56	4
21. Uttar Pradesh	-	-	-	-	4525	94	401	24	-	-	-	-
22. West Bengal	-	-	-	-	-	-	-	-	1179	26	287	7
23. Andaman & Nicobar Islands	-	-	-	-	-	-	-	-	-	-	-	-
24. Arunachal Pradesh	84	2	30	-	93	2	29	1	-	-	-	-
25. Chandigarh	-	-	-	-	-	-	-	-	-	-	-	-
26. Dadra & Nagar Haveli	-	-	-	-	-	-	-	-	-	-	-	-
27. Delhi	-	-	-	-	-	-	-	-	379	12	52	4
28. Goa, Daman & Diu	-	-	-	-	174	3	30	-	-	-	-	-
29. Lakshadweep	-	-	-	-	-	-	-	-	-	-	-	-
30. Mizoram	153	1	29	1	147	3	29	1	-	-	-	-
31. Pondicherry	-	-	-	-	128	4	29	1	-	-	-	-
Total	5814	148	1022	30	17406	420	2478	112	8415	241	1486	44

M: Males,
F: Females.
Source: Election Commission of India, New Delhi.

TABLE - 6.4

REPRESENTATION OF WOMEN IN SELECTED SERVICES FROM 1985 TO 1987

Sl. No.	Service	*Number of Personnel in Position as on 1 January*								
		1985			*1986*			*1987*		
		M	*F*	*Total*	*M*	*F*	*Total*	*M*	*F*	*Total*
1.	Indian Administration Service	3973	311	4284	4061	329	4390	4209	339	4548
2.	Indian Police Service	2325	18	2343	2349	18	2367	2418	21	2439
3.	Indian Foreign Service	485	50	535	483	51	534	480	53	533
4.	Indian Customs & Central Excise Service	997	53	1050	1114	55	1169	1053	59	1112
5.	Income Tax Service	2238	174	2412	2223	181	2404	2244	195	2439
6.	Indian Audit & Accounts Service	531	52	583	547	59	606	530	59	589
7.	Indian Postal Service	438	45	483	461	48	509	454	52	506
8.	Indian Economic Service	591	50	641	593	52	645	481	71	552
9.	Indian Statistical Service	543	22	565	548	29	577	645	32	677
10.	Indian Forest Service	1368	6	1374	1565	8	1573	1773	10	1743
11.	Central Information Service	687	63	750	778	67	845	770	69	839
12.	Central Secretariat Service	1004*	31*	1035	1014	34	1048	976	34	1010
	Total	15180	875 (5.45)	16055	15736	931 (5.58)	16667	15993	994 (5.83)	16987

Note: Figures in parenthesis represent percentage of females w.r.t. total in the respective year.

* Figures pertain to the year 1984.

Source: *Women in India: A Statistical Profile.*

Women in Local Government

The concept of participatory development, the importance of intermediaries, e.g., voluntary action groups and educational institutions were recognized as important instruments to achieve the developmental goals for women. Participatory development through group organizations has been successfully attempted in several innovative projects carried out by women's organizations. The contribution of the voluntary organizations has been considered as particularly significant in demonstrating the effectiveness of participatory development as a process of empowering women, to articulate their needs, to take part in decision making and in following their own vision. In this regard, the participation of women in the Panchayati Raj institutions, which were considered to be the most effective instruments for realizing the goals of economic betterment and social justice for the least privileged, was felt essential. The CSWI report suggested the establishment of All-Women Panchayats at village level, with autonomy and resources of their own for the management and administration of welfare and development programmes for women and children, as a transitional measure to break through the traditional attitudes that inhibit most women in articulating their problems or participating actively in the local bodies. The Empowered Committee, while examining the recommendations, suggested that the subcommittee, while examining the subjects relating to management and administration of programmes for women and children should have the power of Panchayat with earmarked funds.

Participation of women in Panchayati Raj institutions has been recognized as a step towards equality. The Committee on the Panchayati Raj institutions, 1978 recommended the reservation of two seats for women in Panchayats and co-opt women in case they did not come through elections. It also suggested that a Committee of women be set up within Panchayats to operate specific programmes for women and children. The co-option of two women members in Panchayats, has not brought any perceptible impact on women's participation in the Panchayati Raj bodies. Co-option is done only in letter and not in the spirit of getting the women involved in Panchayat activities. The participation of women in Panchayats as it is today hardly gives any scope for women members to participate effectively and independently in democratic and political processes or to influence decision making.

The Minister of Agriculture, in a recent circular to the State Governments, asked the States to take measures for increasing effective representation of women in Panchayats. The examples of Karnataka and Andhra Pradesh have been cited where 25 per cent and 30 per cent seats respectively have been reserved for women. Enhanced representation is likely to remove the isolation of women and give them visibility and strength to be more assertive and to take part in decision making.

Performance of Women Members in Legislative Houses

Contrary to the normal expectation that women members in Parliament as well as the State Legislatures take little part in the proceedings and remain silent spectators, they have been very active and are found to take a lively part in the debates. Apart from subjects of direct relevance to them like welfare, child development, removal of dowry and social malpractices, education and health, centre-state relations, security, food and civil supplies and other specialized and sensitive subjects have drawn the attention of many members. There are numerous instances during the years of their participation in debates and in helping to move resolutions for legislative measures and bills. On their part, they have been feeling that the media coverage is inadequate for them as it is generally focused on men. Women have also taken part in, and in some cases initiated, calling attention notices and adjournment motions, in the Parliament and in State Assemblies, and made a mark with significant and well-articulated contributions.

On women's issues, women MPs have participated actively in the debates on dowry and influenced the government to make changes in the existing dowry laws. They have also given useful suggestions such as having a National Commission on Women, having women judges on family and special courts for hearing cases of dowry deaths. On various occasions, they have raised questions regarding the common civil code, immoral traffic in women, dowry deaths and rape cases.

Women in the Political Parties

Besides participation in the general elections/contesting elections is a very important dimension of participation through political party. As far as political parties are concerned, although at election time declarations are made of granting 15-20 per cent seats to women, no party has been able to achieve the target. In fact many studies have shown that before the women's decade, political parties were not even stressing on women's issues, in their campaigns or in mobilizing rallies. In the last decade all political parties have shown great interest in women's problems as a result of various developments but primarily due to the pressure of women's groups. Parties in their manifestos promise to women all opportunities for increased participation in social, economic and political life. Yet, the record of most of the parties is poor so far as women are concerned. Though exact figures are unavailable, it can be safely presumed that membership of women in parties does not exceed 10 to 12 per cent of their total membership. Parties hardly make a sincere attempt to reach out to women or to put them in positions of authority. To take the example of Congress (I), Mrs. Indira Gandhi and Mrs. Sonia Gandhi (present) have been the only woman Presidents of the Congress Party in the post-independence period. Sheila Dixit has been recently appointed as the Chief Minister of Delhi, strengthening the role of women in politics. Though it was stated that "women have a special role to play in the party and in the shaping of a new society", yet women have not really been able to make their presence felt at the decision-making levels. There have been a few illustrations of women placed in decision-making positions as in the Congress Centenary Celebrations Committee or in the Nehru Birth Centenary Committee. In a few State Congress Committees, women have been Presidents and at the AICC level, it has been a practice to have at least one woman as the General Secretary. To protest against this continued neglect, the State convenors of the women's front at their meeting convened in January, 1985, passed a resolution requesting the Congress President to issue instructions to include women as state convenors in the state election coordination committees and to allot at least one Assembly seat in each parliamentary constituency to women.

A number of political parties have strong women's wings spread all over the country, but advocate revival of traditional values, encourage fundamentalism, eulogize mythological women characters and generate communal sentiments. Some other struggle around issues such as economic demands, world peace, atrocities against women, secularism, national integration, price rise, etc.

On the whole, it would not be correct to state that the women's decade has forced all political parties to be alter to women's problems. The major contention of the left parties that women's problems will get solved once a classless society is established, still continues. However, under the pressure of women members, at least the inclusion of women's issues in their manifestos has been feasible. Yet, access to significant decision making positions in political parties continues to elude women. Today, very few women hold crucial positions. In fact, one of the main reasons for the growth of autonomous women's groups is the disillusionment that arises, owing to a consideration of women by some political parties as peripheral elements, in spite of their involvement in day-to-day political work. This is not a problem on the Indian scene only, but is a global issue, which could only be solved with the growing awareness and rightful assertion by women.

Women in the Trade Union Organization

Participation of women in the trade unions has been a topic which has acquired significance during the last two or three decades. Studies have shown that though it might be difficult to participate in day-to-day activities of the trade unions, women have provided very great strength during crisis periods, such as strikes. A recent study on the more than a year long textile strike of Bombay in 1982 proved that without the support of both women textile workers and the wives of male textile workers, the leaders would have found it difficult to continue.

A distressing fact is that the prevalence of patriarchy prevents men colleagues from accepting women's crucial role. In a recent conference on the problems of working women and their participation in trade unions, a scholar noted: "Today after more than a decade of our struggle we find to our satisfaction that the question and problems of working women and women in general are being discussed widely in our country by various organizations, individuals, press and also by the Government. The question is also being highlighted in international forums." Despite these efforts, many trade unions in the country are yet to pay adequate attention to women's issues and joint efforts have to be made to make a common cause to fight for the demands of working women. The scholar has also documented a number of struggles of women workers from different states indicating the militancy and tenacity of women who were involved in struggles of Adivasis, contract workers, women coal miners, plantation workers, etc.

A recent report also gives the picture of the women membership in the CITU and the proportion of women office bearers in some of the States. Of course, the picture is very dismal. The total membership has been around 10 per cent in 1986, and an infinitesimal proportion as office bearers.

The issues which concern women most, such as equal wages, non-provision of maternity benefits and child care facilities, retrenchment of women workers in the wake of Equal Remuneration Act, have not been taken up seriously by trade unions suggest that there are instances where they expressed their concern regarding these issues by passing resolutions and holding consultation but there is hardly any evidence that trade unions agitated or called a strike to meet these demands nor have their journals taken cognizance of these minor efforts. In this context, it has been even suggested that a separate women's cell or a union for women would ensure more participation of women. It was also strongly felt that one of the major tasks is to orient the male leaders to remove their gender bias and incorporate more and more women in the decision-making bodies.

An analysis of the problems of women working in the unorganized sector throws light on the sexist attitude of mainstream trade unions. It is well known that women constitute a majority of the unorganized labour force. The working conditions in this sector are abysmal. There is no job security, no fair wages, no facilities and no rights to demand for the improvement of their situation etc. It goes to the credit of grassroots level organizations such as WWF and SEWA and the researchers who have highlighted the problems of these women, that attempts are now being made to create some kind of structure to ventilate their problems. In the absence of support from the official trade unions, the women workers are turning to some of the women's organizations for pressing their problems is a very striking trend.

Studies have shown that whenever women took up issues such as low wages, inhuman working conditions, and health hazards by organizing meetings, putting up posters, etc., women workers were harassed and victimized. They were threatened with arrest and rape, and all kinds of pressures from parents, in laws were used to demoralize the women. Employers preferred to use the 'putting out' system and 'price rate' system to enrolling women on their pay rolls. The recently published report of the National Commission on Self-Employed Women and Women in Unorganized Sector, has made several recommendations to ensure the inclusion of women in the unorganized sector in the entire gamut of trade union activities.

Informal Participation of Women

Political participation, viewed from a broader perspective, includes participation in any organized and deliberate activity that seeks to influence or alter the character/function/structure/policies/assumption/behaving of any institution or the power structure in any of the above spheres. In order to assess women's political participation, one has thus to look at their involvement in different types of mobilization such as movements and struggles. The question that needs to be investigated in depth is the one to ascertain women's participation in mass struggles and protest movements and not necessarily in formal political bodies ranging from village level to Parliament.

The history of women's large-scale participation in the nationalist movement is well known and in fact, one can go back to 1905 when women freedom fighters showed immense courage in fighting the British rulers. Of course, more strikingly, mass participation of women was recognized during the Civil Disobedience Movement in 1930 and also during the Quit India Movement of 1942, when thousands of women courted arrest. Some women participated in the revolutionary movement as couriers distributing literature, risking police repression, imprisonment and even capital punishment. Similarly, in the Tebhaga Movement for land reform, which took place during 1946-51 in West Bengal, it has been reported that women participated at all levels. There was a Nari Bahini (Women's Volunteer Force) which would help guard villages at night. Studies have recorded many stories of women's courage, militant spirit and innovation during these struggles. Investigations into the role of women in the Telangana and Naxalite movements subsequently have revealed that women not only gave shelter to the revolutionaries and served as liaison among various groups but also took leading part in direct political action.

One of the most significant events which dramatically brought to the forefront women's issues in the last decades has been the re-opening of the Mathura rape case in the Supreme Court which triggered off a woman's protest movement. A series of rallies, campaigns, *morchas*, *dharnas* and demonstrations were held to protest against rape, wife beating, dowry deaths, molestation of women, media distortions, foeticide and other issues.

Women from various castes, communities and regions have participated voluntarily and together, to raise their voice on important issues. Current rural struggles in Bihar, Himachal Pradesh, Marathwada region and five Tamil Nadu districts centre on various issues ranging from expropriation and redistribution of the land of a Bodhgaya *mahant* in Bihar, the politics of liquor licensing and government water supply in Himachal Pradesh, to struggle for canal water and public lands by untouchable poor peasants in drought prone Marathwada, and struggle for self-respect, employment and justice among Tamil Nadu landless labourers.

In this narrative of women's participation in mass movements, the illustration of the Chipko Movement stands out prominently. There is a feeling that a genuine mass based women's movement can grow out of the grassroot participatory organizations of women. Through such participation will emerge political consciousness of women. The Chipko Movement initiated in 1972-74 is an example of the powerful impact that women's initiative can have on the power brokers, contractors and family members. Where women shoulder major burdens and the drudgery of bringing fuel, fodder and water from long distances, any action which affects these sources of livelihood adversely, will surely bring sharp resentment among them. In this struggle, women have not been merely supporters of an ongoing struggle but have functioned as initiators of the movement with a farreaching impact on gender relations in Garhwali society. As mentioned in the report on the State of India's Environment. "Women acting entirely on their own rose up on the spur of the moment. While in Rani (Chamoli District) the protest was against a timber contractor, in all other areas the protest was against their own cash hungry men who could not care less if the forest was destroyed while their women had to walk for many miles to collect their daily load of fuel and fodder".

Thus the record of women's participation in political processes other than the formal has been quite creditable. Of course, while women have been visible in mass movements, group upsurges and protest struggles, their presence is not felt in structured decision making institutional settings. Even in the structures where women's participation is substantial, they have not been given positions of power. However, it can be stated that protests made by women activists and scholars have resulted in their role in the grassroots level movements being recognized.

Issues Needing Attention

During the last decade, and particularly in the last two years, certain deliberate efforts have been made to implement some of the decisions taken at the Conference of Non-Aligned and other Developing Countries, in April, 1985 and at the Nairobi World Conference in July, 1985 as Forward Looking Strategies for the Advancement of Women. Even then, it has not been found possible by political parties to field the number of women candidates that they had planned, and by elected governments in the Centre and States to appoint the minimum number of women to ministerial positions. One significant step has, however, been the formation of the Department of Women and Child Development which is part of the Ministry of Human Resource Development. The Constitution of a separate Department of Women has helped in focussing programmes for women's development. Efforts are also being made to reach out to the women in the poverty sector through various welfare schemes and programmes.

The incorporation of Equality for Women as No.12 in the Twenty-Point Programme of development enunciated in 1986, and certain special schemes like Legal Literacy Programmes, Awareness Generation Programmes, Prevention of Atrocities Against Women are evidences of conscious attempts made by the government to empower women to handle complex situations. The setting of the National Expert Committee on Women Prisoners and the National Commission on Self-Employed Women are significant steps in the right direction. The most formidable hurdle in the programmes and policies of the Government has been non-implementation or very limited implementation of these measures. Before recommendations to remedy the situation are suggested, it would be useful to have a brief discussion on why women's participation in political affairs is limited.

Reasons for LimitedWomen's Participation in Politics

As mentioned in the Non-Aligned Document, "understanding of obstacles to women's effective participation in political life has generally been clouded by various assumptions regarding women's behavioural pattern, their backward consciousness, lack of interest in public issues, or biological differences in their mental make up. An assessment of the situation at the end of Decade with all the shortfalls in reliable data suggests that, while the visibility of women in the political and developmental process has increased because of greater efforts to obtain first-hand information, the search has also helped to identify powerful, sometimes hidden forces of resistance that obstruct the march towards the goals of the Decade."

On the question of peace, since women are one of the most vulnerable groups in the region effected by armed conflicts, special attention has to be drawn to the need to eliminate obstacles to the maintenance of peace. Women's equal role in decision making with respect to peace and related issues should be enhanced and encouraged at all levels. Women should be able to participate actively in decision-making processes related to the promotion of regional, national and international peace and cooperation.

Nonetheless, it should not imply that women's ability to support causes is restricted only to pacifist issues.

One of the arguments for non-participation has been that the women wilfully place themselves in marginal positions towards matters "political". The crucial problem is that women find themselves being judged and judging themselves by two standards. One standard is of feminity, of the private world which regards them as nurturant, passive, emotional, home oriented and subordinate to men. The other standard is that of their modern role which is the standard of the public world which expects women to be rational, active, achievement oriented, ambitious and competitive. Women in such a situation have two options. Either they follow the rules of the game of politics and are called unfeminine or act in politics guided by the standards of feminity and are seen as peculiar.

A very strong reason explaining women's limited participation has been the theory of women's "backward consciousness". However, it has been seen that in non-formal mass movements, women responded with great enthusiasm and responsibility on crucial themes. Whether it is a movement against foreign government under Mahatma Gandhi's leadership or it is a protest against vested interests in economic or political spheres or confronting the oppressive landlord or contractor, women have not hesitated; they have made sacrifices and suffered repression along with men.

The observations that women when elected do not participate in the debates or women elect those candidates whom their men wish to support, have been proved wrong with more and more research findings. Women do raise relevant issues on a wide range of subjects, and studies on voting behaviour suggest that the secret ballot system helps considerably in exercising individual preference, though these findings / revelations are underplayed by policy makers and political scientists due to gender biases.

Subordination of women in society acts as a structural constraint to their participation in political activities. Owing to the gender-based division of labour in the family, women have to bear the full responsibility of household chores. It is the woman's duty to bring fuel, fodder and water and to cook. They have to look after the rearing and education of children besides socializing. These constraints operate more or less for all classes and communities of women.

Another significant deterrent factor is that of the political culture which prevails today. Not only have the political processes become complicated but many decisions are made behind the scenes. It has also become very expensive and difficult for women, who have little control over resources. Further, the atmosphere of growing violence, character-assassination and unscrupulous struggles for power, have been a serious deterrent to women's participation in an effective manner.

In mass movements which are issue-oriented and aim at achieving concrete objectives, women are able to participate, leave the chores of the house to someone and suffer the hardships and privations of political confrontations. But when an activity requires routine, continuous work which is often complicated to follow, women find it difficult to participate due to lack of supportive structures.

Another important factor which has to be considered is that much of the political participation today requires information, knowledge and exposure to the various experiments, strategies and models. In a country where only 24.82 per cent of women are literate and where only 3 per cent of women in the age group 17-21 are in the higher education stream, it would be futile to expect women to participate effectively. An understanding of political-policies, strategies and actions requires some training, education and constant interaction. This requirement is very difficult to be fulfilled even by men in a poor illiterate society. It is a much more challenging task for women. If women's participation has to be encouraged, a more conscious and deliberate effort to educate them politically has to be made. The working of international events, the interrelationships of various systems in society, implications of political actions and policies and many such issues need to be explained to women so that they participate intelligently and consciously.

If women have to become integrated fully into political life, cultural change is necessary. In the past few centuries, the world has been divided into the separate spheres of the public and private. While women are no longer restricted to "private" activities related only to their families, their outside activities are "privatized" by men and society at large. Another prerequisite for women to be active participants in decision making activities, is the provision of facilities, like education, training, information and above all, economic security.

In conclusion, it may be said that during the Women's Decade, there has been some achievement in making women visible in the political sphere. There has been more positive action on the part of the government to integrate women in the decision-making process. It appears that the operation of larger politico-economic forces generate a political culture that women find difficult to get involved in. Women through the Constitution have been allowed to enter politics but there is a vast difference between allowing and integrating. As a scholar puts it "Toleration is not an active principle, it is a passive one. It places a premium on the elimination of tangible barriers but makes no commitment to a positive value of inclusion and membership. Political liberation of women, therefore, would mean that women would be seen not as deviants or even as welcome strangers". In short, women's real active political participation will necessitate changes both in value and in the social structure.

Recommendations

1. It has been observed through various studies, that education of citizens not only builds up knowledge and information but also helps the citizens to understand the complexities of political process. It is, therefore, recommended that the programme of free universal education up to the age of 14 should be vigorously implemented. Further, serious attention needs to be paid to the content of education. The courses of studies and the textbooks should inculcate values of gender equality, self-respect, courage, independence, etc., which would help develop the personalities of women.

2. In order that women are able to participate fully, it is necessary to spread legal literacy not only among the general community, but also among elected representatives. Modules can be included in existing non-formal educational programmes for this purpose.

3. The working of international events, the interrelationship of various systems of society, implications of political actions and policies, economic and other such issues need to be highlighted to women.

4. Men and women in positions of power should be sensitized to women's issues.

5. Government should effectively secure participation of women in decision-making processes at National, State and local levels. This would imply use of special measures for recruitment of women candidates:

* More women need to be inducted in ministries at the centre and in state governments and they must be allowed to function in areas suitable to their capacities and not be restricted to 'soft' sectors.
* The Planning Commission and all ministries and government departments must have a Women's Cell.
* All government delegations to international meetings must include at least one or more women members.
* Wherever a Committee or Commission is set up by Government for any purpose, 30 per cent of its representation must be of women.
* The Union and all State level Public Service Commissions must have women representatives.
* The Planning Commission and State Planning Boards must have adequate representation of women.
* 50 per cent of all grassroots functionaries must be women. To facilitate its implementation, relaxation of minimum educational qualifications is needed, which can be supplemented by short training courses for women.
* Reservation should be made of 30 per cent seats at Panchayat to Zila Parishad level and local municipal bodies for women. Wherever possible, higher representation of dalits/tribals, women of weaker sections should be ensured.
* 30 per cent of executive heads of all bodies from village Panchayat to district level and a certain percentage of chief executives of Panchayati Raj bodies at lower, middle and higher levels must be reserved for women.

* A more effective step would be to declare a certain percentage of constituencies in the lower tier of Panchayati Raj as exclusively women's constituencies and all executive positions in a certain number of territorial jurisdictions reserved for women candidates.

6. All women members of Panchayats and other executive bodies must be trained and empowered to exercise their authority. Both men and women members must be sensitized to women's issues. A committee should be formed to look into the training needs of women Panchayat members and to help in designing modules separate allocation may be made for this purpose. Particular attention must be paid to the development of interpersonal communication skills among the trainees/ community leaders.

7. Conscious efforts are needed to elicit participation of women through establishing links between the elected representatives and the development functionaries as being experimented in Rajasthan through the Women's Development Programmes (WDP). The whole experiment is based on a decentralized administrative structure. Plans of action should be formulated through frequent meetings and discussions. Further the prime need is to see that the representatives have to be made answerable to the electorate. WDPs in other States must also be linked with Panchayat / local functionaries for more effective participation of women in development.

8. Standing Advisory Committees at Central, State, District, Block and wherever possible at village level should be formed consisting of representatives of important women's organizations.

9. Executive bodies of trade unions must include more women.

10. One of the greatest hurdles in contesting elections is the exorbitant expenditure. This factor not only makes it difficult for women, who have very limited independent resources to participate, but completely eliminates women in the poverty sector from entering the arena. This situation leads to prominence of upper castes, upper classes, urban women in the political sphere. To counteract this inequitous situation, serious steps must be taken to reduce election expenditure. Further, enormous amounts needed

for election, lead to corruption and various nefarious practices. If steps are taken to decentralize the political machinery, then unnecessary expenditure in reaching out to a very large electorate could be avoided.

11. A major step needed to facilitate women's participation both in formal and informal political processes is provision of support services. In all kinds of public participation as well as in seeking opportunities for self-development, the primary responsibilities of women for looking after home and children always come in the way. Unless arrangements are made for child care and other domestic responsibilities, sustained participation of women in the public sphere is impossible without the integration of men in the private sphere. This not only means that men share the familial responsibilities but a new value needs to be given to this joint sharing both in public and private spheres which would ultimately lead to a better quality of life.

12. In a democracy, political parties have a very significant role to play. The parties should take such measures which would facilitate participation of women. All political parties must be urged to ensure that at least 30 per cent of the candidates fielded for election are women till such time as women can stake their claim to nomination as equals. It should be examined if the Election Commission can be empowered to enforce this.

13. It is the bounded duty of political parties to provide political education to the people. They should organize study circles in which not only political understanding of the complex situations is provided, but controversial issues having implications on gender relations is also analysed.

14. Women members of the political groups should be vigilant about their rights and contributions. Whenever sexist attitudes are exhibited or sex discrimination is practised, women members should build up solidarity and oppose such practices. They should also press for implementing whatever has been promised to women; whether the question is of allocation of seats or of providing a creche or taking a stand in Parliament.

15. In generating a participatory political system, the role of voluntary organizations or non-governmental organizations is very crucial. There is evidence that when NGOs are active and play the

role of pressure groups, the representatives also become alert. Through raising the awareness of the community, NGOs can help in fielding candidates who are responsible to the people. They can focus the attention of the people on crucial issues facing women and elect members who understand those issues and are working towards it. Organizations and grassroots women's groups have in fact effectively drawn the attention of the government to atrocities perpetrated on women, to custodial rape, to harassments for dowry, to plight of the women in the unorganized sector, and so on. NGOs can also provide training for future women leaders. They can organize legal literacy programmes and study circles for political education as well as develop participatory methods of working, and thus serve as a practical training centre for effective political participation by women. They should not adopt a beneficiary or 'welfare' approach while working with their target groups. Even if a few NGOs play their role adequately and with courage, a new climate of commitment and responsibility could be generated.

16. NGOs should work as pressure groups or political action groups to press for the fulfilment of promises. They should also provide support to the elected women representatives, when they are presenting women's cases in the deliberative bodies. In short, there should be a very strong link between women representatives and those organizations working with the community.

17. Media should play a productive role in enhancing women's participation. It should give wider coverage to various activities and measures taken by women, and should highlight the problems of women. In order to project women's issues and achievements, perhaps mainstream media may not be adequate and, therefore, it is necessary to develop an alternate media system that could portray women's struggles and experiences, help generate values which encourage gender equality and justice, and build up a positive image of women participating in public life.

18. For politicization of women, networking and creation of pressure groups representing genuine issues and felt needs are essential.

19. A massive awareness campaign aimed at eliciting the support of electors (both male and female) around causes will have to be undertaken.

Policy for Child Development

India is the seventh largest country in the world with a population of 846 million (1991 census) belonging to varied religious and cultural groups, spread over a diverse geographical area. As human development debate, child development issues are gradually emerging as major challenges.

The population of India is young, with nearly 36 per cent consisting of children below 15, thus, two out of every five persons are below 15 years. The total child population in India in 1991 was about 304 million, which is more than the total population of many countries of the world. India considers development of its human resource as its key concern, the foundation for which must necessarily be laid down in the early stages of life. It also believes that in the ultimate analysis, it is childhood that holds the potential and sets the limits of future development of a society.

Much before the UN Convention on the Rights of the Child became law in 1990, the Indian Constitution provided a framework within which provisions were available for protection, development and welfare of children. Article 24 prohibits employment of children in any factory or mine or in any other hazardous occupation. Articles 39(3) and (F) lay down that the State shall direct its policy in such a manner that the tender age of children is not abused and children are given opportunities and facilities to develop in a healthy manner and childhood is protected against exploitation and against moral and material abandonment. Education of children has been recognized as a sine qua non for the growth of children. Accordingly, Article 45 lays down that the State shall provide free and compulsory education to children up to the age of 14 years.

National Policy for Children (1974)

As a follow-up to this commitment, Government of India adopted a National Policy for Children in 1974 which reaffirms the constitutional provisions and declares that it shall be the policy of the State to provide adequate services to children both before and after birth and through the period of growth, to ensure their full physical, mental and social development. This commitment towards human resource development is reflected in programmes focused on maternal and child health, nutrition and education which have occupied an important place in India's efforts to raise the living standards of its poor. Successive Five-Year Plans have provided the wherewithal to deal with these issues.

India has been fully involved with successive reaffirmations of global commitment to the cause of children. The UN Convention on the Rights of the Child in November, 1989, the World Conference on Education for All at Jomtien in March 1990, the Global Consultation on water and Sanitation in September, 1990, the World Summit on Children in the autumn of 1990 and the SAARC Conference on Children soon after the World Summit were all part of this reaffirmation process which transcends national barriers. India is a signatory to the World Declaration (September 1990) on Survival, Protection and Development of Children and the Plan of Action for implementing it.

By endorsing 27 survival and development goals for the year 2000 laid down by the World Summit, India firmly reaffirmed its commitment to advance the cause of children in India. The Department of Women and Child Development (DWCD) under the Ministry of Human Resource Development, in pursuance of this, formulated the National Plan of Action (NPA) for Children in 1992.

National Plan of Action

The National Plan of Action has been worked out keeping in mind the needs, rights and aspirations of 300 million children in the country and set a quantifiable time dimension to India's Charter of Action for Children by 2000 AD. Mid-decade goals, in selected areas have also been adopted. The priority areas in the NPA are health, nutrition, education, water, sanitation and environment. The Plan gives special consideration to children in difficult circumstances and aims at providing a framework, through the goals and objectives for actualization of the convention in the Indian context. The NPA also lists out activities to achieve these goals. To make the goals, objectives and activities of the plan more need-based and area-specific, the Central Government has urged all the State/UT governments to prepare plan of Action for children for their State/UTs, taking into account the regional disparities.

Accordingly, almost all the major States have adopted State Plans of Action for Children (SPAC). The mid-decade and decadal goods are being monitored by a high-powered inter-ministerial committee in DWCD.

The Government of India has also ratified the convention on the Rights of the Child on December 2, 1992. Accordingly, the government took various initiatives to review the national and State legislations to bring them in line with the provisions of the Convention and is developing appropriate monitoring procedures to assess progress in implementing the convention.

Integrated Child Development Services

Our journey towards providing protection and care, welfare and development of children began with the formulation of the Constitution and the launching of planned process soon after we achieved Independence. However, with the adoption of the National Policy for Children in 1974 and launching of the Integrated Child Development Services (ICDS) in 1975-76, the era of special thrust on children's needs began.

The ICDS Scheme aims to improve the nutritional and health status of vulnerable groups including pre-school children, pregnant women and nursing mothers through providing a package of services, including supplementary nutrition, pre-school education, immunization, health check-up, referral services and nutrition and health education. In addition, the scheme envisages effective convergence of inter-sectoral services in the Anganwadi Centres (AWC). The scheme targets the most vulnerable groups of population, including children up to six years of age, pregnant women and nursing mothers belonging to poorest of the poor families and living in disadvantaged areas, including backward rural areas, tribal areas and urban slums. Identification of beneficiaries is done through surveying the community and identifying families living below the poverty line.

The ICDS Scheme was sanctioned during 1975-76 in just 33 Blocks of the country. Since 1975-76, the Scheme was gradually expanded and up to March, 31, 1992, i.e., by the end of the Seventh Plan and two Annual Plans, the Scheme had covered 2,791 community development Blocks and 235 major urban slums. The

Eighth Plan laid considerable stress on child development and improving levels of nutrition in the country. On account of the special thrust in the Eighth Plan, the period saw an accelerated expansion of the ICDS Scheme, bringing the total coverage of Child Development Blocks under the Scheme to 3,702 up to March 1995. Further, the ICDS Scheme was universalized during 1995-96 and the Government is committed to cover all the 5,320 Community Development Blocks and 310 major urban slums in the country.

Alongside gradual expansion of the scheme, there has also been a significant increase in the Central Government's spending on implementation of the scheme during the Eighth Plan period. As against the expenditure of only Rs.1,190.21 crore during 17 years, i.e., 1975-76 to 1991-92, the expenditure during the Eighth Plan period amounted to Rs.2,259.19 crore representing 176 per cent of the original plan allocation during the period. The number of beneficiaries under the ICDS Scheme have also significantly increased during the Eighth Plan period. As against 1.66 crore beneficiaries up to March 1992, there are at present 2.41 crore beneficiaries.

The programme provides an integrated approach for converging basic services through nearly 4,00,000 trained community-based Anganwadi (AW) workers and an equal number of helpers, supportive community structures / women's group through the AW centre, the health system and in the community. Besides this, the AW is a meeting ground where women's/mother's group can come together, with other frontline workers, to promote awareness and joint action for child development and women's empowerment, both in rural areas and urban slums.

The impact of the programme is evident from the remarkable improvements made in child survival and development indicators, *viz.*, decrease in prevalence in malnutrition among pre-school children, improved immunization coverage in ICDS areas, decrease in Infant Mortality Rate (IMR) in ICDS areas, improvement in school enrolment and reduction in school dropout rate in ICDS areas.

The most important impact of the Scheme is clearly reflected in significant declines in the levels of severely malnourished and moderately malnourished children in the country as also in significant decline in infant mortality rate. The percentage of children suffering from severe malnutrition have significantly declined from 15.3 per cent during 1976-78 to 8.7 per cent during 1988-90 (figures published by National Nutrition Monitoring Bureau). The IMRs have significantly declined from 80 per 1000 live births in 1991 to 73 during 1994 (Sample Registration System).

Convergence of Programmes of Various Ministries

In order to achieve better results and maximize output of various programmes and schemes aimed at development of women and children, convergence of these programmes has been initiated with various concerned ministries/departments. The Ministries of Health & Family Welfare, Rural Development, Food and Department of Education, have also agreed for convergence of their services under the ICDS programme. They have issued instructions to their respective State Departments for appropriate and necessary action. The State Governments/Union Territory Administrations have been requested to pursue this with relevant Departments in the States/UTs.

Monitoring is done on a regular basis and programmes are reviewed from time to time to improve effective implementation. The non-existence of services for adolescent girls, especially school drop-outs in the rural areas, was identified as a shortcoming. The scheme of adolescent girls was introduced as part of ICDS Scheme for the benefit of 4.5 lakh adolescent girls in the age group of 11-14 years in 507 Blocks. Baseline survey had also been commissioned to enable an effective and meaningful evaluation so that these results are kept for further expansion of the scheme. Mobilizing women for their own health, nutritional well-being and self-development as well as that of their children is the underlying principle of ICDS. With a view to formalize the strategy of convergence of services, the Indira Mahila Yojana (IMY) was launched in 200 ICDS projects. New possibilities are unfolding for ICDS to promote processes for women's empowerment and for integrating the services of development of children with empowerment of women for total development of the family and community. The IMY has three components: convergence of inter-sectoral services; awareness creation; and income generative activities.

Innovative Models for Child Development

One of the important features of the ICDS has been flexibility in approach which has encouraged implementation of programmes and take initiatives to meet the special needs of children and community in different areas.

Some interesting models are outlined here, only to illustrate emerging principles of action, etc., through varied experiences in different areas. The Ramakrishna Mission Project in Narendrapur, West Bengal, where youth clubs have mobilized community support for ICDS with the felt needs of safe drinking water and environmental sanitation focused on the need for convergent community development activities.

Similarly, in Uttar Pradesh, Nehru Yuvak Kendras and other NGOs have been identified and Division/Districtwise tagging attempted, with youth groups taking up area cluster of AWC and mobilizing community support for qualitative improvement. Activities include Shramdan to improve the environment of the AW, conduct *Padyatras, Prabhat Pheris, Kalajathas* for community education on key themes, e.g.., early childhood education and nutrition, reinforced by mobile advocacy teams.

Another interesting initiative has been that of Tarang in Gujarat where the joyful play/learning continuum across the child's life is being reinforced through use of the playway activity-based methodology in school readiness interventions and teaching/learning approaches in Class 1 for achieving minimum development and learning outcomes, in collaboration with the State Resource Centre in ECE.

The Poriyawadi-Jhabua-Experiment

Jhabua is a tribal district in the south-western part of Madhya Pradesh State bordering the States of Gujarat and Rajasthan. The district has the highest proportion of tribals (86 per cent) as compared to that of the State (23 per cent) and is economically and socially underdeveloped. The ICDS has been implemented in all the 12 Blocks of Jhabua district for more than two decades. However, these efforts had limited impact on the health, nutrition and development status of children and women, since the scattered village population spread over a difficult terrain posed a major constraint of access to services (some of the villages have very small habitations where only six to eight families reside).

After a detailed district survey, the Panchayat approached the District Collector for additional mini AWCs to provide effective access to these scattered and at risk groups. Thus, the Poriyawadi (Children's wadi) mini community based child care centres were launched with financial contribution from the Panchayats. There are approximately two Poriyawadis linked to each AWC with local women volunteers being trained as Poriyawadi Workers. At present, 2000 Poriyawadis have been initiated in Jhabua district to create community capacity for child care and development and access to services. Poriyawadi workers function as social animators, enabling communities and women to improve caring and feeding practices, conducting playway activities and improving utilization of existing services, e.g., ante-natal care, immunization, and Vitamin 'A' supplementation. Some function as ORS Depot holders and have also been involved in mobilizing communities to use iodized salt, monitoring this at community level, using salt testing kits.

Alleppy Model

This new model of development evolved in Kerala enabled successful operationalization of anti-poverty programmes by organizing women's groups from poor communities themselves. Planning and implementation of anti-poverty programme is decentralized and delegated to a newly created structure called a community development society (CDS), which is a formally registered society of women from poor families, within the jurisdiction of the *nagar palikas* / Panchayats. Poverty eradication is the goal and poverty is defined in an alternative way, on the basis of risks index. Poor families are identified by community members themselves at a high risk of malnutrition and ill-health. The programme is implemented as women's programme for achieving goals of improved health and nutrition of families, focusing on the mothers and children. It is targeted to the family as a unit, incorporating basic day-to-day concerns of the poor.

The organizational structure of CDS enables women from poor families to plan, implement and monitor programmes for their own benefits. The CDS structure is a three-tier system. The basic units are the neighbourhood groups (NHGs), consisting of women from 25-40 families at the ward level; the area development society (ADS) and the CDS at the Panchayat level, which forms the apex body. The ADS and CDS are each represented by elected committees-governing bodies. At neighbourhood group level, macro plans are made, based on analysis of local problems and elimination/reduction of impact of risk factors. The NHG plans are consolidated into ward plans, which are finally integrated to form the action plan for the CDS.

The CDS mobilizes funds from banks and NABARD, from poor families themselves, through beneficiary contribution and thrift and credit societies, in addition to pooling resources under various existing anti-poverty and development programmes. The CDS represents people and women-centred sustainable development. It is linked to both the formal government and local body system.

The Alleppey model has been expanded to the rural sector in the entire Malappuram district in Kerala. One hundred and eleven CDS have been registered totally in Malappuram district with one CDS in each of the 106 Panchayats and five towns. Five Departments have joined together to implement this massive project, viz., local administration, health, social welfare, rural development and education.

In all, 1,66,500 women from poor families defined on the basis of the nutrition risk index or poverty index have been organized into 4,760 NHGs, 850 ADSs and 99 CDSs. A District CDS has been formed as an apex body at the District level. A Thrift and Credit Society has been formed with a membership of 50,000 and Rs. 50,00,000 has been collected so far as savings. In all 4,760 community health volunteers have been trained in health and nutrition by the PAC doctors and the health workers.

The CDS model highlights how child development can be promoted in the longer term through participatory convergent community development models for sustainable development.

Chengelpattu Experiment

The Spastics Society of Tamil Nadu has successfully experimented with a "Linkage Model of CBR in Early Interventions in five Blocks in Chengelpet District of Tamil Nadu. The range of activities start at the pre-natal stage through identification of high risk pregnancies and continue up to integration of disabled children into schools and Balwadis. Prevention, awareness creation, community-sensitization, early identification (within one week after birth) and home-based training are the other major service areas. In two years, 14,000 children, (including 6,000 newborns) have been served by a multidisciplinary staff of 12 rehabilitation professionals.

One of the most important aspects of this model, and indeed its very foundation for sustainability, is the area of skill-transfer to local grassroot workers of the existing government infrastructures. The major partners in this model are the ICDS and the primary health centres. About 400 ICDS, AWWS, VHNS, CHNS, SHNs have already been trained in detection and intervention. In two years' time, services in each of the five Blocks have become fully community integrated to the local PHCs.

The focus in Tamil Nadu and Kerala has been expansion of the prevention, early detection and community based rehabilitation approaches to childhood disability through involving ICDS and health sector functionaries in both states and to initiate a network of NGOs in Tamil Nadu to expand the approach to more districts. The critical breakthrough has been acceptance of the health sector in both states in their key-role particularly in prevention and early detection of disabilities. Further, in Tamil Nadu, a State Plan of Disability has also been drawn up.

The experience of ICDS during the last two decades indicates that it has the potential of bringing about a silent revolution — a profound instrument of community and human resource development.

Challenges Ahead

The young child is placed first on the agenda of development, recognizing that the child's needs must be met and rights fulfilled today and that early child development is the foundation of human development and cumulative life-long learning. The promotion of early development and a joyful play/learning continuum across the young child's life is viewed as a key strategic element for promoting the child's right to development, more so towards the year 2000 and beyond, when considerable progress would have been made in achieving goals for child survival, health and nutrition.

Recognizing the unique contribution of the holistic approach of ICDS and in view of its effective universalization, the emphasis will be on consolidation and content enrichment to enhance programme quality, impact and sustenance. The community base of ICDS is to emerge as the major convergent interface between disadvantaged communities and unreached groups and government sectoral services and programmes for children and women and anti-poverty/other development programmes. ICDS will constitute the crucial link between disadvantaged communities and the health and primary education system and together, this will constitute the core of state/district plans of action for child survival, development and protection. Priority will be accorded in these to promoting concerns of the younger child and the adolescent girl.

Shifting Emphasis to Child Development and Protection

Developing on the gains made in the Eighth Plan period, the Ninth Plan will entail a shift in emphasis from promoting only child survival and growth to child development and protection. While the Eighth Plan viewed children as the nation's future human resource, the perspective in the Ninth Plan is to view child development not only as a desirable societal investment for the nation's future, but as the right of every child to achieve full development potential, where combatting mortality and morbidity is not enough.

Child development and improved nutritional outcomes in both young children and women are the result of complex biological and social processes as well as intervention in different sectors. Inadequate dietary intake and disease are the immediate causes or determinants of malnutrition. Inadequate dietary intake and absence of disease require adequate access to food (household food security), adequate care of children and women and access to health services and a healthy environment. While these conditions may not in themselves be sufficient for individual nutrition security, it is likely that these will be adequate to control diseases and ensure nutritional well-being at a macro level. For this purpose, the human economic and organizational resources need to be put together through convergence of sectoral services and interventions to address issues related to care of children and women, household food security, access to healthy environment, women's control over resources, and to promote young child's, survival and development. This would entail strengthening convergence with the ongoing schemes of rural development and poverty alleviation programmes. Efforts are being made under the Ministry of Welfare for prevention and early detection of childhood disability and creating awareness in community for making appropriate referral and collaboration with the Department of Education on early childhood education so as to promote enrolment, retention and learning in early primary grades — especially of girls. Similarly, the ICDS needs to be further integrated with urban basic services, particularly after the universalization of both UBSP and ICDS. In the health sector similarly, the ICDS can be further linked with RCH, immunization and creche programmes as well as in achieving the nutritional goals outlined in the National Nutritional Policy of 1993.

Issues of Free Compulsory Education, Elimination of Child Labour, etc. *(At the time of the United Front Government)*

The Common Minimum Programme (CMP) of the United Front Government attempts to crystalize an alternate form of governance with emphasis on social justice, respect for human freedom and dignity. The CMP represents a commitment to the empowerment of the underprivileged and deprived sections in the community. It attempts to extend to their logical conclusion earlier efforts a social engineering by committing the government to eventually reserving one-third of the elected membership in Parliament and State legislatures for women. It similarly commits one-third of all employment opportunity in government for women. The right to free and compulsory education is sought to be included as a fundamental right and enforced through suitable statutory dispensations.

The government is also committed to conferring ownership rights to slum dwellers, ownership rights in respect of minor forest produce to Scheduled Tribes and other weaker sections who work in the forest, the launching of an attack on poverty, and guaranteed 100 days employment for all, implemented through Panchayati Raj institutions, protection of labour in the unorganized sector, revamping of the public distribution system with special focus on the poor by providing them potable drinking water and primary health coverage and universalization of the mid-day meal scheme. Child labour in all occupations and industries gradually be eliminated.

Finding Adequate Material Resources

All the above have major positive implications for the situation of the child. The real challenge would be to apportion adequate material resources on a sustained basis to achieve the desired goal within a time-bound framework.

The redeeming feature is that India presently has an infrastructure available which has immense potential to ensure development of children. The basic strategy of development, therefore, is maximum utilization and mobilization of both material and human resources. The national planning process, thus, is also focused at different aspects of economic development to achieve optimal human resource development.

All these efforts in the field of child development are a testimony to the commitment of the country to the cause of children. These mandates have resulted in planning of appropriate actions aimed at child-centred development, where children are not just recipients of benefits of service and programmes but the focus of development itself.

The National Plan of Action for Children (NPAC) is an important tool with the government to monitor the progress of its own commitment. Concerted measures are being taken to achieve targets within the stipulated time-frame. Some of the goals are well within reach, while in case of others much more needs to be done. With competitive demands from other sectors, resource scarcity is going to impose a serious constraint in achieving goals. Optimal utilization and mobilization of internal and external resources is, thus, being attempted. The measures to be adopted for achieving these goals require multi-pronged strategies to be initiated simultaneously. The process has already begun; it includes sharpening of strategies, strengthening of the implementation process, convergence of services, coordination, and decentralization of development activities.

Unless the life of the child in the family and community get improved, all efforts would be meaningless. Hence, the focus is on development and empowerment of women whose role is perceived as crucial to the development and growth of the family and community.

Towards Empowering Women

The realization that real development cannot take roots if it bypasses women, who not only represent nearly half of the country's total population (accounting for 407.1 million in absolute numbers, as per the 1991 census) but represent the very kernel around which societal reorientation takes place has been the guiding principle in the formulation of our plans from the very beginning. The government has made concerted efforts towards removing various gender-biases in order to ensure women equal status in the real sense as enshrined in the Constitution of India.

Constitutional-Legal Provisions

The Constitution of India guarantees both rights and privileges to women through Fundamental Rights and Directive Principles of State Policy. Article 14 confers on men and women equal rights and opportunities in political, economic and social spheres. Article 15 prohibits discrimination against any citizen on grounds of religion, race, caste, sex, etc., alike. Article 15(3) makes a special provision enabling the State to make affirmative discrimination in favour of women. Similarly, Article 16 provides for equality of opportunities, Article 39 (a) mentions that the State shall direct its policy towards securing for both men and women, equally, the right to a means of livelihood, Article 39 (c) ensures equal pay for equal work. Article 42 directs the State to make provision for ensuring just and humane conditions of work and maternity relief. Above all, the Constitution imposes a fundamental duty on every citizen through Article 51(A)(e) to renounce practices derogatory to the dignity of women.

In order to safeguard the various constitutional rights, the State has enacted many women-specific and women-related legislations—such as the Equal Remuneration Act of 1976, The Hindu Marriage Act of 1955 as amended in 1976, The Immoral Traffic (Prevention) Act of 1956 as amended and renamed in 1986. An amendment brought in 1984 to the Dowry Prohibition Act of 1961 made women's subjection to cruelty a cognizable offence. The second amendment brought in 1986 makes the husband or in-laws punishable, if a woman commits suicide within seven years of her marriage and it has been proved that she has been subjected to cruelty. Also, a new criminal offence of 'Dowry Death' has been incorporated in the Indian Penal Code. The Child Marriage Restraint Act of 1976 raises the age of marriage of a girl to 18 years from 15 years and that of a boy to 21 years and makes offences under this Act cognizable. The Factories Act of 1948 (amended up to 1976) provides for establishment of a creche where 30 women are employed (including casual and contract labourers). The Medical Termination of Pregnancy Act of 1971 legalizes abortion by qualified professionals on humanitarian or medical grounds. Amendments to Criminal Law 1983 provide for a punishment of seven years in ordinary cases of rape and ten years for custodial rape cases. The maximum punishment may go up to life imprisonment. The enactments of (Prevention) Act, 1987 have been passed to protect the dignity of women and prevent violence against them as well as their exploitation. The National Commission for Women Act, 1990 was passed to set up the National Commission for Women (NCW), a national apex statutory body to review the constitutional and legal safeguards for women and recommend remedial legislation. The 73rd and 74th Constitutional Amendment Acts passed in 1992 provide for reservation of one-third of seats in rural Panchayats and urban local bodies for women as Members and as chairpersons. A new legislation, i.e., the Pre-natal Diagnostic Techniques (Regulation and Prevention of Misuse) Act, 1994 has been enacted to prevent misuse of sex-determination tests and resultant abortions.

Seven

Development of Women Through Five-Year Plans (1951-56 to 1997-2002)

Women's development began mainly as a welfare oriented programme in the First Five-Year Plan (1951-56). The Central Social Welfare Board (CSWB), set up in 1953, undertook a number of welfare measures through the voluntary sector. The Second Five-Year Plan (1956-61) organized women into Mahila Mandals to act as focal points at the grassroot levels for development of women. The Third, Fourth and other Interim Plans (1961-74) accorded high priority to education of women and introduced measures to improve maternal and child health services, including supplementary feeding for children and nursing mothers, etc.

The Fifth Plan (1974-78), saw a shift in the approach for women's development from 'welfare' to 'development' to cope up with several problems of the family and the role of women. The new approach aimed at an integration of welfare with development services.

The Sixth Five-Year Plan (1980-85), marked a landmark in the history of women's development by including a separate chapter and adopting a multidisciplinary approach with a three-pronged thrust on health, education and employment.

In the Seventh Plan (1985-90), the development programmes for women continued with the major objective of raising their economic and social status to bring them into the mainstream of national development. A significant step in this direction was to identify/promote the 'beneficiary-oriented programmes' for women in different developmental sectors which extend direct benefits to women.

The Eighth Five-Year Plan (1992-97), which was launched in 1992, marked a shift from development to empowerment in approach to women development schemes. It promised to "ensure that the benefits of development from different sectors do not bypass women" and women must be enabled to function as equal partners and participants in the development process.

In the Approach Paper of Ninth Five-Year Plan (1997-2002), two major steps towards gender justice have been taken for the first time in the history of planning. Their first is the listing of empowerment of women as a major plan objective. The other is to propose inclusion of a Women's Component Plan in the Plan of all Central Ministries/Departments and State Governments/Union Territory Administrations.

Policies Advocating Women's Concerns

In addition to the women-specific and women-related policies enunciated in various Plan documents, the government has been creating an enabling environment in which women's concern can be reflected, articulated and redressed by the governments, the voluntary sector and the corporate world. As part of this effort, many policy instruments have been brought forth over the years, leading to Action Plans and programmes in several spheres. Some of the important policy-guiding documents include The National Plan of Action for Women, adopted in 1976, which became a guiding document for development of women till 1988, when a National Perspective Plan for Women was formulated. The National Perspective Plan for Women (1988-2000) drafted by a core-group of experts is more or less a long-term policy document advocating a holistic approach for development of women. Shram Shakti — the Report of the National Commission on Self-employed Women and Women in Informal Sector (1988) examines the entire gamut of issues facing women in unorganized sector and makes a number of recommendations for the betterment of women in the informal sector relating to employment, occupational hazards, legislative protection, training and skill development, entrepreneurship development, marketing and credit, etc. The National Expert Committee on Women Prisoners (1986) examined the condition of women prisoners in the criminal correctional justice system and made a series of recommendations relating to necessary legislative reforms, prison reforms and reforms of other custodial institutions and rehabilitation of prisoners insofar as women prisoners are concerned. The National Policy for Children adopted in 1974 considers children as country's supreme assets. Therefore, the State accepts their nurture as its own responsibility. Further, it also recognizes child development as an important step in building up human resources which are pivotal to the economic and social progress of the country. The National Nutritional Policy articulates nutritional consideration in all important policy instruments of Government and identifies short-term and long-term measures necessary to improve the nutritional status of women, children and the country as a whole. The National Plan of Action for the Girl Child (1991-2000) is an integrated multi-sectoral decadal Plan of Action for ensuring survival, protection and development of children with a special gender sensitivity built for girl children and adolescent girls. In addition to these women-specific policies, there are many more women-related policies, like National Health Policy (1983), National Policy on Education (1986), National Population Policy (1993), which have been influencing the welfare and development of women and children in the country. The National Policy for the Empowerment of Women has been drafted after nationwide consultations to enhance the status of women in all walks of life on a par with men and to actualize the constitutional guarantee of equality without discrimination on grounds of sex.

Impact of Plan, Policies and Programmes on Status of Women

The various developmental plans and programmes over four developmental decades (1951-1991) have brought about perceptible improvement in the socio-economic status of women in the country. Important achievements have been made in major thrust areas.

In the field of health, significant gains in respect of women's health status have been achieved. Expectancy of life for females at birth which was 31.6 years in 1951 was estimated to rise 59.7 years in 1989-93. The infant mortality rate for females declined from 131 in 1951 to 75 in 1993. Similarly, the sex differential which was quite high in the 70s has now been bridged. However, the 0-4 age specific mortality rate, even though it has significantly declined from 55.1 in 1970 to 24.8 in 1993, continue to show higher female mortality. The maternal mortality rate in rural India still continues to be uncomfortably high at 324 per 1,00,000 live births although it showed a declining trend from 468 in 1980 to 324 in 1989 (*Source*: RG's Office, 1991).

Similarly, in the field of education, a number of steps were taken up for promoting women's education and equality in line with the National Policy of Education, 1986. The main strategy for education was a distinct orientation in favour of women's equality and empowerment. There is considerable improvement in female literacy as it came up to the present rate of 39.19 per cent from 8.9 per cent in 1951. The enrolment rate of girls in primary schools has also improved from 24.8 per cent in 1950-51 to 92.6 per cent in 1994-95. The drop-out rates amongst girls at primary level showed a continuous decline from 62.5 per cent in 1980-81 to 37.8 per cent in 1994-95. However, the higher decadal growth rate of female literacy (66 per cent) as compared to male literacy (43 per cent) provides some consolation.

In the field of employment, the female work participation (total workers) has grown from 19.7 per cent in 1981 to 22.3 per cent in 1991. This could be to some extent, due to the special efforts made by the nodal department of women and child development to capture women's work in the informal sector and, thus, remove their present invisibility. Similarly, number of women in the organized sector has also risen from 12.2 per cent (27.9 lakh) in 1981 to 15.4 per cent (42.3 lakh) in 1995, recording an increase of 51.6 per cent. Of the total 42.3 lakh women in the organized sector, public sector accounts for 61.5 per cent while the private sector accounts for 38.5 per cent.

Further, employment of women in the Central Government has also been rising steadily from year to year. Women's share has grown from 3.64 per cent in 1981 to 7.58 per cent in 1991 reflecting a change in women's participation in the government. At the senior and middle management levels, though limited at present, their participation has increased marginally from 875 in 1985 (based on the data related to 12 selected all India and their allied services) to 1,511 in 1995-96 (8.4 per cent). Women's participation in decision-making in the government (taking the IAS, IPS and IFS services into account) has also increased from 379 in 1985 to 631 in 1996 showing an increase of 66 per cent over a period of 11 years.

Empowering Strategies and Governmental Interventions

Creation of Separate Nodal Agency—Department of Women and Child Development

The first step initiated by the government to strengthen the national mechanism and focus on women's development was the setting up of an exclusive Department of Women and Child Development (DWCD) under the Ministry of Human Resource Development in 1985 and designating the same as the national machinery for the advancement of women in India. The support structures of the national mechanism, as instituted over a period of time include — the Central Social Welfare Board (CSWB), a charitable company registered under Section 25 of the Indian Companies Act, 1956 assisting both in promoting voluntary action and implementing programmes fully funded by the Department; the National Institute of Public Cooperation and Child Development (NIPCCD), a society registered under the Societies Registration Act, 1860 extending both research and manpower development services to the Department; the National Commission for Women (NCW), a statutory body set up in 1992 for safeguarding the rights of women; the Rashtriya Mahila Kosh (RMK), set up in March 1993 to extend credit to poor and assetless women through the intermediation of NGOs; the National Children's Fund to support projects of NGOs for Child Development/Welfare and the National Creche Fund to extend assistance to NGOs to open new creches.

In March 1997, Joint Committee of Parliament on Empowerment of Women has been set up with the functions of examining measures for women's equality and considering the reports of NCW, among others.

The Department, in its nodal capacity, formulates policies and programmes, enacts/amends legislations affecting women and coordinates the efforts of both governmental and NGOs working to improve the lot of women in the country. The programmes of the Department, which are women specific, include - employment and income generation, welfare and support services and gender sensitization and awareness generation programmes. These programmes play the role of being both supplementary and complementary to the other women related development programmes in the sectors of health, education, labour and employment, rural and urban development, etc., being implemented by different sectors. Some of the important on-going interventions of the Government of India are detailed below.

Women Development Corporations (WDCs)

In order to give the necessary thrust to development of women in the states, Women's Development Corporations (WDCs) were set up in 1986-87. The major objective of the scheme is to play the role of catalytic agents to create sustained income generating activities for women to provide better employment avenues for women so that they can become economically independent and self-reliant.

The functions of WDCs are to identify women entrepreneurs; to prepare a shelf of viable projects and provide technical consultancy services, to facilitate availability of credit through banks and other financial institutions (through the scheme of marginal money assistance); to promote and strengthen women's cooperatives and other organizations; and to arrange training of beneficiaries in concerned trades, project formulations, financial management, etc., through existing institutions, such as women's polytechnic and ITIs.

So far, such WDCs have been set up in Andhra Pradesh, Goa, Gujarat, Haryana, Himachal Pradesh, Jammu & Kashmir, Karnataka, Meghalaya, Orissa, Punjab, Tamil Nadu, Uttar Pradesh, West Bengal and Union Territory of Chandigarh. As per the decision of the National Development Council, in its meeting held in December 1991, the scheme stands transferred to the State sector in April 1992.

Rashtriya Mahila Kosh (RMK)

Rashtriya Mahila Kosh was set up as a registered society under the Registration of Societies Act, 1860 in March 1993 to meet credit needs of poor women, particularly in the informal sector who have little or no access to formal credit institutions.

The policies and procedures for lending to women borrowers through the intermediation of NGOs and other women organizations like cooperative societies, WDCs, etc., for which suitable eligibility criteria, such as lending/credit management experience, sound financial management, etc., have been prescribed by the governing board of the RMK.

An amount of Rs 31 crore was released to the Kosh during 1992-93 as the corpus fund. Short-term loans and long-term loans per borrower are extended through the medium of NGOs, and other eligible organizations. Since inception, total sanctions of Rs 3,355.99 lakh have been issued to benefit 1,88,146 women through 154 agencies as on March 14, 1997.

Mahila Samriddhi Yojana (MSY)

In pursuance of government's policy to empower women by raising their socio-economic status, an innovative MSY was launched on October 2, 1993. The scheme aims at promoting self-reliance and a measure of economic independence among rural women by encouraging thrift.

The DWCD implements the scheme through 1.32 lakh rural Post Offices working under the Department of Posts.

MSY has received a very enthusiastic response from both rural and tribal women, including those living in the remote areas of the country. Since inception of the scheme, 2.46 crore women have opened accounts with a total deposit of Rs 265.10 crore, till March 1997.

Indira Mahila Yojana (IMY)

In order to coordinate and integrate components of all sectoral programmes and facilitate their convergence to empower women, IMY was launched as a strategy on August 20, 1995. It proposes to bring out a mechanism by which there could be a systematic coordination and a meaningful integration of various programmes of different sectors to meet women's needs and to ensure that women's interests are taken care of and provided for under each scheme. This mechanism will be operated at the district level as a 'sub-plan' for women to percolate down to the village level appropriately through the Indira Mahila Kendras (IMKs) at village level and Indira Mahila Block Kendras (IMBKs) at Block level to be established as a registered society and supported by mechanisms at both State and Central levels. The ultimate objective of IMY is to empower women by ensuring their direct access to resources through a sustained process of mobilization and convergence of all the on-going sectoral programmes. The IMY will be operated as a Centrally sponsored scheme.

The major objectives of IMY include: (1) to ensure convergence of sectoral service at the local, Block and district levels through active involvement of women and sectoral departments; (2) to optimise utilization of scarce resources in speeding up of process of mainstreaming of women in development; (3) to create awareness in women through provision of information on different developmental programmes and issues of specific concern to women; (4) to initiate a process of awareness generation/education to enable them to understand and analyse their problems and find solutions through their collective interaction; and (5) to help women become self-reliant and independent by their economic empowerment through income generation activities and active participation in decision-making at various stages.

The IMY has three basic constituents, namely, convergence of inter-sectoral services; income generation activities; and sustained process of awareness generation/education. Under the proposed convergence of inter-sectoral services, IMY will provide the umbrella cover and all sectoral programmes aimed at women's welfare, including non-formal education, training, formal primary education, skill development, health, family welfare programmes and other minimum needs programmes like drinking water, sanitation, housing, roads, electrification, etc., would converge at the village level as per the needs, demands and requirements articulated by the IMK. Income generation activities include creation of employment opportunities through group-dynamics and participation in a broad range of economic activities suited to the local requirements and use of thrift and credit services to expand the income-generating activities. Under a sustained process of awareness generation/education, IMY seeks to create a general awareness among women through ensuring information specific to equality of social status, legal rights, like those to property and inheritance, constitutional safeguards and on different development, programmes/issues of concern to women.

In addition to amount of Rs 5,000 given by the Government of India to the corpus fund of the IMK, each member of the IMK shall contribute Rs five as membership fee and will continue to contribute Re one per month to the Kendra. Such nominal contribution by each member will create a corpus of fund and ensure their effective and continuous participation in the group activities. The corpus so formed will be used as a revolving fund for small credit requirements of the individual members and send money wherever necessary, and for expenditure on holding of awareness generation camps and any other activity resulting in furtherance of the cause of IMY.

The IMY has been taken up in 200 Blocks of the country, on a pilot basis and will be extended in the subsequent years. Selection of these Blocks will be decided by the States keeping in mind the need to ensure maximum convergence of services; care will be taken to ensure that the Blocks are compact and not dispersed over a number of districts. The IMY will initially be sanctioned for a period of seven years starting from 1995-96. The number of IMBs registered is 113 and the functional Indira Mahila Group (IMG) is 13,717, till March, 1997.

Special Thrust on Employment and Training for Women

In line with the Eighth Plan strategy, the nodal DWCD has reset its priorities to accord special emphasis on employment and income-generation activities for women. The ultimate objective in all these efforts is to make women economically empowered and self-reliant. For this purpose, the Department implements some programmes directly through voluntary organizations and interacts with other departments/ministries to ensure flow of benefits to women through their programmes.

Support to Training and Employment Programme for Women (STEP)

The STEP scheme launched in 1987, aims to upgrade the skills of poor and assetless women, mobilize, conscientize, provide training and subsequently employment on a sustainable basis in the traditional sectors of agriculture, animal husbandry, fisheries, handlooms, handicrafts, sericulture, social forestry, wasteland development, etc. In addition to the training and employment support, the programme advocates gender sensitization, women in development (WID) inputs and provision of support services.

Since inception of the programme 61 projects benefiting 3.32 lakh women, have been launched in various states. Dairying, handlooms, handicrafts and sericulture have been some important areas, since inception of the scheme till March 1997, it has provided employment opportunities for 3.32 lakh women with a total expenditure of Rs 94.13 crore. In 1996-97, 12 projects to benefit 76,875 women were sanctioned with a total expenditure of Rs.17.00 crore.

Training-cum-Employment-cum-Production Centres

The second major programme of Training and Employment, which is commonly known as 'NORAD assisted Training Programme for Women', extends financial assistance to public sector undertakings/corporations/autonomous bodies/voluntary organizations to train women in non-traditional trades, like electronics, electricals, watch assembly and manufacturing, computer programming, printing and binding, handlooms, garment making, weaving and spinning, hotel management, fashion technology and beauty culture, tourism bakeries/confectionery and office management, etc.

During the Eighth Plan, an expenditure of Rs 38.28 crore has been incurred benefiting 79,797. Since inception in 1983, 1,10,002 women benefited with training for employment. In 1996-97, 275 projects to benefit 50,000 women/girls were sanctioned with a total expenditure of Rs 19 crore.

In the recent past, there was a progressive shift and increased attention on the most up-coming modern trades, like computer operation, electrical appliances, bakery and confectioneries, fashion technology, beauty culture, ANM training, canteen and hotel management, tourism, etc. This programme not only plays a preventive role in keeping the young and adolescent girls away from early marriages but also keeps them gainfully engaged with economic independence and self-reliance.

Condensed Courses of Education and Vocational Training (CCE&VT)

The CCE&VT scheme, in operation since 1968, has been revised from time to time to provide educational qualifications and relevant skills to needy women so that they become eligible for identifiable remunerative work opportunities.

Under these programmes, voluntary organizations are given grants to conduct courses of two to three years duration for women of the age-group of 15 and above for passing primary/middle/ matric and secondary level examinations. Under the Vocational Training Programme, grants are given to impart training to needy women of 15 year age-group in different vocations leading to wage/self-employment. Under these programmes, 5,823 courses have been sanctioned during the Eighth Five-Year Plan and a sum of Rs 39.07 crore was sanctioned to benefit about one lakh women. In 1996-97, 598 courses were sanctioned with the total expenditure of Rs five crore.

Socio-economic Programme, Welfare and Support Services

The Central Social Welfare Board had started the socio-economic programme (SEP) in 1958. Under this programme, financial assistance is extended to voluntary organizations to undertake a wide variety of income-generating activities providing opportunities of 'Work and Wage' to needy women, like widows, destitutes, disabled, etc., particularly those coming from economically backward and underdeveloped areas for setting up industrial units, handlooms and handicraft units, dairy units, and other allied economic activities like piggery, sheep and goat rearing, poultry, etc.

During the Eighth Five-Year Plan (1992-97), an amount of Rs 30.33 crore has been released to 2,457 units to benefit about 20,100 women. In 1996-97, 13 units have been sanctioned with the total expenditure of Rs six crore.

The national machinery has spread a wide network of a large number of welfare and support services for women and children belonging to lower economic strata through voluntary organizations. These support services represent an important plank for empowerment of women as they reduce the burden of child care and employment related problems, as detailed below.

Support Services

Hostels for Working Women

In order to promote greater mobility for women in the employment market, the Department launched a scheme of hostels for working women in 1973 to provide 'safe and cheap' accommodation to single working women who come to the cities/towns for the sake of employment. Under this scheme, financial assistance is provided to the extent of 50 per cent of the cost of land and 75 per cent of the cost of construction of the hostel building to voluntary organizations. Assistance is also extended towards purchase of ready-built buildings. Besides, voluntary organizations, public trusts, local bodies, women development corporations, universities, schools/colleges of social work also are eligible for financial assistance programme. Working women, whose consolidated income does not exceed Rs 5,000 per month, are eligible for accommodation. A resident is allowed to stay in the hostel for a maximum period of five years. Up till now 805 hostels with attached day-care centres have been sanctioned to be constructed all over the country to benefit about 56,195 working women and their dependent children numbering about 7,558. In 1996-97, 28 hostels were sanctioned to benefit 3,122 women/girls with the expenditure of Rs 8.25 crore.

Creches for Working/Ailing Mother's Children

The Central Scheme of creches for working/ailing mother's children is under implementation since 1975-76. The scheme is implemented through voluntary organizations. The scheme envisages day-care services for children of the age group of 0-5 years. Service include health care, supplementary nutrition, sleeping facilities, immunization and play and recreation for the children. The creche workers are employed to look after the children. The scheme of running of creches is being implemented by the Central Social Welfare Board through voluntary social welfare organizations and by two other national level voluntary organization, viz., Indian Council for Child Welfare and Bhartiya Adimjati Sevak Sangh, all over the country. There are 12,470 creches in action all over the country benefiting 3.12 lakh children. Because of paucity of funds, the scheme has not been expanding and is stagnating at this number since 1988-89. In 1996-97, a total amount of Rs.19.75 crore has been sanctioned. In view of the increasing number of working women even in small towns and rural areas, there is a need for mobilizing community to provide services of creches on a self-sustaining basis without financial burden on governments, etc.

Short Stay Homes for Women and Girls (SSH)

The SSH scheme for women and girls, launched in 1969, extends temporary shelter and rehabilitation to those women and girls who are in social and moral danger due to family problems, mental strains, social ostracism, exploitation or other causes. The services extended in these homes include medical care, psychiatric treatment, case-work services, occupational therapy, educational-cum-vocational training, recreational facilities, etc.

Under the scheme, grants are given to voluntary organizations to run short stay homes in various parts of the country. As per the approved schematic budget, each SSH receives an annual grant of Rs 1,87,300 towards recurring expenses and Rs 25,000 as one time grant to meet the non-recurring expenditure.

National Creche Fund (NCF)

The NCF was set up on March 21, 1994 with a corpus fund of Rs 19.90 crore made available out of the Social Safety Net Adjustment Credit of World Bank to meet the growing requirement of opening more creche centres.

The scheme envisages that 75 per cent of the centres to be assisted by the Creche Fund would be general creches and 25 per cent centres would be Anganwadi-cum-creche centres. The general creches assisted by the Fund would be on the pattern of the Creche Scheme of the Department of Women and Child Development and would provide children below five years, services which would include day-care facilities, supplementary nutrition, immunization, medical and health care and recreation. Children of parents whose monthly income does not exceed Rs 1,800 are eligible for enrolment. The voluntary organizations/ Mahila Mandals selected for opening the creches are required to open creches in schools or in places close to schools, in rural areas and urban slum areas dominated by SCs/STs. The creches have a maximum of 25 children and normally work for eight hours a day. The voluntary organizations/Mahila Mandals are encouraged to involve the community in the implementation of the scheme so that the creches become self-supporting.

The target for the year 1996-97 was to sanction 450 creches and 150 Anganwadi-cum-creche centres. The number of the creches sanctioned up to December 31, 1996 is 14,313.

Gender Sensitization and Awareness Generation

Great deal of importance is attached to efforts which trigger changes in societal attitudes towards women. An integrated media campaign projecting a positive image of both women and the girl child through media and film is the most important component of the government's communication strategy. A large number of TV spots, quickies, documentary films, radio programmes with positive messages about the girl child and women, have been produced by the department to undertake publicity and coverage.

Gender Sensitization

The Women's Development Division (WDD) of the NIPCCD, New Delhi organizes training programmes with a focus on gender issues under the DANIDA Bridging Arrangement as well as its regular activities. These training programmes were organized at national, regional and state levels. Some of the important programmes include para legal training; training of elected women representative of Panchayats; leadership of organization; training of voluntary agencies reaching women; awareness and gender sensitization programmes; incorporation of gender issues in development programmes, etc. The participants of these programmes include government officials, representatives of voluntary agencies, academic and technical institutions.

Under legal literacy, para legal training programmes were organized by the WDD in collaboration with these agencies working for women's emancipation. The major objective of these training programmes were to sensitize the participants about the constitutional, political and legal provisions relating to rights of women; to inform participants about legal structure and procedures; to create awareness about existing support schemes of government and non-governmental agencies and to conscientize them about the scope of rights, their potential to act as pressure groups, to access the entitlements of women. These programmes were organized in West Bengal, Delhi, Himachal Pradesh, Bihar and Haryana.

In the field of training for Panchayat members, training programmes were organized for women elected representatives of Panchayats in Orissa, Karnataka and Madhya Pradesh. About 300 elected women members were trained. The main objectives of these training programmes were to sensitize the leadership qualities among elected women members, to enable them to understand the structure, function and responsibilities of Panchayats and make them aware about various development programmes implemented at the grass roots level.

Besides, the WDD also organized training programmes on leadership and organization of grass roots level women, incorporating gender concerns in Prime Minister's Rozgar Yojana, courses for superintendents of remand homes/jails on custodial justice to women and children sensitization programmes for law enforcement machinery, media campaign on pilot project on gender issues in credit and support services, orientation training programmes for police personnel on atrocities against women, issues and interventions, consultation on women in human settlement development, awareness generation on constitutional and legal rights for women, consultation on violence against women, etc.

Awareness Generation Projects for Rural and Poor Women

The programmes of Awareness Generation Projects was introduced in 1987-88. It aims at identifying the needs of rural and poor women and generating awareness among them of their status in the family and society and to activate them to work for achieving their rights and to deal with social issues, like community health and hygiene, technology application and environment, etc. The camps organized under the programme provide a platform for rural poor women to come together, exchange their views and ideas and in the process develop an understanding of their problems and come out with ways to tackle them.

Education Work for Prevention of Atrocities Against Women

The programme of Education Work for Prevention of Atrocities Against Women, started in 1982, extends financial assistance to research and academic institutions like universities, colleges/women's study centres and institutions of higher learning, etc., and voluntary organizations for various items of education work, propaganda, publicity and research work such as production of publicity materials, research studies on particular aspects of violence/atrocities against women; awards for best films, short stories, poems and other creative efforts, etc. Dissemination of information/publicity materials in regional languages is also envisaged under this programme. The focus is on those women who are subjected to deprivation, brutality, extortion and exploitation.

Integrated Child Development Services (ICDS)

The ICDS - gift to millions of children and mothers living in the most backward rural, tribal areas and urban slums all over the country — aims at improving nutritional and health status of pre-school children, expectant and nursing mothers and adolescent girls through a package of services, viz., supplementary nutrition, immunization, health checkup, referral services, treatment of minor illnesses, pre-school education and nutrition and health education. Started in 1975-76, with 33 projects, the scheme has expanded gradually and reached, by June 30, 1997 to 5,614 ICDS projects by covering 3,663 Community Development Blocks and 260 major urban slums. Of the 5,614 projects, 3,397 are under Central sector projects and the rest of the 510 projects (including 316 TINP projects) are in the state sector. These projects benefit around 198.44 lakh (19.84 million) children and 35.37 lakh (3.54 million) mothers/women.

Of the total 5,614 ICDS projects, around 1000 projects located in Andhra Pradesh, Bihar, Madhya Pradesh and Orissa are receiving assistance from World Bank to enrich the services with innovative activities.

It is proposed to universalize ICDS at the earliest to cover all Child Development Blocks/urban slums. Of these, 500 Blocks/slums are being taken during the current year, while the balance of over 1400 Child Development Blocks/slums are proposed to be covered during 1996-97 or in future years depending on the resource position and capacity of the States to operationalize the new Blocks.

Scheme for Adolescent Girls

For the first time in India, a special intervention has been devised for adolescent girls using the ICDS infrastructure. The scheme of adolescent girls focuses on school drop-out girls in the age group of 11-18 years and attempts to meet the special needs of nutrition, education, literacy, recreational and skill development of the adolescent girls. It attempts to make the adolescent girl a better future mother and tap her potential as a social animator. The scheme for adolescent girls has been sanctioned in 507 Child Development Blocks and, when fully operationalised, would benefit about 4.50 lakh girls.

Special Initiatives

National Commission for Women

In January, 1991, the government constituted a statutory body called National Commission for Women (NCW) with a specific mandate to study and monitor all matters relating to the constitutional and legal safeguards provided for women; review the existing legislation to suggest amendments wherever necessary; and to look into complaints involving deprivation of the rights of women. Similar Commissions have also been set up in nine States. The NCW has taken up a number of activities which include: (a) Setting up of 11 expert committees to tender advice on various women's issues; (b) conducting *Pariwarik Lok Adalats*, to which nearly 35,000 cases were referred; (c) Complaints and Pre-litigation Cell; (d) Legal awareness; (e) Welfare of women prisoners under trials; and (f) Action on issues of women and children.

Legal Literacy Manuals

Ten legal literacy manuals were brought out in 1992 to educate women about the laws concerning their basic rights. These manuals have been written in a simple and illustrated format so that even semi-literates and neoliterates are able to comprehend them. They cover a wide range of subjects, namely, laws relating to working women, child labour, contract labour, adoption and maintenance, Hindu, Muslim and Christian Marriage Laws, including right to property, dowry, rape, kidnaping and police procedure. The manuals have been distributed to State governments and NGOs for wider dissemination and are being translated into many of the Indian languages.

The National Plan of Action of Children (1992) and The National Plan of Action for the Girl Child (1991-2000 AD)

The two Plans of Action are both integrated and multi-sectoral in their approach to ensure survival, protection and development, of children with an ultimate objective of building up a better future for children. While the Girl Child — being an integral part of the total target group of children — is expected to derive full benefits from the general Plan of Action, her gender-specific needs will be taken care of by the Plan of Action for the Girl Child with a focus on the adolescent girls.

National Resource Centre for Women

Government is also finalizing a proposal to set-up the National Resource Centre for Women and three State Resource Centres for Women which will act as an apex body for promoting and incorporating gender perspectives in policies and programmes of the government. A pilot project to test the concepts and methodologies underlying the National Resource Centre has been successfully implemented.

Gender Sensitization of 1991 Census

For the first time in the history of demographic records, an attempt was made to capture women's work in the informal sector in 1991 census. The provisional data of 1991 census on 'Workers and their Distribution', has shown that there was a substantial increase in the female work participation during 1991 census compared to that of 1981.

Reservation of Benefits for Women Under Poverty Alleviation Programme

Under various poverty alleviation programmes of rural development sector, 40 per cent of benefits have been reserved for women belonging to the below poverty line groups (families whose annual income is about Rs 6,000 to Rs 11,000).

Reservation for Women in Grassroots Democracy

The (73rd and 74th) Constitutional Amendment Bills passed in 1992 by the Parliament marks a holistic event in the lives of Indian women as amendments ensure one-third of total seats (33.3

per cent) for women in all elected offices in local bodies whether in rural or urban areas. As a result of this, women have been brought to the centre-stage in the nation's efforts to strengthen democratic institutions at the grassroots level. About 0.8 million women have emerged as leaders/decision makers at grassroots level and entered into public life through the existing 0.23 million local bodies all over the country. Of these, about 76,200 are chairwomen at the village, Block and district levels.

Training in Leadership Development

A massive country-wide training programme was launched in 1993 to extend leadership training for eight lakh women Panchayat members/chairpersons, emerging as a result of the elections to Panchayats and urban local bodies since 1993 when the 73rd and 74th Constitutional Amendment Acts came into force.

Voluntary Action

India has a rich tradition of selfless voluntary action. While the governmental interventions in this sector are operationalized largely through NGOs, the initiatives that the latter have themselves developed are rich and diverse. These efforts have often demonstrated success of alternative models of empowerment and development. Whether it is in the field of credit of poor women or women's health or women's awareness generation or women's literacy, or participatory rural appraisal involving women or organizing women's self-employment groups in traditional and non-traditional sectors of the economy. The Central Social Welfare Board, which is an apex agency of voluntary organizations at national level promotes voluntary action and community participation through its country-wide network of more than 12,000 voluntary organizations at the grassroots level. Besides these, there are many more voluntary organizations working at block/district/state levels in the field of women and child development.

Future Approach

Holistic Development

The major approach for the future will be to bring in holistic approach for women's development. This underscores harmonization of various efforts in different fronts — social, economic, legal, political and cultural. This calls for consolidation of various programmes and efforts in different sectors of the Government, and their integration in a logical fashion to converge various services and facilities required by women. A Sub-Plan approach to package all relevant resources and benefits for women's development will be laid down to ensure their systematic focus on women.

The over-arching strategy component for women's development in the Ninth Plan will comprise mobilization and convergence orchestrated by women's groups and supported by Panchayati Raj institutions. The organization of women will by itself empower them and provide them a forum for articulating their needs and contributing their perspectives to development. This will also give them experience in participatory decision-making, thereby building up a cadre of grass root leaders, capable of effective participation in institutions of local government.

This capacity building has to start in the womb, without any deprivation, for the mother of the child, particularly the girl child. Her survival, protection and development as identified in the National Plan of Action for the Girl Child (1992) has to echo through all sectoral programmes. Access to education, health, information and resources are, therefore, the vital areas of concern, that need to be effectively addressed in future to attain many of the goals for the next millennium.

The thrust in the future has to be on identifying traditional sectors of employment that are shrinking due to technology changes or market shifts, and retrain the women to take up jobs in the new and expanding areas of employment.

The provision of support services is another critical input that can greatly improve women's enhanced economic participation. Promoting women's labour market mobility through an expanding network of working women's hostels, the provision of toilet facilities for women in places of work and widespread provision of creches for working parents are essential if women are to derive maximum benefits from the economic liberalization process.

Areas of Priority

Future Programmes for Consideration for Women's Empowerment

Keeping in view the aforementioned experiences, the following specific programmes could be considered for adoption in the future: (i) Expansion of education and training among women; (ii) EDP training; (iii) Provision of child-care support facilities for men and women workers so that either parent can avail of this facility at the workplace and not make it a cost on women's employment; (iv) Provision of hostel and residential facilities to enable women take up employment away from home; (v) Special employment and placement services which should seek to promote employment of women in non-conventional sectors through dissemination of information, counselling, etc.; (vi) Legal protection and legal aid services; (vii) Promotion of women workers organizations through voluntary effort; (viii) Protection against flexibility. Considering the new trend towards economic liberalization such protection cannot be ensured through statutory means and should, therefore, be attempted through negotiations and collective effort. The State, the employers as well as the workers must have separate layers of protection against loss of employment; (ix) Introduction of flexitime, multi-entry, conducive personnel policy on leave, transfer and promotion and training opportunities, to help women retain their jobs or move to new and higher areas of work; (x) Conducive credit policy to access credit to women through appropriate organizational and institutional mechanisms including, self-help groups, and (xi) Improvement of the bargaining strength of women workers by encouraging their participation in trade unions.

Separate Mahila Plan Component in all Central Plans

The DWCD has recently launched the IMY, which is intended primarily to mobilize the women around an integrated delivery system. IMY is a major step towards participation of women in the planning and development processes of their areas. It is also a mechanism that can establish a system of coordination and integration of the sectoral activities. In order to put the need perceptions and the sequential priorities of these women into the Sub-Plans, women would be organized into groups and empowered to participate in the planning process. A sub-plan, consisting of the women's components, would emerge through an interactive process of discussions at the district, block and Panchayat/local levels.

Different developmental schemes and programmes already have quantified components of SCP and TSP. In a like manner, these schemes and programmes could also have a "Mahila Plan" component. It will, therefore, be helpful if all Central Plan schemes/programmes, Centrally-sponsored schemes/programme, State plan schemes/programmes and non-plan schemes/programmes identify a Mahila Plan component, with both physical targets and financial outlays. For plan schemes/programmes, such a component should exist for both the Annual and Five-Year Plans.

The basic approach to women's development and empowerment should continue to be based on the theme of convergence, i.e., convergence of the development programmes of different departments of the government to target women through a single delivery system as well as convergence of the efforts of both the government functionaries and community or NGOs in achieving a common objective.

New Targets for Women's Empowerment

Shyamala Shiveshwarkar

This Women's Day there was reason to rejoice. The ninth Plan draft document has said that 'empowerment of women' is one of its prime objectives. While this is significant, what is also important is the sub-Plan that was evolved in the run-up to the preparation of the Plan, the fact that a think tank of women was set up to evolve a document that spelt out the specific demands of women in the country. Way back in 1974, the report of the Commission on the Status of Women had called for a sub-Plan, one that would address gender inequities but it was not taken seriously. So while some attempts were made in subsequent Plans to give women a place in the developmental process, it tended to be sectoral and haphazard.

The think tank, comprising academicians, activists and researchers held consultations with the Planning Commission, the

Department of Women and Child Development, various ministries and women all over the country. The focus was on building consensus with a view to understanding what women wanted and what is perhaps even more important on what was working for women and what was not.

The concerns voiced were varied, but the key ones were the right to information about changes, opportunities, options, schemes, services and technologies, the gender sensitization of government functionaries particularly the police and the local administration in the areas of health, agriculture and animal husbandry, and the right to work and employment guarantee schemes.

Liberalization, it was pointed out, is here to stay but women were losing out and will continue to lose out because they have neither the skills nor the legal safeguards to be included.

Other important demands were gender analysis and gender audit of all plans, policies and programmes, the elimination of violence against women and girls through the strengthening of institutional capacity and legal provisions and the decentralization of democracy so that decisions can be taken at levels that are *ipso facto* more accessible to women.

Happily, if one is to go by the Ninth Plan draft, there is a veritable sea change in Plan perspectives. Until now women's development, to quote the document, was primarily 'welfare oriented'. The focus was always on health, nutrition, education and in the early nineties, on training for employment. Demands that they be recognized as participants in development made little headway. The approach was patronizing and chauvinistic.

The draft is therefore significant promising, as it does, "to create an enabling environment where women can freely exercise their rights within and outside homes as equal partners along with men". It goes on to add that "this will be realized through the early finalization of the 'National Policy for the Empowerment of Women' which lays down definite goals for targets and policy prescriptions along with a well-defined Gender Development Index to monitor the impact of its implementation in raising the status of women from time to time. Also significant is the fact that the Ninth Plan directs both the Centre and the States to adopt the 'women's component plan' through which no less than 30 per cent of funds and benefits are earmarked to the women-related sector.

To quote Madhu Dandavate, Deputy Chairperson of the Planning Commission "Women have moved from 'footnote' to an 'objective' in the ninth Plan" but a lot more will have to be done to ensure that policies are evolved along the lines of the Plan initiatives. Perhaps, as Anita Anand, a member of the think tank suggests, an autonomous body on the lines of the National Organisation of Women in the USA should be set up. Bandhs and dharnas will no longer suffice and a much more sophisticated approach is required in which people with expertise in policy analysis and advocacy will lobby for change. In fact, it must work in tandem with the Planning Commission to ensure the economic and political empowerment of women and gender sensitizing of issues.

The tendency all along has been to direct jobs, resources, political positions, credit et. al., to men especially in the macro sector. The assumption was that the benefits would percolate down to the women and children but, in actual fact, it has only further marginalized them. Panchayati Raj will of course go a long way in remedying these aberrations. Since the passing of the 72nd and 73rd amendments four years ago, almost a million women have come into local politics and in Haryana and Kerala there are all-women Panchayats. But, the issues raised by them at the grass roots level will have little success if women's representation in the upper echelons of democracy remains low. Studies conducted in the US on disparities between the blacks and whites have shown how important it is to have a 33 per cent reservation. Anything below this has proved to be ineffective. This is why it is absolutely imperative that the 81st Amendment Bill providing for 33 per cent reservation for women is reintroduced and passed in the next session of Parliament.

Eight

Women and Mass Media

The mass media can either reflect existing values and serve to strengthen and reinforce traditional ideas and the status quo or they can be used positively as forceful motivators of social change. Throughout history communication media have been powerful agents of social influence. In the early days, the story teller, the songster, the actor and the puppeteer were all using their art to record and preserve their culture. Not only this, they also used it to define the norms of their culture and to inform people about their society's nature, it's goals and it's imperatives. Modern journalism, be it in the form of newspapers or magazines, still serves these basic goals. But in the last few years new technologies have been introduced which have greatly magnified the communication media power and the importance of media in shaping the mores of societies has increased in proportion.

The focus of this study is on women who influence the mass media, women as depicted by the mass media and women as influenced by the mass media. The methods by which the mass media can be used to further the cause of women's development and consciousness would also be discussed in this study.

Traditional forms of Media and Women

Traditional media in all societies have been the folk songs, stories, puppet shows and dramas. Women have played an important role in these traditional forms of entertainment. Some aspects of folk-lore have dealt exclusively with women and their problems. For example, in northern India there is a whole folk-lore based on women's longing for husbands who have gone away to earn money or the fears of a young bride leaving for her husband's village and so on. Traditional folk stories also contain a large number of portraits of women who have very strong personalities.

Traditional folk-lore generally reflects traditional attitudes to women. Traditional media portray women in the old framework of wife/or mother or daughter which still continues to be the basis of media presentation of women today.

Women, who have gone against the stereotype role are rarely remembered, for example, in Indian history, a truly valiant woman ruler, Razia Sultana of the Slave dynasty has been almost forgotten and has no place in folk-lore. Perhaps the only exception in the Indian context is Rani Laxmibai of Jhansi, but it is worth recording that her story was popularized by a female poet, Subhadra Kumari Chauhan.

Women who Influence Modern Mass Media

Women are playing a big role in mass media nowadays. They participate in it in diverse fields. These havve been listed as follows:

Films

They are film directors, producers, writers, music directors, dance directors and lyricists.

Advertising Firms

Proprietors, executives and designers. Though no exact figures are available. Women have played, and are playing, a very limited role as shapers of mass media. The women employed by these organizations are mainly in low skill, low prestige jobs. Admittedly, there have been some reputed women in controlling position in the media, but on the whole it is a field dominated by men.

TV and Radio

Woman directors, producers, writers, announcers and media executives.

Newspapers and Magazines

Proprietors, editors and journalists.

There is only one exception and that is in the case of a women's magazines. These magazines, both in the west and in the Third World, tend to have woman editors and executives, if not proprietors. But the target group of these magazines has been the traditional house-bound, housewife and the magazines have been churning out the usual *pot pourri* of recipies, beauty hints tips on how to please the husband or boss, etc.

Women as Depicted by the Mass Media

Films

The commercial films produced in the Third World countries have had a tendency to portray woman in the stereotyped traditional roles of good wife, good mother and good daughter. As opposed to these 'virtuous' women, the stereotype of the 'bad' woman is offered. Interestingly enough this 'bad' woman is generally portrayed as westernized, liberated, scornful of tradition. There have been very few films which have portrayed women as individual personalities different from the normal stereotypes of the society in which the film was made. A few films which portrayed women as strong individuals have always been careful to portray them within the traditional framework of mother, sister and wife relationships. This is specially true of the big Indian film industry. There have been very few attempts to break away from this stereotype except in a few "new wave" films.

Advertising Industry

In the present urban context, perhaps it is the advertising industry which has the single biggest impact after films. The advertisements which we see either show the harassed housewife magically transformed by a new brand of tea, cleaner or gadget, or a worried mother being told how best to look after her children or an attractive young girl wondering how to hook or keep her men. These advertisements are aimed at selling products bought by women. There is another category of advertisements dealing with products being sold to men. These generally show pretty girls drooling over a particular man, because he is wearing brand 'X' suitings, shoes, tie, riding brand 'Y' cycle, scooter, car, smoking brand 'Z' cigarette *ad infinitum* and *ad nauseum*. The general strategy of these advertisements being to catch male attention by showing pretty girls, no matter whether the product being sold is in any way related to women or not. The sexual identity alone of a woman's personality is emphasized, thus distorting her image, role and status in society.

TV, Radio, Newspapers and Magazines

These media are apparently used normally as a means of communicating to men. There are special times or places, set apart to deal with women's problems, somewhat similar to the childrens sections. The underlying assumptions seem to be that women are not interested in the general issues but would prefer to learn about beauty hints, recipies or new knitting designs. These things are of course of interest to women, but to set these items apart as special enclaves as different from the interests of the general public denies the fact that 50 per cent of the 'general public' is female.

There is very little attempt to identify or discuss the immediate problems of women in our changing societies. Outrageous acts of brutality, for example, dowry deaths in Delhi or sale of women in Dholpur are exceptions but common problems like sexual molestation of women, wife beating and unequal pay for equal work, get very little attention. Sensationalism is the key to media approach to woman's problems.

The entertainment provided, i.e., serials, plays, features, short stories, etc., all generally portray women within the traditional framework and unquestioning acceptance of this is taken for granted. (The few new women's magazines started recently in India, e.g., *Manushi*, *Vama* are in honourable exception). The usual woman's magazines though very different in quality or presentation, etc., show general acceptance of the *status quo*.

Cartoons and Comics

This part of the mass media has become increasingly popular so much so that no newspaper or magazine is complete today without its daily cartoon or weekly or daily comic strip. The foolish woman and the nagging wife, or mother in law are dominant themes while the male is normally shown in sympathetic light *vis-a-vis* the females.

Women as Influenced by the Mass Media

(i) The mass media is very much a part of the socializing process and in this role, the media is being used to reinforce the traditional stereotypes of women. More than that, the distorted image of woman as a sexual being alone is being emphasized out of all proportion.

(ii) The second point is a corollary of the first. The coverage of women as participants in economic activity as leaders and as general participants in the developing process of our changing societies has been wholly inadequate.

Thus an impression is given that women have no role to play in the economic life of the community. This impression thus conveyed is false in as much as the total work force of the country consists of at least 20 per cent females. This figure does not include the unpaid labour of housewives or of rural women's dairy and farming activities in their own homes. The media thus gives an erroneous impression of women as consumers and dependents (mostly through advertisements, cartoons, etc.) Rather than producers.

(iii) The media is attuned mostly to a male audience and caters basically to this audience. Woman's viewpoint on general issues is normally not sufficiently represented.

Thus women tend to see things mostly from a male point of view and are thus conditioned to accept the male world view rather than to evolve one of their own.

Discussion

1. The mass media specially through the advertising medium is influencing women more and more towards a consumer society in which the latest and the best must be acquired immediately. Due to prevalence of mass poverty, these cannot be had by most women and thereby it causes frustration and social disharmony.
2. How can participation of women as decision makers in media be increased?
3. At present no organization exists which can monitor media performance in regard to presenting woman's viewpoints on general issues. How could woman's organizations act as pressure groups to monitor media content and analyse and review media performance?
4. How to carry out dissemination of women's problems to the media?

5. How can traditional media be used to change traditional stereotypes of women?

Nine

Role and Influence of Mass Media on the Status of Women

We have seen that religious tradition as well as some features inherent in the social structure have perpetuated certain stereotypes and myths about women. Although their virtues and merits have at times been extolled, the principal social role assigned to a woman is essentially one subordinate to man. The social norms, attitudes, and values sustained by such stereotypes are deeply entrenched. To eradicate them would need determined and purposive effort. Education and the mass media of communication could be important in bringing about changes in attitudes, but both have limitations. Like education, mass communication is a necessary but not sufficient condition of change.

The role and influence of the mass media on the status of women can be considered from the following angles:

(a) a content analysis of the media and their treatment of women;
(b) the influence of the media on their audience;
(c) the influence of the media on women themselves.

Studies have revealed that the mass media have made and make a great impact on social change. Changes in a society's attitudes, are the result of historical growth, the gradual spread of education, the work of social reformers and charismatic leaders and so on. However, modernizing societies have come to rely increasingly on the mass media for spreading messages.

The media provide information and guidance and create awareness. They can assist changes in attitude by reinforcing ideas and providing real or ideal models or behaviour and can raise aspirations for better standards of living. The media can thus contribute towards the development of skills, tastes and images current in a society.

The content of communication at any given time reflect the pattern of values of a society. The way subjects dealing with women are treated indicates to a great extent, the prevailing attitudes of that society towards its women. This could work both ways, to improve, or lower women's status in the society by introducing new, or reinterpreting old ideas.

In any country, women who are half the total population are often half the audience. The success or failure of development plans, in education, family planning, community development, health and nutrition depends upon the involvement and participation of women. Our investigation shows that compared to men, women are underprivileged in many ways and suffer from serious disabilities. Since formal education is a costly and a long-term process, it is essential to harness the mass media for the eradication of illiteracy and to speed up the spread of basic education among women and girls. The National Council for Women's Education emphasized the potential significance of the mass media to generate public opinion in rural areas in favour of girls' education. The Family Planning Programme is making intensive use of the mass media to inform and create awareness among the people.

Incidental studies on the impact of mass media indicate, however, that women's exposure to the media is often very inadequate, and unsatisfactory. It appears that the mass media has not been an effective instrument to inform and prepare women to play their new roles in society. The committee's investigations indicate a general lack of awareness about rights, problems, opportunities and responsibilities among both men and women. Since the government controls a significant section of the mass media, it should set the pace. May be there is little that the private sector can be forced to do, but there is need for pressure groups within society itself to spearhead changes in the role of the media.

A proper assessment of the present role of the media in regard to the status of women will require detailed surveys and studies. Due to the want of empirical data, our comments on the influence of mass communication media on the status of women is based mainly on expert comments and views, and discussions with individuals in various walks of life.

The most significant factor in mass communication is that in India, where 80 per cent of the total population is still rural, the mass media is concentrated in urban areas and emanates from there. The themes are mainly urban and are concerned largely with the educated elite. The communicators themselves are from the urban areas. Starting with the Press, which has a powerful role to play in moulding public opinion, almost all the newspapers are published from the major cities and towns and give emphasis to political and urban news.

Role of the Press

The serious press in India has by and large not degraded the status of women. News items highlighting the role of women have been published whenever possible. Some noteworthy achievements by women in different fields appear in daily newspapers from time to time and the major dailies and almost all the Indian language dailies carry a weekly women's section. A content analysis of this section would be needed before any comment can be made on the subject matter of the sections and their views on the role and status of women.

A citizen should be able to appeal against misuse of his or her name by the press. For instance, in report about rape, abduction or other such incidents, the press should not mention the name of the girl, or of her relatives. The press is supposed to exercise restraint and not publicize news which may affect a woman's reputation.

Recently there has been some protest against the use of the female figures in advertising. As far as the press in India is concerned, the revenue from advertisement sustains a large number of dailies. The discretion, if any, in the selection or rejection of advertisements is exercised by the owner or staff of a paper and could be heavily influenced by financial considerations and not the subject matter of the advertisement. The present tendency of advertising agencies to over-emphasize the female form has resulted in number of complaints to the Press Council of India about exploitation of sex in advertisements.

Among the powers and functions of the Press Council, the following two have bearing on the status of women:

(a) To build up a code of conduct for newspapers, news agencies and journalists in accordance with high professional standards.

(b) To ensure the maintenance of high standards of public taste and foster a due-sense of both the rights and responsibilities of citizenship.

An examination of the complaints made to the council during 1972-73 showed that there were quite a few from individuals complaining against the photographs of female figures in advertisement and otherwise.

It is interesting to note that out of a total of 103 complaints made to it in 1972, the Press Council considered 24 complaints about objectionable writing. Of these 9 dealt with obscenity. One ruling about the publication by Blitz of two photographs of women said that, as they served no purpose, "they could easily have been avoided by the Blitz, which was a serious paper". A number of other complaints dealt with undue exposure of the female figure in advertisement and film journals.

The debate on the use of the female figure in advertisement continues unresolved. While the Board of Advertisers are supposed to maintain high standards, it is the responsibility of the general public and particularly women's organizations to complain or protest against obscenity. The Press Council has already given a ruling on this subject and until there is more vigilant watch on advertisements, hoardings and posters, the present stress on near nudity and sex to sell goods and attract cinema audience may continue. It is commonly complained that cinema advertisements tend to use for display scenes cut out by the censors.

On a complaint that a soap advertisement was exploiting sex, the Press Council observed that such complaints reflect the confusion in values and attitudes prevailing in our society, because the woman in the picture was not less modestly dressed than several modern women one might see in the streets, at parties and at shopping centres. On saying this, the Council was not oblivious of the fact that many women appeared in public fully clad, without exposing anything below the neck, or above the ankle, with blouses up to the elbow. However, the norms of dress followed by a large number of other respectable women might not measure up to the requirements of the puritan.

The Council had this group in mind when it referred to the dress of the modern women, since in judging contemporary society it had also to consider the mores prevalent among this section. They were an integral part of Indian society, and "signified the contemporary ethos."

Referring to this controversy in the foreword to the Seventh Annual Report, 1972, the Chairman of the Press Council observed, "The next aspect of journalistic propriety I wish to refer to is the increasing number of papers resorting to the publication of barely clothed female figures. These appear in advertisements and are sometimes published even when they seem to serve no apparent purpose. This criticism copied from the other societies which are more permissive, hardly, if I may say so, fits in with our culture." While the Press Council can fulfil a watch dog function it cannot lay down any positive guidelines to form new attitudes towards role of women.

Role of Radio

By its reach and impact the radio provides the most powerful mass communication. It is specially important as a medium of information and education in a vast country like India where the coverage of the press is not extensive. All India Radio operates under the administrative control of the Ministry of Information and Broadcasting and is the sole broadcasting organization in the country. Its special women's programmes are broadcast regularly from all stations of the AIR, at least twice a week. In 1971, women's programmes occupied a total of 3729 hours and 06 minutes, i.e., 1.4 per cent of the total broadcasting time and in 1972, they took 3,746 hours, i.e., 1.5 per cent. Special broadcasts are also put out by the Farms and House Units of AIR for rural women. These programmes, specially meant for rural women, provide education and entertainment and are broadcast in the regional languages at a time most convenient for women to listen. In each State, women's welfare organizations of the State Governments organize listening clubs with follow up discussions in the Mahila Mandals. Two mass communication researchers, Mathur and Neurath, who studied village radio broadcast in India found that such broadcasts had effect where listening clubs were organized and suggestions were followed.

Nutrition is a subject of recent interest to wives and mothers in villages and towns. UNICEF has provided 5,000 transistor sets to enable Mahila Mandals to listen to programmes about nutrition. Women also participate in broadcasts of cultural and entertainment programmes. Programmes for women range from 30 to 45 minutes twice or thrice a week. Discussions and talks on the topic of interest to women are also included.

Under the commercial services of AIR, started in May 1970, radio programmes are used for advertising. A code of conduct guides the staff and advertisers and ensures that commercial programmes are not only in good taste, but also in conformity with the national interest and with public welfare. The Family Planning Units of AIR plan and produce family planning programmes for rural areas, industrial workers, women and youth, projecting a broad based social movement closely linked with maternity and child health and nutrition. While the Government of India has laid stress on family planning instruction, national integration, nutrition, new agriculture practises, just how much has been achieved in a positive way to emphasize the new role of women in present day society remains unsure. The Audience Research Unit might be able to provide some feedback. It is important to study the existing programmes and their impact which may indicate gaps in programme content and coverage and indicate guidelines for future women's programmes. It is important to remember that with the high percentage of illiteracy, higher among females, radio is the medium with a vast potential for educating the illiterate. An administrator with long experience of work in the AIR said at the Asian Region Seminar for the International Alliance of Women New Delhi in November, 1973 that, "Village housewives have been badly neglected. AIR's programmes for women are for the urban middle-class women and have no relevance to the working women in the village. Programmes on family planning have to be directed to peasant women, along with programmes on hygiene, nutrition, etc., through those in the village whose voice can command respect.

Role of Television

The development of television as a medium of mass communication is still at a pioneering stage. Apart from the Delhi Television Centre set up in September, 1959, television facilities have recently been extended to Mumbai and Amritsar and will also start functioning in Calcutta, Madras, Jullundur and Lucknow with relay centres at Pune, Bhatinda, Kanpur, Karnal and Mussoorie.

Two relay centres to be set up in Calcutta will serve Kharagpur and Durgapur/Asansol areas.

Apart from special educational and farm programmes, the television service from Delhi provides a varied programme mix to viewers including programmes for women and children. Few specialized programmes so far have been aimed at popularizing better agricultural practices under the 'Krishi Darshan' programme. The total duration of the transmission is more than three and a half hours daily apart from the school television broadcasts.

The weekly women's programmes include discussions about social problems, but the typical programme is likely to contain subjects of interest to housewives only. An assessment of the number of these women's programmes and their impact will have to be made before ways and means of utilizing this medium can be recommended.

Role of Literature

In the early part of the twentieth century, a large number of books on fictions were written. The aim of authors like Rabindranath Tagore, Sarat Chandra, Prem Chand and others was definitely social reform. They dealt with a number of social problems affecting the status of women and attempted to portray even prostitutes in a sympathetic light. A cursory glance at popular book stalls of fiction which is voraciously consumed by college students and others these days, however, shows a depressing lack of taste. In adherence to the western trend of sex and violence, modernity in Indian fiction seems to mean imitation of western themes. While a few playwrights have attempted to highlight social and economic problems, their books are still not best sellers. Romance and pornographic literature is still popular, perhaps because it is cheaper in price and readily available. Gandhiji criticized distasteful descriptions of the female form in popular fiction and condemned writers for dwelling on them with the "sickly sentimentality". Political leaders have also from time to time expressed their views on the new role of women in a developing society but these have not been adequately publicized. The Publications Division of the Ministry of Information and Broadcasting has brought out a few books on women of India.

Role of Youth Magazines

There are a number of recent publications of magazines aimed at youth. A brief examination of typical youth magazines shows that they do not provide much food for thought. They imitate their western counterparts and the emphasis is on fashion, music, films and sex. It remains to be assessed what that impact of such magazines may be on the minds of impressionable boys and girls and whether they are, in any way, preparing the future generation for accepting the new role women are expected to play in society.

Role of Films

Film exerts a tremendous influence on the audience because of its vivid and powerful impact. All cultural media like theatre, art, architecture and films project a pattern of moral values as well as reflect established patterns. The influence of these media on social values and modes of behaviour is thus a two-way process. The cinema makes a much wider and deeper impact because in the modern industrial and mechanized State, the cinema is more easily available.

India is one of the largest producers of films in the world. In 1971, India produced 433 feature films and 414 in 1973. Out of these respectively 146 and 134 films were produced in Mumbai, 250 and 243 in Chennai and 37 in both years in Calcutta. The Film Division of the Ministry of Information and Broadcasting, produces a large number of news and documentary films annually. The Division has produced more than 3,000 films in the last 25 years. Most of the films are in English and 14 regional languages. In 1971-72, Films division produced 90 documentary films through its own units and 23 through outside producers. In addition, 65 newsreels and 43 documentary films were produced by State Governments. These figures indicate the enormous scope of the film industry in India. An interesting fact is that out of the total number of feature films produced, as many as 283 in 1971 and 273 in 1972, were on social themes, the next highest category being crime films, which have shown a steady increase since 1961 when 30 crime films were produced as compared to 82 for 1972.

The Government appointed an Enquiry Committee on Films Censorship in April 1968 to enquire into the working of the existing procedure for certification of films for public exhibition in India. The Cinematograph (Second Amendment) Bill 1973, was prepared after taking into consideration the recommendations of the Committee. The report highlights the attitude of the film maker and film goers. The average Indian film goer is well aware of what usual themes in the films are likely to be and the box office usually demands a star-caste and dances and night club scenes, though not all witnesses and members of the Committee agreed with this observation. The contents of the bulk of Indian movies are sex and crime and "they follow the base motive of the lower type of American movies with inartistic plots, vulgar dances and songs and dialogues in a disgusting tone. Even the titles of the films are objectionable and the posters which advertise them are improper and vulgar." The sole aim of the film industry is to make money. The Vice-President of the South Indian Film Chamber commented, "The Chamber did not award any prizes for films of outstanding merits, nor did it discourage the production of low quality and vulgar films. The aim of the Chamber was solely to protect the industry." A film critic and social worker said that we knew instances of some girls who had deviated from the path of moral rectitude on seeing excessively erotic films. A lady member of an examining panel thought that producers should come to some kind of mutual agreement not to project on screen scantily dressed girls and women. The general opinion appears to be that there is a rapid increase in the emphasis on sex themes in films. The ambivalent attitude of the Indian film producer is illustrated in his projection of the heroine who is supposed to embody all the virtues but is usually immodestly dressed and the hero, who is otherwise a 'good man' behaves in a very vulgar fashion on meeting the heroine. The usual Indian film has by and large exploited sex to attract audience and has degraded the image of the Indian woman.

The cinema exercises a tremendous influence on the juvenile and uneducated mind. In 1957, a survey was made covering Greater Bombay, and large number of young persons and adults were questioned. The investigators noticed a marked tendency particularly among adolescents to imitate patterns of behaviour shown in the films. Four types of unhealthy influences noted were in habits of living and spending, manners and mannerisms including fashions in clothes, hair dressing, speech and behaviour towards the opposite sex and immoral and anti-social practices like stealing, prostitution, etc.

Another survey conducted by the Indian Institute of Mass Communication for the Enquiry Committee on Film Censorship in 1968-69, revealed that out of the total sample, nearly 88 per cent were film goers, with youths forming the majority. Categories of films preferred and generally viewed by women were: (i) films on family life, (ii) musicals and (iii) devotional films. Girls preferred: (i) Western films (ii) musicals (iii) romantic and (iv) tragic films. The least preferred films were on contemporary themes. Questioned as to what should be the chief aim and purpose of films produced in India, 31.11 per cent of the men said that it should be to educate. 42.40 per cent of the women emphasized the development of social, cultural and religious values in society. 37.65 per cent of the college boys laid emphasis on entertainment. As regards the treatment of sex and love in films and details of reactions to the nude human form in painting or sculpture, 36.60 per cent women regarded it as objectionable and 38.40 per cent as indecent, 34.47 per cent of the college girls regarded it as unobjectionable and 25.88 per cent as aesthetically satisfying. In regard to objectionable and undesirable elements in films, one out of ten adults considered a film undesirable when it dealt with violence, crime and horror, while one in twenty youths said so. Nearly half of the men and one-third of the youths considered films dealing with sex and violence to be undesirable, while seven out of ten women considered such themes as objectionable. 41 per cent of the adult sample and the 36 per cent of the youth sample agreed with the statement that 'sex and violence are the predominant themes of a large number of Indian and foreign films' and that there was a growing tendency to expose the artists' body for either aesthetic purpose or dramatic purpose or merely for commercial exploitation. 71.67 per cent of the men and 36 per cent of the women agreed that this exposure served only commercial exploitation. The study indicated further that 32.90 per cent of the sample did not agree with the statement that the present day film goer will lose interest in Indian films if these did not have cabaret or night club scenes showing scantily dressed girls.

Among the grounds on which a film may be refused a censorship certificate are those involving 'indecency and immorality'. The Central Board of Film Censorship has head-quarters and regional offices which review and censor films. This is one measure of possible control, though there is a great deal of debate as to the extent of control in censorship particularly regarding sex and violence. The legal aspects of film censorships have been discussed in the report of the Enquiry Committee on Film Censorship. Article 15 Clause 3 and Article 39 (f) which empower the State to make a special provision for women and children and to protect childhood and youth against exploitation, are thought to be wide enough to authorise any law or regulation to protect children and young persons from the influence of certain type of film.

In 1960, Government of India set up a Film Finance Corporation, which provides loans for films with valid cinematic values, which eschew the box office formula. The Government also gives national awards to films of high ethical and technical standards and of social, educational and cultural values.

Reviewing the role and influence of the Indian films, it may be observed that in its content and treatment of women, it has laid more emphasis on sex to draw audiences. The stress is on the physical attributes of the heroine. In most social films she is invariably assigned a subordinate status in relation to men in all spheres and thus continues to perpetuate the traditional notion of a woman's inferior status. Very few films have endeavoured to project the new role of women in present day society. These films have not attempted to educate women regarding their rights, duties or responsibilities and have ignored reality. A few film makers have made films on contemporary themes and problems.

But even these have not attempted to change traditional or conventional images of women and tend to perpetuate the status quo.

Images of Heroine

In the earlier thirties, film themes were largely based on adventure, religion or myth with emphasis on a virtuous heroine who remained devoted to her love. During the period between 1939 and 1945, escapist films with light music, stunts, plenty of dances and physical display, made the heroine more a symbol of sex rather than devotion. Elements of crime and adventure were also thrown in.

This period was followed by revival of interest in moral and social themes and films by young directors like Raj Kapoor, Guru Dutt, Chetan Anand and others dealt with problems like casteism and prostitution. "The liberal inclusion of love and sex, dance and music and humour as concessions to the requirements of the box office have led to the vulgarization of serious themes in such films". Love and sex form a dominant theme in most Indian films and there is a full quota of amorous sequences. Women are treated only as an object of sex. The 'other girl' is a stock character who is responsible for disturbing the development of a love affair between the hero and the heroine and is usually portrayed as a 'vamp' or woman of easy virtue. The other stock character is older woman, who may be the mother-in-law and she depicts the conflict between the younger and the older generations. She is usually of a shrewish temperament. Recently, western cinemas have greatly influenced Indian films, particularly in the physical display of love and of the human body especially female. Recent Indian films are becoming more sexy, in their content." The bedroom, bathroom, cabaret and rape sequences are common formulas for box-office hits.

Ten

Women, Media and Communication

The contents of communication are reflective of the values of society which, in turn are nurtured and sustained through communication. The treatment meted to women and girls in different modes of human communication, mirror the prevailing attitudes and values towards women in a particular society. Image portrayal through communication reinforces reality.

In India, the dominant stereotype images of women and girls are that of: (i) Less competent human beings; (ii) Instruments for exploitation by men; and (iii) Key to commercial success in this age of advertising.

To break the vicious circle of existing 'undesirable' images and project the reality of the lives of women and girls would need an overhaul of the content of existing communication messages through a well thought out National Communication Policy on Women and Girls.

Any nation on the path of development cannot relegate nearly half its population to be "wasted assets" or to utilize their potential only by half measure. The success of all development plans and programmes including those relating to education, small family norms, health and nutrition, etc.; depends upon the active involvement and participation of women.

Human resource development necessitates equipping women and girls with information, knowledge and skills to facilitate their active and equal involvement and participation in the nation's development programmes and activities. Formal education as the path of human development is both costly and a long-term process.

Thus, in a developing country like India, it is critical to harness mass media and other forms of communication, including traditional folk forms of entertainment. This becomes imminent as new obscurantist revivalist forces are at work in society that negate women's right to equality. These claim legitimacy and distort old cultural tradition, religious practices and community rights. Thus it is critical for educating the masses and inculcating new values so as to give practical shape to the constitutional guarantee of equality of status and opportunity to both men and women.

Both common experience and several systematic research studies, reveal that the mass media so far have not been effective instruments to inform and prepare society about women's new roles in national development. This is largely due to the very limited reach of mass media among women and girls, especially in rural areas. Even the limited exposure is mainly in the form of entertainment films or film-based programmes providing little opportunity for education about new values tasks or skills.

Media content and production also leave much to be desired in terms of making educational programmes meaningful or attractive enough for the common men/women. In these circumstances, the expansion of media facilities, especially of electronic mass media like television, is both an opportunity and a risk in the case of women and girls.

Used wisely on the basis of a well thought out communication policy for women and girls, mass media like the television can be a great instrument for social transformation towards women's greater participation and equality.

Situational Analysis

In India, media facilities have expanded enormously over the years since Independence (1947). In recent years, there is a definite policy shift in favour of adopting new communication technologies to accelerate the pace of development and change in the country. The country is on the threshold of a new communication revolution of which satellite, computer, television and video are major manifestations. The whole country is technically knit together through satellite and television and can have common experiences of joy, grief, information and aspirations. The communication scene in India is changing in such fundamental ways that many social scientists term it as the dawn of the "Information Age".

The number of journals and newspapers at the end of 1986 was 23,616 of which, 1,978 were dailies. Newspapers are published in 92 languages. The combined press circulation is about 54 million copies. Nearly 93 per cent of the total sale of daily newspapers, however, is in large towns with a population of over one lakh which account for only 10 per cent of the country's population.

The radio is by far the most extensive network. Technically, the radio signals cover almost the whole country. However, on an average there are only 4.4 radio/transistor sets per 100 persons. Not only this, of the nearly 30 million radio sets in the country, 80 per cent are in urban homes, leaving only about 6 million sets with the 525 million rural population.

Television expansion in recent years has been phenomenal. As on August 1987, there were 210 transmitters covering nearly 70 per cent of the country's population. However, only eighteen centres have television programme production facilities. Further only 9 million television sets are estimated to be in the country. But the growth rate for TV sets is expected to be three million annually in the next three years, promising rapid expansion of television in India. Most of the present 9 million TV sets are in metropolitan cities and towns. To facilitate viewing in villages and urban slums, community sets have been provided in villages and tribal areas. In 1987, the number of community TV sets was estimated to be about 22,250. Despite this, the viewing in rural areas continues to be very limited.

There are about a million videos in the country. The video has reached many small town restaurants, long route buses and even remote villages in some areas, serving as a new status symbol and a source of ready entertainment, mainly films, for a very large number of people in the country. Although until now, video is largely used for entertainment, it has the great potential of being used for education as well.

Like the television and video, films also have a limited outreach. Although India is the largest producer of feature films, about 992 annually, the cinema houses in the country are limited, about 11,200, with approximately 11.5 lakh seats, i.e., 7.4 seats per one thousand population. Most of the cinema houses are in metropolitan cities and large towns.

On the whole, the reach of mass media in India is rather limited especially in rural areas, among women and slum dwellers. This is mainly due to four mutually reinforcing factors. These are:

(1) Low literacy (about 35 per cent); (2) Low purchasing power (about 40 per cent of the population lives below poverty line); (3) Poor means of transportation for timely delivery of newspapers, or maintenance of radio/TV sets; and (4) Lack of relevant information, if purposive communication is the aim of mass media.

Studies reveal that there is a noticeable association between backwardness or underprivileged condition and deprivation of communication resources. A study of the 'rural poor', who are the largest beneficiaries of the Integrated Rural Development Programme, revealed that the overwhelming majority were not exposed to any of the mass media. Only five per cent of the underprivileged regularly listened to the radio.

In sheer monetary terms, the mass media are of limited relevance to the masses, especially those who are living below the poverty line. They can barely meet their essential needs of food and clothing, etc. Buying a cheap transistor set is a luxury they cannot afford. Newspapers and periodicals are out of the question. Thus the access to media and to media exposure can hardly be expected among the rural people, the slum dwellers, and other deprived sections of the society. In the circumstances, the mass media in India are essentially 'class' media. However, it has far-reaching consequences and can be an effective vehicle for social change. Media ascribes prestige and status to new values norms, and practices which they portray. Further, to an extent, interpersonal channels and folk forms of communications make up for the limited outreach of mass media.

The National Plan of Action for Women drawn up in 1976 was clear about communication priorities and provided sufficient direction for subsequent media planning. Its recommendations linked mass media to the priority action spelt out for a mass education programme which stressed the need for special extension education activities, publicity campaigns, and innovative use of non-formal learning facilities. Almost every section of the Plan urged "vigorous campaigns of education and action" so that the plan goals could come within the reach of women everywhere. However, there were ambiguities within the Plan which must have been confusing for communicators. Among others, there were obscure references to "the needs and interests" of girls and women, without clarifying whether this meant existing felt needs of these submissive and inarticulate persons, or those to which they could aspire, for realizing which, they could demand attention. As a result, the years that followed saw a quantum increase in programming for women but not so clearly a qualitative progress. A welcome infusion of analytical programming only came in the mid-1980s, and that too only in some parts of the media.

Policy enunciations in the Sixth Five-Year Plan (1980-85) were more precise. A separate chapter on women and development was incorporated in the Plan for the first time. Significantly, it spoke out clearly the need to integrate objectives for women's development with broader national objectives; it called for re-examination of school curricula, school books, teacher training as part of the needed drive to build awareness and provide necessary knowledge to girls. It also urged the provision of home science education to both men and women so that the concept of "symmetrical families" could be fostered. In referring to the need for an improved data base regarding women, it also implied the need to invest in developing feedback mechanisms to monitor the worth of communication and education efforts. While, the Sixth Plan pronouncements on women's development sustained the emphasis of the previous Plans on women's orientation for better child care and for family planning, the Plan strategy for rural development made special mention of the need to effectively involve the rural women — as a farmer and agrarian worker — if programmes for transformation of rural society were to succeed. In doing so, the Sixth Plan gave real meaning to educational and other objectives suggested in parts of the 1976 blue print of Action. This also gave clear guidelines to State media services on what the content of their communication should be.

A flawed argument that coloured the Sixth Plan and earlier references to women's health and nutrition, was the inference that these were important for the survival and well-being of their babies, and not as their human right, even apart from the special needs of pregnancy and lactation. This bias has persisted and is faithfully reflected in the mass media. It indirectly continues to undermine that aspect of nutrition education which could motivate women to feed their girl children, let alone themselves.

The summary statement of the Sixth Plan chapter on women and development made a very important and pace-setting observation on the broader advocacy required: "Programmes relating to education, health, nutrition and employment would no doubt go a long way in the removal of social disabilities facing women. However, the improvements in the socio-economic status of women would depend to a large extent on the social change in the value system, attitudes and social structure prevailing in the country". This frankly posed the question: What would the State say to the people, through the means and channels at its disposal or response to the guidance to initiate this desired and quite radical-change, and to vigorously carry it forward? The Plan chapter on Communication, Information and Broadcasting contained only an oblique promise to use research in order to provide 'more imaginative intermeshing' of the various programmes elements (VI Plan, Chapter 18, pt. 22). The Ministry of Information and Broadcasting reports of the Plan period, by and large, continued to list programmes for women along with those for selected backward sections of society.

The Seventh Five-Year Plan (1985-90) reflects even clearer thinking on what the real issues of women's development are. From the Sixth Plan focus on employment, economic independence, education and health, the Seventh Plan moves on to an essential intangible of the desired change: "The long term objective of the development programmes for women would be to raise their economic and social status in order to bring them into the mainstream of national development ." And elsewhere, "...The basic approach would be to inculcate confidence among women and bring about an awareness of their own potential". This section goes on to list among key strategies 'extensive utilization' of the various mass media, and the adoption of an integrated multi-disciplinary thrust encompassing employment, education, health, nutrition, application of science and technology, etc., as well as the changing of educational programmes and schools curricula 'to eliminate gender bias'. In the listing of major programmes that should involve and benefit women, agriculture, livestock farming and horticulture, rural and urban small-scale industry and training in technologies related to these are given high priority. While the policy statement of intent on education is quite liberal, the section on health once again stresses mothers in connection with Plan objectives for reduction of maternal and infant mortality, although the appraisal of women's health earlier in the chapter does indeed state the challenge more comprehensively. The chapter also mentions about wage imbalances and of the special needs of women headed households, as well as the increasing displacement of women workers because training in new technologies relevant to their work still bypasses them. This is a detailed manifesto for communication.

The Seventh Plan chapter on Communication, Information and Broadcasting picks up some of these cues. Listed priorities refer to raising the level of people's consciousness, enriching the social and cultural life and making them better-informed citizens. It commits the media to bring a 'vehicle of education and extension' to narrow information gaps faced by different target groups. It lists youth, women, children and 'weaker sections' as key target groups for special programming. The Information and Broadcasting Ministry reports of the past two years refer to such programming.

Issues Needing Attention

Women have been recognized by India's policy-makers as the largest oppressed group in Indian society. Broadly assessed, this oppression has the effect of limiting their capabilities, both in the conventional role of home maker, wife and mother, and in the wider roles of productive resources and responsible citizens of a free nation. Poor access to knowledge, social and cultural barriers to a choice of options, and a low level of confidence in seeking and using knowledge have inhibited, and continue to inhibit, women's potential to overcome these limitations.

A confining image dictated by centuries of rigid social norm has been absorbed, internalized and perpetuated by generations of Indian women and men. It has not been dislodged, even though women have themselves begun to question it. It prevails as the persistent image and self-image of most Indian women and girls today. It constrains them from equipping themselves for their own good as well as that of the community. It inhibits them from receiving and accepting knowledge that could lift them out of their present condition. By the same token, it makes them receptive and responsive to communication that reinforces the image that our society has traditionally encouraged them to accept.

Notwithstanding various directives, woman's image has gone through several unjust projections at the hands of the media. The passivity of female characters in film/television is a major cause for concern. Rarely is a woman shown as capable of solving her problems, standing up to indignities or violence, facing challenges on her own, or taking decisions. The image of the educated woman is typecast as insensitive, self-centred, and uncaring. The economically independent woman is shown as domineering and ruthless. The woman is ideal only when she is in her nurturing roles and as a supportive supplement to man. The portrayal of children in the media especially films and television is also very disparaging. Girls are always shown as cooking, and looking after the younger siblings and imitating the nurturing role of their mothers, whereas boys seek adventure, solve problems, and follow the role model of their fathers. Women specific programmes on radio and television perpetuate sex stereotypes and cater to women as housewives and mothers, rather than provide knowledge and skills for their role as economic contributors.

The print media has perpetuated the neglect of and damage to women. All magazines/newspapers have special columns/pages for women. In addition, there are exclusive magazines for women in almost all Indian languages. Invariably, their fiction sections glorify patriarchy and women's roles as housewives, mothers and dependents. Atrocities against women, from eve-teasing to wife beating, are portrayed in neutral terms. The emphasis remains on embroidery, cooking and home management skills.

The advertising world continues to use women to peddle its products, and to present women as a sexual object. Advertising also reinforces house work as the sole responsibility of women, with household equipment advertisements addressed only to women.

The media has given tremendous spurt to indecent posters and hoardings which are displayed everywhere, and are crude reminders of distorted images and attitudes to women. In an attempt to curb this, a Committee of prominent persons comprising of film personalities, social workers and police officers headed by the Police Commissioner has been constituted in Delhi to remove vulgar and obscene posters/hoardings and initiate legal action against offenders. The Government has tried to tackle this problem by enacting the Indecent Representation of Women (Prohibition) Act (1986) under which, indecent representation of women is deemed an offence punishable with a maximum imprisonment of two years. The Act recognizes that what is obscene or indecent is not readily definable. Nor is it easily enforceable or comprehensive. But it should serve as a constructive step forward in protecting women's dignity.

To give a new direction to communication and media, accent has to be placed on reviving supporting indigenous folk media. Particularly in respect of women, literature, art, music, theatre, dance and folk forms like Harikatha, Burrakatha, Yakshagana have been effectively used by women's groups to communicate messages to the masses. Child marriage, wife beating, ill-treatment or abuse of women are condemned through these media forms and widow remarriage, right to property and respect for the woman's dignity and person are upheld. Such innovative parallel media, especially in the regional languages, offer considerable potential to harness low cost communication strategies towards empowering women and project positive alternative images/roles and attitudes towards women.

It is the latter positive, social and personal image of the Indian women and girls that should be the essential theme and focus of any worthwhile initiative to make communication and media policy and practice exert a more positive influence on what people think, know and believe, not merely for the sake of women, but to further national development objectives and benefit the nation as a whole. This perspective is in consonance with the new and progressive precepts of human resource development which India has adopted as cornerstone of its development philosophy.

Such a communication policy would support and promote the mainstreaming and integration of women, and their conscious participation in national life at all levels rather than single them out as a weak, secondary and dependent group deserving help, but with only a few given functions to perform. It would have to be a courageous and clear-minded policy, capable of setting normative standards, offering new images and ideas, and encourage an honest examination and healthy debate among men, women, youth, children, in many structures and institutions that constitute today's Indian setting.

Such a policy must also link firmly and substantively with the policy directions being set for education, and for the proposed development of culture, the creative and performing arts and the new forums being encouraged for their further growth. If it does, then new ventures in communication and media use can provide leverage to women's own efforts to be more informed , responsible and self-reliant both inside and outside the home setting. If it does not, it will not be able to bring about the pace-setting changes that are now both necessary and possible. Nor will it have enough impact on the sources which provide the content of what passes through the various media channels operating in society.

An important underlying premise for such a communication perspective is that the emerging image of the Indian woman and girl would seek to illustrate an egalitarian ideology. Far from projecting the woman's role as nurturer of the child, it could surely focus on the fact that she is one of the two parents, and that 'parenting' is the task of both. Far from advancing her role only as a homemaker in life, it would surely emphasize that she should be nurtured from childhood as a person capable of conscious choice and allowed to learn about responsible citizenship as well as responsible parenthood. It is implicit in such a policy that communication resulting from it would not be addressed to women only but to the society and that a matching initiative would have to be made to remedy what is communicated for and about men and boys, who are equally the products of a defective social system.

What national policies must now propose is therefore, comprehensive and inclusive rather than exclusive. That would still require considerable affirmative and specific attention to the special needs of girls and women, without contradicting the fundamental point of equality in development and thus in motivation for development. Nor does it ignore the special challenges posed by culture, religion and the allocations of duties and activities to one or the other sex.

Recommendations

1. In order to change the attitudes towards women and girls and raise the social consciousness of the country, a conscious strategic change is required in national media and communication efforts.

2. Setting up of an Expert Group on women's issues for radio, television and other government media, including print media is urged. This group will work towards operationalizing a Communication Policy for Women particularly, on drawing up a framework on roles/images projected of women. They should also examine media strategies for combating revivalism and obscuritism that denies women constitutional equality. The group may also consider the possibility of a national voluntary code to govern the projection of women in advertisements.

3. The communication policy for women and girls needs constant monitoring and reappraisal as the question of communication and image portrayal of women and girls is a sensitive and complex one. For this purpose, a 'Media Advisory Committee' consisting of eminent social workers, writers, social scientists and media practitioners may be constituted. The committee besides operationalizing the communication policy will keep constant vigil on media contents of other social communications. The committee may also approach research organizations and individuals to undertake relevant studies and analysis including feedback about the new media inputs.

4. A balance must be struck between the nation building and revenue earning potential of at least TV and Radio services. The proposal to inject 'Vividh Bharati' channels with public interest education and information packages must be pursued in a professional manner, with high quality content and entertainment value that will compete with the best commercial standards. It is recommended that serious consideration be given to scrutinization of the Chitrahaar and Chitramala programmes and their content must be firmly vetted.

5. Media personnel, including originators of information in all media forms including AIR, Doordarshan, Print Media, etc., must be sensitized to women's issues particularly to the projection of positive images of women. More sensitized women need to be inducted for producing information programmes, films, etc., in

the national media. Positive role models of women as cultivators, producers, managers, etc., must be forcefully projected.

6. A scrutiny of all existing Censor Board rules regarding indecent representation of women in the media must be made and redefined. Particular attention must be paid to the distinction between 'pornography' and 'obscenity'. Women could comprise at least half the membership of all Censor Boards and media monitoring cells and all persons selected for membership should have awareness of the issue involved.

7. Alternative media forms such as folk theatre, puppetry, etc., need to be widely encouraged, especially where existing electronic and print media have no/or limited outreach. Already as suggested by the National Commission on self-employed women, fairs/*shibirs*, health camps/*jathas* can also be organized to reach poor women.

8. The lyrics of songs broadcast on the radio and scripts of radio plays must be scrutinized. The existing guidelines of AIR should be consciously applied and reviewed where necessary. It is recommended that the government's media channels should not be used to perpetuate counter-productive messages couched in these entertainment items. Special programming on women on specific subjects should not stop but should be complemented with a planned increase in family programmes. Suitable timings for putting these across on TV and radio should be determined through field studies.

9. Initiatives for quality control must be taken in respect of commercial and popular films and serials. Guidelines should be developed for their evaluation. A short discussion should precede the screening of films which endorse traditional stereotypes. Advertisements which are either degrading to women or endorse the stereotypes should be banned.

10. Textbooks in use in the formal and non-formal education system and at other levels of education and training should be carefully assessed for removing negative images and references to women.

11. Research and analysis should be undertaken to assess the ways in which the various communication channels reach and affect women and girls.

12. The outreach of different media by age, sex and occupation should be assessed.

13. Reasons for the very low exposure of women to mass media must be identified.

14. Reaction of the target group must be much more extensively researched and analysed. Feedback, should not only be about communication programmes and activities, feedback monitoring studies should accompany the transmission of communication programmes in all media channels. The competing or complementary influence of other social and commercial media should also be closely watched and assessed.

15. Feedback information should be actively encouraged in universities and other research institutions. Besides, it should be a compulsory component of the syllabi of mass communication and journalism training institutions.

16. Theatre writers and directors should be encouraged to evolve new trends and develop new plays, deriving ideas from the rich theatre heritage of the country. The staging of these should be linked to open ended audience discussion. Some experimental work has been done in this sphere which should be studied and appropriately encouraged to expand and diversify. This project should be experimentally applied through the new programming activities flowing from the zonal cultural centre programmes of the Government of India.

17. There should be "Resource Centres" at the Centre and State levels for identification, collection, dissemination and documentation of material related to women's issues.

Eleven

Blue Print of Action Points

Legislative Measures

The existing legislations should be reviewed so that equality and social justice can be ensured to women of all communities and creeds. Where this involves amendments to existing personal laws of minority group, initial efforts should be concentrated on arousing a desire for change from among the members of such minority groups. A vigorous campaign should be made to educate women about their rights, and to generate among all communities, a desire for a common civil code, to be achieved by the end of the UN Decade for Women in 1985.

Legal aid should be organized for women in need with the active assistance of the Bar Councils.

The setting up of family courts should be considered for speedy and effective adjudication in all cases concerning the family. Women, particularly in rural areas, should be protected against harassment.

The practice of dowry should be eradicated. The legislation should be strictly enforced. This is a social evil which requires sustained action not only on the part of government agencies, but also on the part of voluntary organizations and public leaders.

The provisions of the existing Child Marriage Restraint Act should be reviewed. Special attention should be given to streamlining the enforcement machinery and involving local authorities and voluntary organizations in the implementation of the Act. Active public support should be mobilized by governmental agencies, voluntary organizations and public leaders against child marriage, particularly in rural areas. Simultaneously, systematic programmes of education and training should be developed for girls till they marry.

Administrative Measures

Education

Education is the greatest known catalytic agent for social change. All out efforts should therefore be made to achieve the goal of universal primary education as early as possible. The ideas of equality between the sexes and participation by women in development should be woven into the fabric of the educational system.

The employment of women teachers should be actively promoted. The existing employment procedures, including those for part-time employment, should be reviewed and, where necessary, relaxations in age, etc., made so that more women teachers, can be employed and husbands and wives are posted in the same schools or at the same station.

The content of education should be strengthened in terms of both life and work relevance. Attention should be given to vocationalization and diversification of courses which should not only be limited to traditional women's vocations but also give emphasis on the preparation of women for participation in modern sectors of industrial production. Polytechnics (including mini-polytechnics) should be started for girls in the smaller urban centres to provide training facilities in trades crafts which will prompt self-employment.

At the stage of higher education special incentives like freeships, scholarships, hostel facilities, and book loans should be made available to girls from rural, backward and hilly areas, from backward classes and from poor families. A greater diversification in the courses offered should be made to enhance work opportunities in non-traditional vocations in modern sectors of industrial production.

Adoption of multiple entry in education, non-formal part-time education facilities, condensed courses for education, correspondence courses and courses for continuing education should be made available in a larger measure to women in semi-urban and rural areas, and to working women in urban and semi-urban areas. Adult education and functional literacy programmes should be vigorously pursued through both official and voluntary agencies.

Employment

Equal Remuneration Act, 1976, has been passed, providing for payment of equal remuneration to men and women workers and the prevention of discrimination on grounds of sex. Special steps should therefore be taken to review recruitment, promotion and other personnel practices in all public and private sector undertakings to ensure that there is no discrimination against women candidates. Women apprentices should be taken without discrimination in industries. Representatives of women's voluntary organizations should be associated in the machinery set up to ensure adequate participation of women in employment.

Village industries which provide scope for the employment of women should be further promoted. Special training services should be organized and credit, marketing facilities, etc., extended, specially in regard to crafts which can have a ready export market, through modernization of design, etc. Integrated pilot projects to cover training, production and marketing should be started.

The existing requirement procedures and employment conditions should be reviewed to encourage the re-entry of women into the workforce. For this purpose, the provisions relating to maximum age of entry into services should be reviewed. Part-time employment of women should be promoted wherever feasible. Refresher courses and training programmes should be organized for adult women to make them fit for re-employment.

Organizations entrusted by the government with the task of promoting self-employment opportunities should develop special women's entrepreneurial training motivation programmes and provide special assistance to women entrepreneurs and to women's co-operative in terms of credit, licensing, etc.

The existing legislation in regard to maternity benefits should be reviewed. It should simultaneously be ensured that there is no consequent adverse effect on the employment of women.

Health Care, Nutrition and Family Planning

Maternal and child health care facilities should be expanded, particularly in semi-urban and rural areas, and coverage provided to high risk pregnant women. Ante-natal and post-natal clinics should be started in every Primary Health Centre and district hospital.

Nutrition supplementation should be provided to high risk pregnant mothers. Simultaneously, nutrition and health education should be given to girls and to mothers through all available media and institutions (school, hospitals, PHCs, etc.).

Family welfare planning services should be expanded and measures intensified to educate and prepare couples to avail them, specifically in rural, backward and tribal areas. The facilities under the Medical Termination of Pregnancy Act, 1971 should be made available in semi-urban and rural areas and information regarding the provisions disseminated among women, immunization facilities should be gradually extended to all children.

Facilities of Working Women

The establishment of day care centres, creches, and *balwadis* should be promoted on a large scale in rural, semi-urban and urban areas to help working mothers and active women social workers discharge their duties, and enable the older children to attend school.

Hostel facilities for working women of the lower income groups should be expanded.

Care for the Socially Disadvantaged

Women without any means of support, and the physically handicapped should be provided services for education, training and rehabilitation so that they can become self-reliant. Old age homes should be opened for the aged and the infirm. Special programmes should be developed for unmarried mothers and their children.

The provision of the Suppression of Immoral Traffic Act (1956) should be reviewed to facilitate their more efficient implementation. Comprehensive rehabilitation programmes for victims of immoral traffic and their children should be developed. Special steps should be taken to prevent vulnerable young girls and women from becoming victims of this social evil.

Promotion of Voluntary Effort

The growth of voluntary organizations, especially in rural, backward and tribal areas and in urban slums should be promoted to mobilize public support for different programmes of welfare. Training facilities should be provided on a large scale to voluntary workers. Leadership training programmes, particularly for women from weaker sections, should be developed so that they can function effectively as agents of change. The establishment of Mahila Mandals should be promoted in every village so that they can function as field level agencies for social and economic transformation. Voluntary organizations have critical role in mobilizing public opinion in favour of equality among men and women and eradicating superstitions, social evils and waste.

A vigorous campaign of education and action should be launched in favour of community sanitation and hygiene. Public utility services for women should be expanded wherever called for.

Machinery for Implementation

In order to ensure that the Resolution unanimously passed by the two Houses of Parliament is acted upon and the implementation of the Plan of Action is ensured, it is proposed that:

(i) A Standing Advisory Committee should be set up at the national level which will review the progress every year so that a report is submitted to Parliament annually. The Committee may be called 'The National Committee on Women'.

(ii) To service the above Committee a special bureau should be set up in the Ministry of Education and Social Welfare (Department of Social Welfare). The Bureau will keep in touch with the implementation of the various programmes by the Central Ministries, State Governments and non-official agencies.

(iii) At the State level similar committees should be set up under the chairmanship of the Chief Minister. These Committees should also have adequate administrative support.

Education

In realization of the importance of education in general and the need for equality in opportunities for the intellectual development of men and women, successive Five-Year Plans have consistently placed special emphasis on the acceleration of women's education. The emphasis with regard to women's education has all along been to equip her for the multiple roles as citizens, housewives, mothers, contributors to family income and builders of the new society. Efforts have been made during the past two decades of planned development to enrol more girls in school; to encourage girls to stay in schools; to continue their education as long as possible; and to provide non-formal education opportunities for women. The Draft Fifth Five-Year Plan has declared that "the outlays for the education of girls will be stepped up..". The fulfilment of the constitutional directive in respect of providing free and compulsory education up to the age of 14 years has been included as one of the components of the Minimum Needs Programme.

These efforts have had a significant impact on the progress of women's education in India. For example, there is a primary school within the easy walking distance from the home of almost all the children. This has resulted in an increase in the enrolment of girls in classes I-V as a percentage of total enrolment in these classes from 28.1 in 1950-51 to 37.6 in 1973-74. In respect of classes I-VIII, IX-XI/XII and university education also there has been an appreciable increase in the percentage of girls' enrolment to total enrolment, between the years 1950-51 and 1973-74. In fact, girls' enrolment is observed to be growing at a faster rate than those of boys.

Despite these encouraging trends and marked progress made in respect of women's education, the educational status of women is still far from satisfactory for the following reasons:

(a) Literacy among women is generally lower than that among men. According to the 1971 Census data, only 13.4 per cent of women in this age group of 25+ are literate.

(b) Enrolment of girls in classes I to V is only 66.4 per cent of girls in the corresponding age group, i.e., from 6 to 11 years; while in respect of boys the relevant percentage is 100.2.

(c) Drop-out rate is also very high in classes I to V. A recent study has shown that the drop-out rate especially accentuated in the case of girls from rural areas and from the less privileged sections of society, is as heavy as 42.85 per cent between classes I and II.

(d) In classes VI to VIII, percentages of enrolment of girls and boys to the total girls and boys in the relevant age group (i.e., from 11 to 14 years) are 22.2 and 48.3, respectively.

(e) At the secondary stage, i.e., from classes IX to XI/XII girls enrolled constitute only 12 per cent of girls in the relevant age group 14 to 17 years as against 31 per cent in respect of the enrolment of boys in this age group.

(f) Enrolment of girls in Post-Matric classes constitutes only 2.3 per cent of girls in the concerned age group 17 to 23 years, while the enrolment percentage of boys in this age group is 7.5.

Factors Retarding the Progress of Women's Education

Girls and women in India have thus not been able to take full advantage of the available opportunities/facilities for intellectual development. This is mainly because of several social and cultural factors in addition to various other reasons. Action plans and strategies for women's education should, therefore, aim at neutralizing the effects of the factors which have retarded the progress of women's education in India. With a view to facilitating the formulation of such a plan of action, in what follows, some of the major reasons which have operated against girls/women in taking full advantage of educational opportunities/facilities are listed below:

(a) General indifference to education of girls.

(b) Social resistance arising out of fears and misconceptions that education might alienate girls from traditions and social values and lead to maladjustments, conflicts and non-conformism.

(c) Early marriage and social inhibitions against girls pursuing education after marriage.

(d) Prevalence of child labour among girls belonging to weaker sections and the hard domestic chores which some of the unmarried girls — even in the middle-class families — are required to perform.

(e) The prevailing notion that the sole occupation of women is to bear children, look after her husband and children, and thus be restricted to domestic work.

(f) Discrimination effected by employers against women labour in both organized and unorganized sectors in matters of recruitment, training and promotion.

(g) Many girls and their parents find that the school curriculum do not conform adequately to their needs and interests.

(h) Unsuitable and inflexible school timings and inadequate facilities for girls in schools, particularly in the co-educational schools.

Major Objective of Women's Education

It should be recognized here that the general objective of any policy towards women's education cannot be different from those relating to men. However, in view of the social and cultural handicaps that have operated against women in general and in view of the multiple role that women are required to play, the need for a set of objectives specific to women's education is imperative. The following major objectives are, therefore, considered here:

(a) Prepare women to fully participate in socially productive work, fully aware of family planning needs with a view to achieving her full integration with the democratic and developmental efforts of the country.

(b) Help break down overt covert biases against women.

(c) Make women aware of the various legal, social and economic rights, provisions and privileges available to them and the way they can take advantage of them, for their advancement.

(d) Enable women to be self-reliant to achieve economic independence.

(e) Impart the idea of equality between the sexes and participation by women in development through the educational system.

(f) And above all, to find full expression for her talent, ability and personality and for this purpose, enable her to adopt a discriminating attitude so that she can escape the bonds of superstition and obscurantism.

Action Plans

Action plans here are evolved within the general framework of major objectives mentioned above. In addition, the action plans have taken into consideration other objectives which are specific of educational categories like elementary education, middle stage education, secondary stage education, university education and non-formal education. For the sake of convenience, in what follows, action plans specific of each agegroup of girls, are all mentioned separately.

Elementary Education-Girls in the Age Group 6-11 years

Girls in this age group constitute the population of girls of primary school going age. Action plans for this age group will need to be in two directions:

(a) To universalize primary education for girls, and
(b) To strive for the retention of girls already enrolled.

Towards this end, the following action plans are suggested:

Administrative and Structural Measures

(i) State Governments should take note of the habitations without primary schools as indicated by the Third Educational Survey and make arrangements for providing primary school within a distance of 1.5 km of all habitations within next five years.

(ii) Mobile schools should be provided for children of all nomadic tribes, migrant labour and construction workers.

(iii) Girls in this age are often required to look after younger children and attend minor household duties, particularly in the rural areas and among weaker sections of the society. As this is one of the major reasons that holds such girls from attending school, special efforts should be made to enlarge the scope and coverage of pre-school education programmes like Balwadis and Anganwadis, where the older girls can be given practical work experience and child care.

(iv) These pre-school education programmes should, wherever possible, be attached to primary schools or at least located in the vicinity of primary schools, as that would help in cultivating a school going habit right from the childhood.

(v) Supervision and inspection of primary schools should give particular attention to the problem of enrolment of girls. their retention, involvement of the community, etc.

Promotional and Motivational Measures

(vi) Special and sustained persuasive and motivational campaign and organizational drives should be undertaken among regions/communities which have shown markedly a low achievement in girls enrolment. Voluntary organizations at local levels like Mahila Mandals and local bodies should be fully involved in this programme.

(vii) Promotion and support to girls' education should also be tackled through a multipronged programme of incentives — both for bringing girls to schools and for retaining them in schools. The incentives can be in the form of mid-day meals, free supply of books and reading materials, scholarships awards, etc. Active collaboration of voluntary organizations may be sought in this regard.

Pedagogical Measures

(viii) The primary teacher training course should undergo a major revision with a view to adequately preparing the teacher for the promotion of girls' education. Emphasis should be more on the use of such non-formal methods of imparting education that would interest and attract more and more girls to attend schools.

Education for Girls in the Age Group 11-14 years

Population of girls in this age group constitutes girls of middle school going age. This group can be divided into three sub-groups:

(a) Girls students attending middle schools;
(b) Girl drop-outs at various stages from classes I to V; and
(c) Girls who have not attended school.

The objectives of education and training are different for each of the sub-groups.

Middle School—Girl Students

Action plans for education of girls in this age group should be concerned about:

(i) encouraging further enrolment of girls at this stage;
(ii) retention of girls already in middle schools; and
(iii) rendering the curriculum more relevant.

The following action plans are suggested:

Pedagogical Measures

(i) The content should be more oriented to the needs of girls in the village communities so that both the parents and the girls see relevance of this education for their own lives. The curriculum of the middle school stage needs to be given a strong work experience orientation, introducing girls to crafts and skills which will be of direct use to them in the family, community and farm, and help them in rural employment and self-employment. It should also introduce girls to scientific knowledge, principles of home-making, family life education, nutrition and diet, environment education and civic education.

(ii) *Women Teachers*: It is very important for the promotion of girls' education to employ women teachers in schools. In fact, the general view is that women are more suited to be teachers and larger number of teachers should be women. However, the problem may come up in different ways. More number of men may be qualified and trained women may not be in a position to accept employment as full time teachers due to personal problems; women also have difficulties in working in rural areas. There has to be relaxation from age restrictions. The States may consider reserving a certain number of posts of teachers for women and where there are not adequate number of trained teachers, untrained persons may be recruited and deputed for training. The question of giving posting to husband and wife both of whom are teachers in the same place may be considered.

It may also be worthwhile in those areas which have schools without women teachers, to select educated women in that area and send them for training and appoint them in the schools in that area. Where educated women are not available for posting in a school, local women may be selected and posted as school *matas* (school mothers) to keep the girl students company and induce parents to send their girls and children to schools. The rules relating to age and qualification of recruitment and service may have to be relaxed in these cases and the deficiency made up through in-service training.

Women should not be discriminated against in matters of recruitment. Selection and recruitment should be made on merit. No qualified meritorious woman candidate should be overlooked. State Governments may contemplate providing for 50 per cent of teachers in schools being women and to look into this aspect while sanctioning grants to institutions.

In single teacher institutions (the exact position will be brought out by the Third Educational Survey), it may be desirable to ensure that where there are two teachers, one of them should be a woman. If locally educated women are available, they can be recruited. Husband-wife teams can be posted.

(iii) The primary teacher training course needs to undergo a major revision to adequately prepare the trainees for their special responsibility for the promotion of girls' education in rural areas, especially in adapting the content to suit the needs and interests of girls, in adopting non-formal methodologies and in linking with community and developmental activities.

(iv) Supervision and inspection of schools should be given particular attention to the problem of enrolment of girls, their retention, factors contributing to wastage and stagnation, revision of curriculum, involvement of the community, working conditions of women teachers, etc.

Promotional and Motivational Measures

(v) School timings should be flexible, as many of the girls in this age group are required to help their mothers in routine domestic chores.

(vi) Adoption of multiple entry and part-time courses is recommended.

(vii) Incentives like mid-day meals, scholarships, free school uniforms, free books and study materials, stipend, awards, etc., should be extended to all girls in the rural areas and slums in the urban areas.

Middle School-Girl Drop-outs

Alternative Measures

(viii) For school drop-outs of girls, pre-vocational training programmes should be organized on an extensive scale to cover all girls in the rural areas and in the slums of urban areas. The objectives of such training should be to render them self-sufficient in home management, and help them to achieve economic independence. With this in view, such training programmes should include courses in sewing, knitting, cooking, nutrition, minor repairs of the house, motherhood, child care, etc.

Girls who never attended schools

(ix) For the non-student girls in this age group, the objective should be to provide adequate preparation in life through a combined three-year course in general education and vocational training. Vocational training should be on the lines of pre-vocational training mentioned above.

(x) Such training programmes should be extended to all girls in the rural areas. In the urban areas, preference should be given to girls in slum areas and destitute girls.

Education for Girls in the Age Group 14-17 years

Girls in this age group also can be classified into three groups:

(a) Girl students with motivation to attend secondary school;
(b) Girl drop-outs from classes VI to VIII; and
(c) Non-student girls, i.e., students who never attended schools.

Girl Students

The action plans under this category should emphasize more on:

(i) facilitating more girls to pursue education at the secondary stage, and

(ii) strengthening the content in terms of both life and work relevance.

The following action plans are suggested:

Administrative and Structural Measures

(i) Separate girls schools or separate sections should be started where the social/cultural environment demands them.

(ii) In co-education schools special attention should be given to the provision of adequate toilet, rest and recreation facilities, separately for girls.

(iii) State Governments which have not yet made high school education free for girls should do so on a priority basis.

(iv) Multiple entry system and part-time education may be provided.

Promotional and Motivational Measures

(v) All courses of training in vocational and technical schools at the secondary stage should be open to both boys and girls. There should be no discrimination in this regard.

(vi) Liberal incentives in the form of book allowances, book-bank facilities, etc., should be extended to encourage more girls in rural and backward areas to pursue secondary education.

(vii) Separate hostel facilities should be provided particularly in rural areas and residential scholarships should be offered.

Pedagogical Measures

(viii) The curriculum should be more diversified taking into consideration the various occupational opportunities available to women and the interests and aptitudes of girls.

Girl Drop-outs

Alternative Measures

(ix) Condensed courses of education started in 1958 were found very useful. Under this scheme women in the age group 13-30 years who have had some schooling are prepared for middle school, matriculation or equivalent examinations within a period of 2 years' duration. The minimum age limit here should be reduced to 15 years. This scheme should be extended to cover all rural areas and weaker sections of the urban community.

(x) The condensed course should be organized for smaller groups, say 5 to 7 persons, using the community resources like girls' high schools and girls' colleges.

(xi) Apart from imparting general education, condensed course should also aim at imparting job-oriented training with the active co-operation of existing vocational training institutions.

(xii) Correspondence courses and self-study programmes may be introduced.

(xiii) Efforts should be made to cover at least about 215 lakh of girls in the age group 15-30 under the condensed courses programme during the Fifth Plan period.

Non-student Girls

(xiv) Fourth Plan introduced a programme of functional literacy with the objective of imparting elementary general education and vocational training-related to the functions performed to men and women in the rural areas who never attended schools. This programme should be expanded to cover all rural areas.

(xv) Apart from imparting general elementary education and knowledge about farming technologies, the curriculum for women should include courses of training in occupational skills like kitchen, gardening, food processing, poultry keeping, animal husbandry; household arts like cooking nutritional values of foods locally available, sewing, knitting, etc., and motherhood, child care and family planning as also electronics and like fields.

(xvi) Similar programmes should also be designed for girls in this age group and under this category belonging to urban areas.

Education for Girls in the Age Group 17 Years and Above

Education for girls in this age group also can be divided into three groups, as in the case of other age groups:

(a) Education for girls at the higher education stage;

(b) Education for girl drop-outs from the educational system beyond the secondary stage; and

(c) Education for non-student girls — girls who never had any education.

In respect of the last category here, i.e., education for non-student girls, action plans are the same as those concerning non-student girls in the age group 14-17 years. Hence, this category is not dealt with separately here.

Education for Girls at the Higher Education Stage

Action plans in this area should aim at:

(a) Making higher education available to the less privileged sections of the society, particularly girls from the rural areas; and

(b) Making the curriculum more relevant and responsive to the cultural and occupational needs of women.

The following action plans may be taken up for consideration:

Administrative and Structural Measures

(i) The general policy here should be to discourage separate institutions for women and to promote co-educational institutions for women and to promote co-educational facilities. However, in areas where separate institutions are required to promote education of women, they may be permitted on the merits of such cases.

(ii) Vocational counselling and guidance services should be organized in a more meaningful way to help girls— in colleges and universities — opt for suitable courses relevant to their talent, interests and needs.

Promotional and Motivational Measures

(iii) Incentives like scholarships, freeships, etc., should be provided to enable girls from rural areas to pursue higher education.

(iv) For girls belonging to weaker sections, in addition to freeships and scholarships, bursaries should also be provided to meet their expenses on food and lodging.

(v) Provision of self-cooking facilities in hostels for girls should also be considered.

(vi) Girls pursuing higher education should be provided

easy access to textbooks and other reference material through book-bank facilities.

(vii) Girls should be encouraged to enter professional courses. If necessary, reservation of seats for girls in professional courses may be considered.

Pedagogical Measures

(viii) Diversification of courses at the junior college level and undergraduate level should be undertaken on a priority basis with a view to preparing the girls for the various employment opportunities open to them.

Education for Girl Drop-outs

Girls in this age group drop-out of educational system for various reasons. Marriage is one of the reasons which force girls in this age group to discontinue further formal education. Economic hardship is another reason which forces some girls to drop-out and seek jobs, with a view to supporting their families. Social prejudices and cultural attitudes also force some of the girls to leave the formal educational system. For girls in this category, therefore, the policy should be to extend non-formal educational facilities on a large scale.

The following action plans are suggested:

(i) Facilities for part-time self-study and correspondence courses should be expanded on a large scale to enable working girls and non-working married and unmarried girls to enhance their educational qualifications.

(ii) In addition to course leading to degree/diploma, short courses in specific subjects through summer schools/ sessions, ad hoc programmes like seminars, laboratory work, workshop experience, etc., should be organized for working girls, with a view to upgrading their professional skills and qualifications. Facilities for further education not necessarily leading to a degree but for upgradation of knowledge and skills could be provided.

(iii) While the initiative for organizing such programmes should be taken by the Central and State Governments, the employees should also be increasingly involved.

(iv) Pre-examination training facilities should be organized on a large scale for educated women from the rural areas and those belonging to weaker sections with the objective of equipping them to successfully compete in examinations for public jobs.

(v) Entrepreneurship development programmes should be organized separately for educated women in the age group 18-30 years with a minimum of matriculation level of education.

The objective of such training programmes should be:

(a) Make them aware of the various opportunities for self-employment;

(b) Motivate them to take up self-employment;

(c) Impart needed skills/training; and

(d) Promote achievement motivation among them.

Administrative Measures

To make the various action plans successful and to achieve a real breakthrough in women's education, there is an urgent need for a matching and effective administrative set up, both at the central and state levels. With this in view, the following suggestions are made:

(i) In the Union Ministry of Education and Social Welfare, a special unit/cell may be set up to be in charge of women's education to review and initiate follow-up action.

(ii) In each State education department, a senior officer should be placed in charge of girls' education in order that it may receive adequate emphasis, execution and co-ordination.

(iii) As the district is the operational unit for all educational programmes and as the needs of girls vary in extent and kind from area to area within a district, a separate cell for girls' educational formal and non-formal — may be created within the purview of the district educational officer at the district headquarters.

(iv) School supervisory system should be staffed with more women.

(v) A suitable machinery may be set up at the Centre and the States to help in the formulation of plans for women's education — formal and non-formal to monitor, co-ordinate and evaluate progress of women's education from time to time, to create public opinion in favour of women's education, etc.

Twelve

National Perspective Plan for Women 1988-2000

The Perspective Plan for Women is an effort at a long term overall policy for Indian Women, guided by those constitutional principles and directives relevant to the development process. It is linked to the national targets determined for the end of the century in respect of certain basic indicators especially of health, education and employment. The Plan views women not as the weaker segment of society or as passive beneficiaries of the development process, but as a source of unique strength for reaching national goals.

The Plan aims at:

Economic development and integration of women into the mainstream of the economy.

Equity and social justice for all women.

These are critical goals for the all round development of women not merely as producers and providers, but also as individuals with a right to human dignity in a society where 'culture', 'caste' and 'class' tend to discriminate against gender.

The overall purpose of this plan is to find the highest common denominator for all national endeavour, curing across the spectrum of class and religion; functions, sectors and disciplines; to harness the resource represented by the people—both the women as well as the men. This renewal of efforts, from the fifth decade of political independence, will have meaning only if the full potential of the silent half-comprising the 331 million women and girls of India, (about 150 million of them in material poverty and many more close to it) is harnessed. The direction and design, priorities and pace of national development, must have direct relevance to their lives and future. Every dimension of development—political, economic and cultural, not just social—has to assist and hasten their generation.

If the results and lessons of the past are any guide, a larger allocation of resources for women within the prevailing patterns and structures of development, does not promise a reversal of trends. A parallel substream of women's development even if possible, will only perpetuate discrimination and subordination. An alternative strategy of national development which will provide not just some additional space for women, but create a democratic, egalitarian, secular, cooperative social structure has to be defined and tried. In such a scheme, it will be necessary to accelerate the women's component of composite programmes, to ensure the integrity of the enterprise as well as a measure of compensatory justice. The goals of holistic human development must not be at the expense of one another and the ascent to equality must be collective.

Situational Review

For outlining a development perspective, a review of the existing situation of the Indian woman is an essential prerequisite. Both, positive indicators as well as negative indices that are a growing cause of concern to policy makers, planners, administrators and activists are projected to present her overall status. A brief review of the Five-Year Plans and the programmes for women launched in the last few decades, is also included.

Among the positive developments affecting women are:

The expectation of life at birth has improved from 44.7 years in 1961-71 to 52.9 years in 1971-81.

The sex ratio has registered a slight rise—from 930 women per thousand men in 1971 to 933 per thousand men in 1981.

The average age at marriage for girls has reached 18.3 years in 1981 as against 17.2 years in 1971, achieving for the first time an average higher than the minimum prescribed age for marriage.

The focus in the programmes for women has shifted from welfare to development. This shift can be perceived in the creation of a separate department for the development of women.

The Programme of Action of the National Policy on Education (1986) lays stress on women's equality and has identified for the first time three areas for special attention, viz. (i) review of school textbooks to remove sexist bias and developing approaches to promotion of the value of equality through school curricula; (ii) reorientation of teachers to promote gender equality through their teaching and (iii) increasing the coverage of women and women's issues in the research and teaching activities of higher education.

Women's Studies and Development Centres have been set up in constituent colleges of several universities with the objective of using students and teachers as resource groups for creating social awareness and bringing about attitudinal changes in society.

There is an effort to sensitize administration to the women's perspective in development programmes, through the introduction of a women's component in training programmes for senior administrators conducted by the Department of Personnel in the Government of India.

There is a special effort launched to involve women at all levels in the planning and implementation process of programmes for women.

There is an increasing emphasis on professionalizing women's programmes by providing technical expertise for their implementation.

For the first time since Independence the elected representation of women in Parliament has gone up to almost 10 per cent of its total membership.

The Prime Minister's office has now identified 27 beneficiary oriented schemes exclusively for women. These schemes though falling under various Ministers are monitored by the Department of Women and Child Development, Ministry of Human Resource Development.

A National Advisory Committee on Women has been set up with the Prime Minister as Chairman.

Several legislative enactments/amendments have come into force to protect the interests of women.

Overshadowing the positive indicators, there are certain distressing negative indices as follows:

Though a marginal improvement has been registered in the sex ratio, the projected ratio for 2000 AD is depressing with 500 million males to 480 million females.

Amniocentesis tests are being misused to determine the sex of the child in the womb, resulting in the female foetus being aborted.

Age specific death rates indicate higher rates for female children and women up to 35 years of age.

As per the 1981 Census, 75 per cent of women are illiterate. This is compounded by the high drop out rate for girls which is estimated at 55.5 per cent at the primary stage and 77.7 per cent at the middle school stage. Enrolment of girls in higher education has been almost static from 1975 to 1985. There are also substantial disparities in the enrolment of girls and boys at the university stage, and in technical and professional colleges.

The work participation rate for females declined in the census decades up to 1981. In 1981, it recorded a marginal improvement.

The fertility rates in 1981 showed only a very marginal decline—average number of children born to a woman during her lifetime being 4.6. There are in addition many incomplete pregnancies. Over 50 per cent of women suffer from anaemia in pregnancy, which accounts directly for 15-20 per cent of all maternal deaths.

Approximately 90 per cent of the women workers are engaged in the unorganized sector. Of these over 80 per cent are in agriculture and allied occupations. In the organized sector women constitute only 13.3 per cent of all employees. In the public sector, they account for 11 per cent of total employment and in the private sector for 17.8 per cent.

The number of female job seekers through employment exchanges increased from 11.2 lakh in 1975 to 51 lakh in 1986. After showing an increase between 1975 and 1982, the percentage of placements declined in the subsequent years, i.e., 1983-86.

Studies show that modernization and mechanization are tending to marginalize women in many sectors. They are either pushed down or out of the workforce. There are also indications that agricultural modernization/industrial growth policies have tended to widen gender disparities.

Estimates of the average hours of unpaid work done by women outside their homes vary from 6.1 and 7.5 hours per day, with some women working up to 10 hours and more. Apart from their domestic duties, women are engaged in agricultural operations for an average of 12 hours a day. Despite this, their access to ownership of land, credit and other productive resources remains negligible.

Recent surveys indicate that, 30-35 per cent of rural households are headed by women due to male migration, neglect, abandonment.

Only 994 women hold senior management/administrative posts as against 15,993 men in similar jobs in the All India Services, constituting only 5.8 per cent. There are only 21 women officers in the Indian Police Service as against 2418 men (0.9 per cent). In the Indian Administrative Services, there are 339 women against 4209 men (7.5 per cent).

Women comprise only 7.5 per cent of the membership of registered trade unions and approximately one per cent of the office bearers and executive committee members.

Proportional representation of women in elected offices either remained stagnant or declined in the last decade. This is not withstanding their increased voting turnout in the general elections.

Crimes against women continue unabated, there were 6668 reported victims of rape in 1987 and 1517 dowry deaths including by burning (provisional figures).

Women in the Five-Year Plans

The First Five-Year Plan (1951-56) envisaged welfare measures for women. To spearhead welfare measures, the Central Social Welfare Board (CSWB) was established in 1953 which symbolized the welfare approach to women's problems. The CSWB was also reflective of the community development approach, which envisaged for the first time, the need for organizing women into Mahila Mandals or Women's Clubs. A number of studies have shown that the community development (CD) worker, perceived more as a harmonizer of interests rather than a stimulator of awareness, worked closely with the rural elite. Moreover, although rural women came within the purview of the CD programmes, they were not specifically catered to as a target population based on economic or other specific class related criteria. A large majority of poor rural women thus remained untouched.

The Second Five-Year Plan (1956-61) was closely linked with the overall approach of intensive agricultural development. The welfare approach to women's issues persisted. The plan recognized the need for the organization of women as workers. It also perceived the social prejudices/disabilities they suffered. The Plan stated that women should be protected against injurious work, should receive maternity benefits and creches for children. It also suggested speedy implementation of the principle of equal pay for equal work and provision for training to enable women to compete for higher jobs.

The Third Five-Year Plan (1961-66) pinpointed female education as a major welfare strategy. In social welfare, the largest share was provided for expanding rural welfare services and condensed courses of education. The health programme concentrated mainly on the provision of services for maternal and child welfare, health education, nutrition and family planning.

The Fourth Five-Year Plan (1969-74) continued the emphasis on women's education. The basic policy was to promote women's welfare within the family as the base of operation. The outlay on Family Planning was stepped up to reduce the birth rate from 40 to 25 per thousand through mass education. High priority was accorded to immunization of pre-school children and supplementary feeding for children, expectant and nursing mothers.

The Fifth Five-Year Plan (1974-79) emphasized the need to train women in need of income and protection. It also recommended a programme of functional literacy to equip women with skills and knowledge to perform the functions of a housewife (including child care, nutrition, health care, home economics, etc.)

This Plan coincided with the International Women's Decade and the submission of the Report of the Committee on the Status of Women in India (CSWI). The overall task of the CSWI was to undertake a comprehensive examination of all the questions relating to the rights and status of women in the context of changing social and economic conditions in the country and problems relating to the advancement of women. The report stressed that the dynamics of social change and development had adversely affected a large section of women and had created new imbalances and disparities such as:

* The declining sex ratio;
* Lower expectancy of life;
* Higher infant and maternal mortality;
* Declining work participation;
* Illiteracy; and
* Rising migration.

The CSWI Report led to a debate in Parliament and the emergence of a new consciousness of women as critical inputs for national development rather than as targets for welfare policies. A second significant outcome was the recognition of women as a group adversely affected by the processes of economic transformation. It was realized that constitutional guarantees of equality would be meaningless and unrealistic unless women's right to economic independence is acknowledged and their training in skills as contributors to the family and the national economy is improved. A major outcome of the CSWI report was the National Plan of Action (1976) that provided the guidelines based on the UN's World Plan of Action for Women. The National Plan of Action (1976) identified areas of health, family planning, nutrition, education, employment, legislation and social welfare for formulating and implementing action programmes for women as called for planned interventions to improve the conditions of women in India.

An immediate outcome of the National Plan of Action was the setting up of the Women's Welfare and Development Bureau in 1976 under the Ministry of Social Welfare, to act as a nodal point within the Government of India to coordinate policies and programmes and initiate measures for women's development. The Women's Welfare and Development Bureau was charged with the nodal responsibility of:

(a) Co-ordinating and collaborating with multifarious programmes in other Central Government Ministries;
(b) Initiating necessary policies, programmes and measures;

(c) Collecting data to serve as a clearing house;
(d) Monitoring programmes for women's welfare;
(e) Servicing the National Committee on Women;
(f) Following up on the recommendations of the CSWI by formulating proposals and providing guidelines;
(g) Working out financial and physical targets;
(h) Liaising with multinational /UN agencies in the field of women's welfare;
(i) Legal issues and problems concerning women; and
(j) Implementing programmes and schemes.

In 1977-78 as an exercise for the Sixth Plan, the Government appointed the Working Group on Employment of women. Two other critical reports on village level organizations and participation of women in agriculture and rural development were prepared as part of the exercise. This plan was undoubtedly influenced by the CSWI Report of 1975. It devoted a whole chapter to Women and Development. For the first time a shift was perceived from welfare to development approaches for women. Influenced by the era that heralded concepts of social justice, the Sixth Plan recognized women's lack of access to resources as a critical factor impeding their development and, among others, the programme providing joint *pattas* (titles) to men and women was initiated. However, though the plan defined the magnitude of women's problems and suggested development strategies, the 'Family' rather than the 'women' remained the basic unit of development programming.

The Seventh Five-Year Plan operationalized the concern for equity and empowerment articulated by the International Decade for Women. For the first time, the emphasis was qualitative, focusing on inculcating confidence among women; generating awareness about their rights and privileges; and training them for economic activity and employment. In keeping with the spirit of the decade which aimed at integrating women into mainstream national development, the Plan emphasized the need to open new avenues of work for women and perceive them as a crucial resource for the development of the country.

The access of women to critical inputs and productive resources such as land (joint title on *patta* scheme initiated in the

Sixth Plan period) were expanded in the Seventh Plan period to include support through credit (or small scale capital), marketing, training in skills/management and technology. At the same time, it was emphasized that technology that causes unemployment or displacement of women must be resisted. Another salient and crucial recognition was the need for organization of women workers and unionization that could:

(a) Make demands for improving legal services to safeguard rights;

(b) Reduce occupational and health hazards.

The Plan acknowledged the long hours spent by women in activities within the household especially in the collection of fuel, fodder, water, etc., as well as their labour on the family farm or in family business. While the Seventh Plan did not call for the computation of women's work in these two areas as part of women's contribution to the GNP, the identification of these hitherto invisible areas was a significant beginning. Complementing the productive endeavour were the supportive services offered to women, especially maternal and child care facilities as part of the total package of services for women.

Existing Programmes

Currently, the Government of India has over twenty-seven schemes for women, some women specific and others both for the male and female population. These schemes are located in different departments and ministries of the Government of India such as Rural Development, Labour, Education, Health Science & Technology, Welfare, Women and Child Development, etc. The total outlay on the women-specific schemes in the Seventh Plan is 2.4 per cent of the total while a gender break-up of beneficiaries or targets is unavailable for general schemes (RLEGP, NREP, etc.)

In 1985 the Government of India constituted a separate Department in the Ministry of Human Resource Development, for the development of women and children. This Department funds the Central Social Welfare Board that has developmental and welfare programmes for women. The Department also plans and executes programmes for women besides monitoring programmes for women in other Ministries/Departments. A number of these programmes were envisaged in the Sixth/Seventh Plan periods—viz., Women's Development Corporations, Support to Training and Employment Programme (STEP), Training-cum-Production Centres for Women, Awareness Generation Camps for Rural and Poor Women, Women's Training Centres or Institutes for Rehabilitation of Women in Distress, Short Stay Homes for Women and Girls, Voluntary Action Bureau and Family Counselling Centres, Free Legal Aid & Para Legal Training, Working Women's Hostels, etc.

Women specific programmes implemented by the Department of Women and Child Development include:

(i) Strengthening and improvement of women's work and employment in agriculture, small animal husbandry, dairying, fisheries, handlooms, handicrafts, khadi and village industries, and sericulture;
(ii) Economic rehabilitation of women from weaker sections of society in the form of training and employment on a sustained basis;
(iii) Better employment avenues for women to bring them into mainstream national development;
(iv) Providing Short Stay Homes for women and girls in moral danger together with counselling, medical care, psychiatric guidance and treatment and services, and development of skills; and
(v) Preventive and rehabilitative services to women and children who are victims of atrocities and exploitation.

The thrust of these various programmes is to provide five principal categories of services:

(a) Employment & Income Generation Services;
(b) Education & Training Services;
(c) Support Services;
(d) General Awareness Services; and
(e) Legal Support Services

Holistic Perspective to the Development of Women

Poverty is a consequence as well as a cause of several factors that limit life. The obstinacy of this self-perpetuating cycle needs to be broken before its grip can be loosened and overcome in the measurable future. The poverty-induced cycle affects all the people but impinges hardest on girls and women. Material poverty starts a chain of consequences, namely, infections, nutritional deficiencies, ill-health, growth retardation, slow learning, small body size, low productivity, repeated child bearing, excess of unpaid and unrecognized work, low earning capacity, unemployment and perpetuation of poverty. The strategic response need not tax the nation's resources and can yield decisive social benefits if it spans the spectrum of needs through the life cycle—the girl's education, food, security, safer environment in the home and neighbourhood, vocational training, support services to save time and energy, income and employment opportunity, safe motherhood, breast feeding and proper weaning, immunity against childhood diseases, management of common illnesses like diarrhoea and respiratory infection, growth promotion and early childhood stimulation as educational foundation leading to full and equal participation in socio-economic life. The process of inter generational (and now intragender,) improvement, which is what development planning is about, has to ascend these steps in an unbroken sequence.

These may not necessarily cover women in specially difficult circumstances such as refugees and migrants, prostitutes and victims of atrocities, the mentally and physically handicapped, etc., as these would require separate and detailed studies as has been done in the case of women in custody. However, for the majority of women, especially the rural poor, an integrated and decentralized approach to planning is envisaged. While the plan perceives mainstreaming as long-term goal, it also realizes that some sector-specific measures will have to be undertaken to elicit higher participation of women in the development process during the interim period.

Recognizing the need for a holistic approach, the Perspective Plan offers sectoral reviews of the situation of women in rural development, employment, supportive services, education, health, legislation, political participation, media and communication and voluntary action, while suggesting interlinked and converging strategies towards a holistic development of women by 2000 AD.

Index